100 Pennies

"When mentally healthy children are born into a family with the disease of mental illness, surviving this insanity is a testament to their resilience and mental health. And yet, it is confusing. They learn to never completely trust themselves.

In her heartfelt and riveting book about living in an environment of rage, alcoholism, cruelty, and deceit, the author tells of a lifelong struggle to survive the hell she was raised in. It tells of her bravery, courage, and belief during her painful years of recovery, moving forward step by step into the unknown world of trust, growth, and happiness.

This book is a powerful voice of healing for all survivors and therapists."

Kay Posillico, LCSW,
Life Center Counseling &
Health Services Huntington,
NY

100 Pennies:
A Journey to Forgive the Unforgivable

by Gaetane Martin

ISBN: 978-0-692-98643-1

Printed in the United States of America

DEDICATION

To my mother, shown here at age 66,
shortly before her death,
and all victims of domestic violence.

Preface

I knew that one day I would write the story of my life, but first, I had to remember it. Even now, my journey remains one of remembering and healing, always with the hope that peace will finally find its way into my mind and heart. Only then, once all the secrets are remembered and told, will the real story begin.

My story is about one little girl who saw love around her; who was determined, tenacious and clear about her purpose in life. She grew up knowing that there was another way to live even if she didn't how she was going find that other life; she knew that she was going to end the generational incest that was part of her day-to-day experience. She had little memory of the events that shaped her; she didn't know about dissociation at the time; the 'not being there" state that affects most victims of trauma. Still, she was convinced that she alone would end the poverty, the hunger, and the domestic violence. She would end it all, for a great injustice is done to children who grow up in families like hers.

So, here it is; written; for all the children of the world and all the families living as victims of poverty, hunger, domestic abuse, and incest. When I'm asked why I wrote it, my answer is because no one should ever live an invisible life.

This book is meant to help all those who struggle with invisibility and overcoming the silence of generational poverty, hunger, domestic violence, and incest. That's why this book had to be written and my story told. There will be no more secrets.

Gaetane Martin

Acknowledgements

First and foremost, I thank God. In the process of putting this book together, I realized the gift of fortitude that He gave me. He gave me the power to believe in my passion and pursue the belief that another life was possible. I could never have done this without my faith.

To my children. You are the best part of me! You are my treasures in this world and I would give my life for you. The work that went into making this book a reality is all because of you! You gave me something to work towards; a better life than I ever had is all I ever wanted for you. I love you more than words can say.

To Jim, my significant other; thank you for your encouragement and support and most of all for giving me space to write this memoir. You are a gentleman; a dignified and a loving man. I love you.

Andrea, my friend, I love how our relationship has continued and grown and I am grateful to have your support! There are no words to fully describe what you mean to me, but I think you have an idea. Remember, love between us is everlasting, even in absence. I've always been and will always be here for you and all my friends in Canada.

To my friends, you became my family: you know who you are. You have given me the most support when you didn't even realize that I needed it! Much love to you all.

To my brothers, Luc, Jacques, and Adam and to my sisters; to Doris, who passed away, and to Antoinette, Grace, Jackie and Eileen. You have a special place in my heart. I raised you. I fed you. I never wanted you to be hungry or hurting.

Jeannine, dear friend, remember when we sat at the beach and I shared a part of my life that I never shared before? I told you about my hunger as a child. It changed my world. Thank you for being an excellent source of inspiration and supporting my creativity.

I would also like to express my gratitude to Linda Lombardo, my special editor and coach, who saw me through this book, bringing it to fruition and into an English version. Thank you for your patience and dedicated professional help and hard work.

Thanks to Elizabeth Rogerveen whose developmental editing services helped me organize and structure the book.

Thanks also to Cathleen O'Connor, PhD who did the interior layout and line editing in addition to writing the marketing copy for the book. www.cathleenoconnor.com.

For a beautiful cover design thanks to graphics designer Shar. Contact at: https://www.fiverr.com/landofawes

To my special mental health professionals, this book would not have been possible without your dedicated help. You helped me and believed that I could find my way out of hell into a peaceful, joyful, healthy life. And yes, I am living the life that I always knew was waiting there for me.

Introduction

One night, like many others, my father came home drunk. He'd warn us before he left. "I'm going out to get drunk and it's your fault because you're all such shit," he'd say. We believed him because he would come home drunk, wanting to kill mom. We were all used to the sound of the door slamming in the middle of the night when my father finally came home, the cursing and stumbling about in the dark as he tried to find my mother, so he could kill her. It seemed she heard him, too and hid. I knew that she'd stay safely hidden until he gave up and passed out asleep somewhere. But, in my young mind, there was always the chance that this time would be different. *What would happen to her if he found her? What would happen to all of us kids if she died?*

This one night, he wasn't even in the house yet. He was still outside, shouting for our mom: "You fucking black crow!" he called her. "Don't even try to hide from me!"

My mother heard him, too; I could tell from her sudden commotion. *Good,* I thought, *she'll hide.* Instead, she came rushing up into the bedroom where all of us children had been sleeping - all of us together in the creaky old iron bed that had pink bubble gum stuck on the rails, which was as good a place as any to keep it if we were going to resume chewing it in the morning and avoid waking up with gum stuck in our hair.

It was wintertime and freezing cold, so we were all under the heavy wool blanket, fully dressed, trying to stay as warm as we could. I sat up in alarm when my mother ran into the room. She came right over to me and spoke in a hushed voice, "Don't tell him where I am. Don't tell him, Gaetane!"

With that, she took off to hide. I was grateful she didn't tell me where she was planning to hide because then I could never tell on her; she left me truly innocent. Later, I learned that she hid in the pantry under the stairs where there was no light for him to see her.

Usually, my father never involved us kids in these middle-of-the-night dramas. *Usually,* he never came up to our bedroom. He would just search for my mother downstairs until he passed out somewhere. Still, we kids were afraid, always on guard.

The door slammed, and the yelling got louder now that he was inside. He was still yelling for my mom, threatening to kill her. "I'm going to kill you, Loreen! Don't try to hide because I'll find you!" His words sent a chill through me.

Suddenly, I heard him come pounding up the stairs in his boots, more determined and steadier than you might expect from a man who was stinking, blackout drunk. I started to shake. My other siblings were wide awake by now and I could feel them shaking, too, under the blankets.

In a drunken rage, my father appeared in the doorway; our room had no door.

I was the only one who saw the gleam of the rifle in his hands. *Oh my God, he has a gun!* How long would it be before someone found us, all murdered by my father, still in our bed with pink bubble gum all over the bedpost? My teeth began to chatter. I could hardly hear him above the chattering! And yet, I could.

"Where the fuck is your mother? Tell me!" He looked like a murderer with his wild eyes and his face full of anger and liquor. "Where is she?" he demanded, "Where is that fucking big cow? I'm going to kill her!" His voice was menacing, enraged.

"She's not here," was all I could say – because I knew if I said I didn't know where she was, he'd keep looking for her. Though I expected we were all about to die at the hands of this madman, I somehow held my ground and refused to tell him that my mother was in the house. "Please go to sleep, she's not here," I pleaded.

"Tu es une christe de manteuse," he growled at me, calling me a fucking liar. "I'll kill *you* if you don't tell me!"

I thought I'm sixteen and I'm going to die. I believed we were all going to die, and in that moment of complete powerlessness, I started praying. I gave my life up to God. I closed my eyes and begged Him to protect us.

And suddenly, my father just turned around and left the room. I could hear him as he thumped back downstairs, still stumbling and angrily cursing.

I waited. After a little while, the cursing stopped. It got so very quiet. I knew he'd stopped looking for my mother or, more accurately, he'd passed out somewhere. And there we were, everyone in the house left paralyzed with fear; us in the old, iron bed and my mother still hiding in the food pantry under the staircase.

The next morning, like so many other mornings, my father remembered nothing of the night before as my mother dutifully cooked him his breakfast.

"To forgive is holy; there must be something bigger than our own pain that allows us to let the pain go and forgive those who harmed us."

Gaetane Martin

Chapter 1

In the early days, my father would be sober for five or six months at a time; but when he drank, he was a binge drinker. He would warn us a few days before the binge, telling us that he was going to get "disgusting drunk" and it was all our fault because we were all *merde*. Shit. Then we knew that we were in for it again. There would be *hell* to pay for *making* him go on a binge! Mother was usually sick or pregnant, and I took care of all my younger siblings - so what did we ever do so wrong that we were all such shit?

He would start with a big bottle of gin or whiskey from his bootlegging family or who knows where with what money, drinking right out of the bottle. When he got that drunk, he didn't eat - not that we had much to eat. Sometimes, when he'd come home, he'd vomit blood - or maybe when he'd vomit blood, that's when he'd come home. I was never sure which came first.

There was talk that, when he'd go out drinking, he'd spend his time with other women; any woman that he could. My father was very handsome and kept himself well-dressed. He could be so charming and seductive on the surface, but most of these women were prostitutes. In addition to his time spent with other women, he'd get into drunken brawls. The fighter in him was ever present.

When he'd get back home, he'd want to *kill* my mother. She'd hide, and he'd hang around the house trying to find her in the dark or by the light of a candle or the fire in the stove since we rarely had money for electricity. He would call her dehumanizing names, animal names. He was a woodsman, after all. He'd call her an ugly, black crow or a fat, lazy cow.

Meanwhile, he was the scavenger preying on everyone. It's true, my mother appeared a bit chubby because she was often pregnant and being pregnant slowed her down, although she was never allowed to stop and rest. He was the predator, seeing things backward and wanting to kill my mother.

The few times he involved we children, I was able to talk him out of killing anyone. I'd tell him that he wasn't well, and he should get some sleep. This one-way conversation would go on until he passed out. Often, we'd find him in the chair by the wood stove in the morning. Because his house had burned down when he was a child, he was afraid that the stove would catch fire. He would feed the stove slowly, so the fire never got high, and, as a result, it was chilly in our house.

And that's where we'd find him in the morning, in the chair by the stove, passed out, looking like hell, like he was going to die any minute - and yet we were the ones who were supposedly sick, we were the ones who were *shit.*

You would think, with a father like this, that I would be happy when he was away. He was away a lot, for long periods of time, because he was a logger; there was this whole culture of lumberjacks in our area of Canada. The town where I was born was originally settled by the French in the 1790's for logging because it was located strategically at the meeting point of the Madawaska and Saint John Rivers, waterways used to transport the logs. Before that, it was a sacred meeting place for native tribes of the Maliseet Nation, the Algonquian-speaking Indigenous people, as they migrated each season. They would use the river to canoe down from their various northern territories and plant summer crops together, then return upriver after the harvest in their individual tribes to hunt caribou and other large game for the winter. By the time I was born, the little logging settlement had grown into a prosperous city, surrounding a federal Indian reservation.

The French colonists originally called this town *Petit-Sault* - Little Falls - for the waterfalls where the two rivers merge. It was renamed to Edmundston after a local military and political leader in 1851. In 1947, I was born in Edmundston because that's where the hospital was. All I know about my birth is what my mother told me: that I came into the world quickly, nearly born on the steps of the hospital. I don't know if there is any meaning to being born that quickly, but I've been full of energy my whole life and I move as if there's urgency in everything. My name was written as Gisele Gaetane Martin on my birth certificate, but I was always called Gaetane. Ironically, the name Gisele has its roots in the Germanic word *gisel*, meaning hostage; and this hidden aspect of being a hostage is how I felt for so many years of my young life.

While Edmundston is a sizeable city, the nearby town I grew up in is called *Riviere-Verte*, Green River, and was much smaller. With a population of less than 2,000 even today, it was more like a village. There were only two streets: the main street, and the back street. It was a small town surrounded by wilderness, nestled cozily on the eastern bank of the Saint John River, often covered in snow. In those days, my little town was known for its French language, Catholicism, and a rural, often poor life. This was my foundation from birth.

The economy was very poor in our village. There were few businesses and jobs, so my father, like his father before him, had become a lumberjack at a young age. His father supplemented the income with bootlegging American cigarettes and moonshine whiskey. My father's family, the Martelles, were very poor - dirt poor with no education. He grew up in an alcoholic household that made its money bootlegging and logging, with a long line of domestic violence, and worse. This was known by others in town.

The story went that there was a time when the Martelles had money. They had owned land - so much land! But they sold it to the local oil company. The revenue from the sale of the land was divided among all the sons, who were drunks and knew nothing about how to manage anything, let alone this huge amount of money that came their way. They didn't bank their money; instead, they hid it in the walls of their houses and under the bed frames until it was all spent; all wasted. All that money disappeared as if it had never happened, and the land, too, with nothing left for their children but poverty and hard work.

I found out that my father was quite smart as a child, but he was not allowed to go to school because his family needed the money he could bring in; a rural mentality that hard work was worth more than an education. Instead of going to school, he was taken to the lumberjack camp with his father and forced to work all day, every day. He was of small stature but was given the job of saddling the huge horses at the camp. He had to stand on a box to reach the backs of these horses - while hoisting a huge, heavy saddle. If he didn't saddle the horses properly, he was beaten. My father never learned to read or write and that frustrated him. He didn't like feeling powerless.

He began to drink the family's bootlegged American whiskey and smoked at an early age because it was all around him and expected of a man. He became a fighter, getting into drunken brawls and womanizing. Loggers and lumberjacks spent most of their time in the remote forests, rarely seeing women. As a result, the competitiveness was fierce among them; there were few rules to curb their aggressive behavior and the riskier the task or stunt, the manlier they were. This led to a promiscuous lifestyle, even for the married men. There was an exaggerated need to show off one's masculinity in both public demonstrations and private ones that were never discussed.

Not every lumberjack or logger acted this way, but most did if they wanted to survive the other men. It was a whole lifestyle for a man to be lumberjacking in rural Canada. Not much changed when my father married my mother except that he had a place to act out his aggression and domination privately in ways that were never discussed. Maybe it was the only place he felt true power. He was abused, and I understand that. But it made him such an evil person; so mentally ill, selfish and cruel. That was the only way my father knew how to be, and he thought he was right about everything – he never showed remorse for anything he did or didn't do. Yes, you'd think I'd be happy when he was away for weeks at a time. But it's a funny thing that happens when you're sexually abused by a parent. Instead of being happy, I cried because I missed him. Ironically, for me, my father was the whole world. I was addicted to my father in those days. Taking him away was like taking away a drug from an addict, and I would go into withdrawal. He didn't pick on me or beat me like he did to my mother and most of my siblings. He just *loved* me.

From a young age, I had many people in my life who loved me. I never questioned that love. Why would I? Not even the love I received from my father. Little children accept what happens around them and to them. I had no idea at my young age that the way he loved me, by sexually stimulating me, was not the normal way a father should love a daughter, though he told me these special times were our little secret. Until I was 11 years old, I had no idea how wrong this was. All I knew in those early days was that I pleased him, I was pleasing to him, I was his favorite; wasn't that love? It was all I knew of the love of a father.

And whenever he left, I felt so abandoned!

I got sick with illnesses that not even the hospital could diagnose, with high fevers reaching 105 degrees at times. I would get severe headaches - there were plenty of those when he was gone. My mom's mother, Grandma Smyde, would come and visit to nurse me back to health. My grandmother's remedy for fever was a raw potato that she'd slice and lay on my forehead. It felt cool against my burning skin! I was burning up with fever and my eyes would burn so much that it was hard to keep them open. All this sickness started because I was crying constantly when my father was gone. My mother and neighbors would shake their heads and say, "Look at Gaetane. Here she goes again with those big tears."

One time, the emotional pain was so strong that I thought maybe if I cut myself it would let the hurt out; my blood would pour out and along with it, the pain. I would be at peace from this torment. I had never seen or heard of this coping mechanism of "cutting" before; it was pure instinct. I was only five years old at the time as I went under the stoop and found a piece of glass. I cut myself just above my wrist on my left hand; I somehow knew not to cut my wrist.

I learned quickly not to ever cut myself again with a piece of glass or anything else - it hurt like hell! Now, I wasn't just in emotional pain, I was in physical pain, too. I felt wretched and cutting myself only made things worse. I cried some more under the stoop. I would have to find another way to deal with this intense pain.

Chapter 2

The first house, we called *la petite maison rouge* - the little red house. There was no indoor plumbing or refrigerator. We had no running water; just the water pump outside. Right inside the little red house was a tiny living area. We didn't have much in there, just a sofa that opened into an extra bed when needed and two worn maroon chairs with metal arms. On one side of the living room was my mother and father's bedroom. There was no door for privacy; only curtains hung in the doorway. I was impressed that there was a window in their room, and the big, heavy bedroom furniture - somehow, I knew that someone had spent real money on it at one time or another.

To the other side of the living room were our kitchen and dining area. It had a linoleum floor, a small table with four white chairs, a couple of cabinets hanging on the wall, a cooking counter and a wood stove that was our only source of heat in the house, the infamous washing machine on rollers, and a back door to a little stoop. There was no toilet in the house; only an outhouse and chamber pots inside the house - "slop pots," we called them. The walls were not insulated, and the house got very cold in winter.

Upstairs was one large bedroom with the big iron bed where all of us kids slept in the summer. We would collect fireflies and put them in a jar. My mother helped us poke holes in the lids. "They need to breathe, too," she'd say. Even with the best intentions and lots of holes in the lids, the fireflies died quickly, often before we even fell asleep. It was disappointing because I loved watching their little lights.

It was impossible to sleep upstairs in the wintertime, though. There was no insulation on the ceiling upstairs, so in the winter, icicles and frost formed on the nails that protruded through the roof into the room. Imagine lying in bed and seeing icicles, like daggers shining in the dark, above your head, waiting to fall on you!

I learned to sleep with my clothes on in the winter, and, in the mornings, it was a struggle to get out from under the covers and expose myself to the cold air in the bedroom. Despite the cold, I couldn't stand sleeping in scratchy socks, so my bare feet would hardly touch the rough wooden floor as I ran to the wash basin in the corner. Pouring water from the chipped pitcher into the old porcelain basin meant breaking the icy crust that had formed overnight. I had to use my fist to break through. *Crack! Crack!* Then I would splash it on my face while my feet danced in response. *Quickly, quickly* - God, it was cold!

When it got too cold to sleep upstairs with the ice and frost, we would close the opening of the stairs with a snug make-shift door and we'd sleep on the pull-out sofa bed downstairs; *all* of us.

We lived in our dirty clothes and we were very cold and hungry. Because we were always dirty, we smelled since there was usually no soap to wash us. My poor mother wore rags and cried. I rarely saw her dressed up.

She was pregnant with another mouth to feed and she wasn't equipped to have more kids, let alone care for all of them. There was hardly any money for food, clothes, or electricity; although there seemed to be money for gambling and alcohol. There were times when there wasn't even money to buy oil, so we would revert to these tiny white candles in the lanterns instead of the very costly oil.

It was such a blessing and luxury that the milkman was my mother's uncle with his own dairy farm. He was such a sweet man, delivering glass bottles of fresh milk to our small stoop, milk that we would never have had the money for. After he lost the dairy farm, we had no milk again.

My mother didn't have one single mean bone in her body. She didn't have the rage that I saw in my father, his father or even her own mother. It was "money" that was such an issue for my parents that they would fight. It was confusing as a child, but I learned that "money" had the power to make my mother cry and my father angry. What was clear to me was that it was dangerous to be without it; dangerous and unsafe. Without money, there was no food, no electricity, no money for bills. They would fight about losing the little red house. We could lose everything if there was no money; it was all that stood between us and the street.

My father would get very angry, and my mother would cry, and hide from him when he came home drunk. She lived her whole life trying to make my father happy or at least trying to keep him at bay; trying anyway she could. My father took out most of his frustrations and anger on my mother, even when she begged and cried; her face beet red from one thing or other because of him.

There was only one time when my mother stood up to my father, only one.

All of us kids were in the kitchen with my mom cooking when my father came stumbling in the kitchen door drunk, nasty and cursing. He was hardly able to stand up yet, of course, the first thing he wanted to do was hit my mother. For once, she didn't run and hide; instead, she beat the daylights out of him.

As he lunged toward her, my mother grabbed a broomstick and whacked him good, right in the face! Once she'd done that, it was as if she couldn't stop! She hit him everywhere she could: his arms, his face, his whole body. We watched every blow as she swung that broomstick and it hit its mark. What a victory! We were petrified but so excited, and we cheered her on so eagerly. He tried to hit her back, but she only hit harder.

After that beating, the brute went to bed and slept for hours. When he woke up, he kept looking at himself all black and blue in the mirror in disbelief because he never remembered anything after getting that drunk. "Where the hell was I?" he finally asked. "Someone beat the shit out of me."

Well, we kids weren't about to say anything. I had even warned my mother not to say anything; to pretend she had no idea what happened.

But my mother laughed at him and said, "*I* beat the shit out of you!" Well, he took off after her and did his best to give her the beating of her life.

I couldn't believe it. The only time my mother defended herself and we all got to see it, and it had changed how I felt about her and the level of respect I had for her. And then she turned around and told on herself and did that to herself, getting such a beating until she was crying again. I was devastated.

My mother went back to just trying to survive, seeming overwhelmed. She worked as hard as she could even when she was pregnant, and we worked right along with her. We had our chores to do around the house from the time we could lift a finger. I cried, standing on the stool in front of the big, white enamel basin because I didn't want to wash dirty dishes; I just wanted to play. Instead of playing, we had so many chores. We made the beds; picked up our clothes, which we didn't have much of; pumped water from the well so Mom could wash the clothes; did the dishes; chopped wood for the stove; and Saturday was the day for the big cleaning.

The only chore I enjoyed was shining the waxed floors, because we did it by putting on our woolen socks, waiting for the wax to dry, and then sliding back and forth across the floor until it gleamed as best it could. This was fun for us kids and was a special treat.

But there was nothing more special than Christmas. My mother made it so special and we all felt so loved. Every year, we would go with my mother to cut down our Christmas tree. We'd have our sleigh, our ax, and our rope, and we'd get the perfect Christmas tree. After we found it and chopped it down, we tied it to our sleigh and pulled it home. I didn't realize the irony at the time, but my father was a lumberjack and he never helped us chop down one Christmas tree; he never helped with anything.

My mother would time things perfectly to put up the tree on my brother's birthday in mid-December, and she made the tree so beautiful. Even without lights, she made it look as if there were lights. She would hang the tinsel strands perfectly, one by one, on the branches, and how the tinsel would reflect the light coming from the wood stove and the candles. That had to do for lights since there was no money to buy anything so frivolous.

Somehow, in the winter, my mom would find some money to make fudge from time to time. It was our favorite; we looked forward to that fudge. If I close my eyes, I can still see her stirring it on the wood stove. It needed to be constantly stirred or it would burn. Then, she'd put it outside, so it would get cold and firm. This was our treat in the winter.

My mom would take us to go see Santa Claus every year. She'd bundle us all up in our navy blue prickly wool one-piece snowsuits and the scratchy wool hats and mittens her grandmother made for us, and off we'd go. It only took a few minutes before I'd start feeling itchy and begin scratching from the unlined wool, but I wasn't complaining - I was going to see Santa! The snow was so high at that time of the year that the streets looked like tunnels. It felt like we were walking through an igloo at the North Pole when we were on our way to see Santa Claus.

We would tell Santa what we wanted for Christmas and he'd give us a piece of candy. On Christmas Eve, we got new pajamas that my mother had made for us; the only pair we had for the winter. We'd try to wait up for Santa, but of course, we'd fall asleep in our new pajamas, which were flannel and so soft. I felt so warm and safe.

We believed in Santa Claus because it was the only time of year that we got toys; it was the one day we didn't feel poor. Things were never wrapped; that was an unnecessary expense even for Santa. The presents just had a tag, like A Gaetane de Pere Noel" As we got older, we questioned why Santa wrote in the same exact beautiful calligraphy handwriting as my mother, but we usually let it drop once we had our gifts to play with. It was no matter that my sister and I would each get the same present, like a doll with a small comb and mirror. My brothers might get a truck each, or cowboy cap guns, and we each got a coloring book with a small box of crayons and a little candy stocking. I wonder now what my mother had to give up creating that day for us.

Mother would wear a special dress on Christmas and looked so pretty with her red lipstick and her beautiful black heeled shoes she so rarely wore. And then we would go visit our grandparents, where we had so much food in abundance at each house. Such feasts - there was even real meat! Venison was the featured meat, along with wild rabbit - but I never liked the wild meats with their tough, gamey taste. You half expected them to get up from the table and run out the door! I often wished they would.

No, what really excited me was what I called the *real* meat: chicken, pork, and beef. All the special recipes that my grandmothers made with real meat were something to look forward to, like the best chicken and dumpling stew. As I write this, I still can taste and smell all the special meals that were prepared for the holidays by my two - very different - Grandmothers.

Even my father seemed cheerful at Christmas. I thought him so handsome with his green eyes as I watched him smile and sing and dance.

Christmas was a time in my life that I was truly happy, and I loved to see my mother so happy at Christmas time. I loved to color, and my mother was incredible at coloring. Sometimes, she would color in my books. She had this soft smile when she colored, and I loved to watch her draw. She would make the most creative drawings of angels and Santa Claus faces! She was an amazing artist and such a creative person.

I felt like Christmas was magic, for it was the only time that I felt my mother's love and felt safe. She taught me how to pray and prayed with me to Jesus each night before I went to sleep, even in the summertime when it was still light out. Especially then, she was the mom I wanted and needed.

Chapter 3

My father's side of the family couldn't have been more different, exact opposites of my mother's family. My mother's family, the Smydes, were educated, professional and affluent, and lived in the next town over from us. They owned lots of land and businesses. It was said that they had owned the first car in town in the 20's. They traveled and were well-known and respected in the area. They were also very religious. Even as a small child visiting my parents' families, anyone could have seen the difference.

My mother's parents owned one of the biggest houses in the neighborhood. They both loved to dance and would travel to Quebec to popular nightclubs. I loved that house. It's still there today; having survived all these years. Back then, it seemed like the most perfect house anyone could ever want because my grandparents not only had running water, they had a toilet and a tub *inside* the house, a refrigerator in a big kitchen, a large living room with a piano where we would sing church songs for Christmas, and they even had a dining room and a central foyer where the pot-bellied stove provided plenty of heat. Upstairs, the bedrooms had heavy oak furniture with fancy mirrors and windows with soft curtains that were so beautiful. In Grandmother Smyde's home, it was all about things - the house, the furniture, the car – it was all beautiful. And they had books, big books, everywhere. They were passionate regarding education and living a proper life.

Because of my mother's family, I came to know the difference between poverty and affluence as a child, and this was the knowledge that eventually saved my life. I knew the difference between what we had as Martelles, my father's side of the family, versus what the Smydes had. I knew what was beautiful and what was ugly. It was all very impressive to me because I knew that it had to cost so much money to buy these beautiful things; extra money, not just the little bit of money for basic food and electricity. That's how I knew the heavy furniture in my parents' bedroom had cost so much money once.

But even with their big house full of all these luxuries and plenty of food, any of which would have made me so happy, Grandma Smyde did not seem to be happy. I couldn't help noticing that she often seemed angry. At what, I could only guess. Maybe she was angry because she lost two of her children; one, my Aunt Gaetane who I was named after, was killed by lightning. It struck her in the kitchen doorway downstairs when she was only five years old. So strange; and at the same time as her little daughter got struck by lightning, my grandma was giving birth upstairs. The second of her six children who died was my Uncle Al, killed ten years later by a car right in front of their house. My grandparents were away traveling when it happened, but my young Uncle Bernard was there and saw the whole thing from the porch. My grandma told me once that she'd had a premonition; a bird flew into the window where she sat, and it died. She knew "it was an omen." She was connected spiritually, so I believed her.

Maybe it was the shoes that cut on her bunions that made her so irritable; I know this was a problem because she'd complain about it from time to time. Whatever the reason, she seemed angry at the world, at her husband, and at us. And she had so many rules she could get angry about! I was afraid of Grandma Smyde back then. She was a vigilant housekeeper, wearing an apron with a rag sticking out of her big pocket that she also used as a handkerchief. She was organized, and everything was to be kept neat and clean, calm and respectful. We were not allowed to run or play indoors, touch anything, or raise our voices. Children were to be quiet; no fidgeting or fighting. We were expected to be polite to guests in her home.

In her kitchen, there was a little kid's table with four chairs. This was where children had their meals, separate from the adults. We ate quietly without making a mess. In fact, if we ever made so much as a crumb while we were eating, grandma would be cleaning around our plates before we even finished eating. She gave us "the eye" that told us we were an unacceptable and unruly bunch even when we were behaving. Still, I loved that beautiful house and I was happy to be there because it smelled good. Grandma was a great cook, especially during the holidays.

We weren't ever hungry there. But we were never good enough, and neither was my mother. We were dirty, we didn't speak properly, and we certainly didn't dress properly. My mother had been my grandmother's princess - who'd chosen a life that was nothing like how she was raised. As a result, we were all a huge disappointment and embarrassment to the Smydes.

My grandmother would lecture us about our mother - "*La Princesse.*" Hundreds of times over the years, we would get these lectures. My grandmother had grown up very poor in a large family with ten children, she made sure we knew. She had to scrub floors to earn money. She got no education. She swore she would pick a good husband and her children would never have a life like this, scrubbing floors. When she married my Grandpa Smyde, she had married into money. My grandparents had six children together, one of whom was my mother, Loreen. They saw to it that Loreen and all their children were educated. My mother had been educated at a private English school and could speak both English and her native French Canadian fluently. She had won many calligraphy awards in school. She was an artist. Her parents had seen to it that she was introduced to many things - skiing, ice skating, travel to all sorts of places – and introduced her to all the right people. She'd had a good social circle of friends and loved being with people. She'd had the privilege of fine fashion and anything money could buy. My mother had never scrubbed a single floor growing up, or even boiled water! In the life that my grandma had planned for my mother, these would have been unnecessary skills to learn.

From my grandma, I learned that my mother had been smart, friendly and creative, with much potential, because she was raised in an environment that valued all those things. According to my grandma, all those gifts were wasted. My mother had been pretty, too. "She was a princess!" my grandmother would say to us kids, so harshly. "I worked hard so that she would not ever have to work a single day in her entire life! She had everything; a privileged life. She could have married anyone, and she married that *tramp*!" My grandma hated my father, and his whole bootlegging family who sold their land and never invested their money. They were just a bunch of dirt-poor, illiterate, violent, womanizing alcoholics.

She would make mom feel like she was not a good mother saying things like, "This is not the life I had planned for you. I warned you not to marry that tramp and now look at you. You can't even take care of your own children properly. They're dirty!" As if that required pointing out. No princess could ever live in our house, she made that for certain. Somehow, grandma believed that she could control or help change others by being mean and putting them down and being so strict with her beliefs about "living right." She was very smart and opinionated and could be so harsh.

I learned that my mother had several boyfriends before my father came along; all of them were very educated and professional businessmen. Her parents had high hopes for their daughter having a suitable marriage - until Loreen met my father. I never found out exactly how my parents met. I thought that they must have met ice skating because my mother loved skating and my father did, too. Otherwise, how would these two very different people come together? My father was so handsome and could be so charming, and my mother was still young when they met, had been so overprotected, and was naïve. Back then, it was her innocence about the world that probably made her such easy prey for my father. After they met, he must have seduced her, figuratively and literally, because she was pregnant when she married him.

This is ironic, because my grandma was very religious and, especially after I came of a certain age, she told us that sex before marriage was a sin; that proper people didn't live that way. She added that it was also in respect of our own dignity that we do not give away our virtue. In addition to her talks about sex before marriage and sin, she'd tell us that if ever a boy touched us, and we felt like we wanted to do something sinful with that boy, one good Hail Mary would make that thought go away. I guess with my mother and father, in the heat of the moment, there wasn't time for a Hail Mary. How could there be, when my mother had no clue about the harsh realities of life that getting involved with a man like my father would bring? Her mother had raised her like a china doll in a dollhouse, so smart about everything except real life.

You would think with all these lectures about marriage and such that my grandma had a happy marriage, but I never knew my grandpa very well, he was gone so much. And he didn't seem at all interested in me until I was of school age. Then, we finally had something to talk about. He would ask me about school; a reminder of how important education was to the Smydes. What I mostly remember about my grandpa was that his big red nose reminded us of Rudolph the Red-Nosed Reindeer - he could light the way with that nose! He was, however, blessed with beautiful teeth, which almost seemed like an apology from God for the red nose. Or maybe his teeth were so nice because he had grown up so wealthy and had the money to take care of his teeth. As if he knew his teeth were his best asset, Grandpa Smyde smiled a lot. He had one gold tooth that, whenever he smiled, flashed at us! This gold tooth was a fascination to us kids. Gold seemed very important to him. Even when he died, he left instructions that we make his headstone of black granite with the writing engraved in gold - and that's how you'll find it today, just as he instructed.

He wore such fancy clothes. His suits were of fine quality and he had a long woolen black cloak and a black felt hat. His black shoes were shiny, and he wore striking ties and shirts accessorized with cuff links that looked like gold to me and probably were. And he had those elastic bands around his arms called garters; I guess this helped hold his shirt sleeves in place, but they were also a high fashion style. His long socks were held up with garters as well. Once, he told us that he'd bought himself pigskin gloves, which were very expensive. He also bought expensive clothes for our Grandma, who herself was very frugal. She'd dress up for him, but she dressed very simply otherwise, with her apron and the rag sticking out, ready for use. I think she dressed up when he was around because my grandpa liked to show off, so she tried to keep him happy.

Grandma had so many beautiful things! She had fur coats made from seal skin, gold rings and pearls. She even gave me a beautiful cameo once. Sadly, I lost it. My grandpa was happiest when he was drunk. He drank a lot of whiskeys; Crown Royal, in fact. It came in a blue bag and we used the blue bags for our marbles. My grandpa would go "North." Sometimes, he'd go live elsewhere for as long as eleven months out of the year. We called it "North" because he'd go into the woods, into a very remote wild area unsettled by people. It was his way of escaping; that was his story.

But there was a story about him that was told to me by one of my uncles. The story went that my grandpa "was often seen at one of the local hotels up North." This hotel was known for its prostitutes, for drinking, and other things. My mother and my uncle had seen my grandpa several times on the porch of the hotel, kissing women who were "not my grandmother." Because the hotel was known for prostitution, it was implied that these women were prostitutes. Once, my uncle commented that my mother would be very upset to see her father on the hotel porch kissing prostitutes; she would be ashamed that he would behave this way.

This was such a contradiction because, according to my grandma, her daughter, my mother, had married "a tramp." That's what she called my father, even when she must have heard the rumors that her own husband ran around with every woman in town; this was the pot calling the kettle black if you ask me. Or maybe she was truly ignorant or in absolute denial. I see it now as a pattern that my mother ended up with someone so very like our alcoholic womanizing Grandfather – but much worse.

But there we would be, in my grandma's beautiful house with full bellies and not a crumb wasted on the spotless floor, not able to fidget, with all these angry lectures. Maybe it was her upbringing in poverty and years of scrubbing floors, her dead children, her princess who fell from grace, her absent husband, or her bunions that made her so angry. Maybe it was all of it. My mom could hardly share her own feelings or side of things; it was always about her mother's point of view. And then there were my Grandmother Smyde's sisters, my great aunts, who were all so different.

My Great Aunt Rose was sweet and soft, very loving, generous, and easy to approach with her beautiful smile. She had lilac trees growing in her yard and gave me some of the branches filled with blossoms. Every time I see a lilac tree or smell lilac, it is a loving reminder of her. I believe the love people share stays on this Earth. It is a comfort to those left behind. My Great Aunt Sarah was very bubbly and full of life and had such bright eyes! She loved music and dancing and danced until she died at 98 years old. She was an independent lady who drove a car, which was unusual at the time for a woman to do. She would bring positive messages to Grandma Smyde, probably because she saw how her sister was so angry, sad, and alone.

But my Great Aunt Mona was a horror; she was filled with what I called "the red rage." The poor thing was also filled with crippling arthritis that was so deforming that she covered her hands with pretty handkerchiefs, so no one would see them. I wanted to feel sorry for her, but she never had anything good to say about anyone or anything, so it was difficult even given her crippling condition. Her husband, my Great Uncle Pat, was also a member of the Smyde family so they had money; you would even call them wealthy. Their children were educated doctors, lawyers, businesspeople, and nurses. They owned many huge farms and owned most of the land in town.

From these different parts of my mother's family, I saw that there was another way to live that was different from my way of life. But the most influential person to me in my mother's family was her grandmother, my great grandma. My mom talked about her grandma so fondly; how she had felt so loved by her since she was little and spent so much time with her as she grew up, how they could talk and talk; they were confidantes.

It was a great day when my mother would visit our great grandma and we got to come along. Great-grandma would be wearing her hairnet, apron and beige cotton stockings when she greeted us. Always. My mother adored her. She was a large woman with a face that showed the lines and hardships of her life, but she had the kindest smile that went right to her eyes.

She suffered from Parkinson's disease, although we didn't know to call it that. We just knew that she shook and had to navigate her way with that additional burden. Her head and hands moved with little tremors. Despite her shaky hands, my great grandma would knit mittens, hats, scarves, and woolen stockings for all her grandchildren, which were many. Although grateful for the best of intentions, those mittens, scarves, and socks stung like stinging nettles because she used a very prickly kind of wool. My mittens were red, and so were my hands and legs after all that scratching! Yes, I got to be warm, but at such a cost! But bless her heart for all that knitting with such a disability.

And I loved to visit because my great grandma lived on a farm that was so special. One of her sons lived there with his family and children, my cousins, and every single person on that farm was a kind person to all of us. I was drawn to the people and places in my life where kindness was expressed. I think all children do that.

And there were animals! My mother was not very fond of animals, but it was fun to visit a farm for us kids and take hay rides. It was our only opportunity to be around farm animals. I will never forget the day my great grandma was milking a cow. I was fascinated watching her milk the cow; fascinated with the process of milking and that there was something warm to drink that came from these large, curious animals. When she finished the milking, she gave me a cup of some of that warm milk, fresh out of the cow. I gulped it down in an instant and immediately got so sick, vomiting all over the place. It was unpasteurized and so rich. I wasn't used to anything so rich. I made such a mess, but she didn't make me feel bad about it.

When we were there, we picked blueberries and other berries and my great grandma made cakes and pies for us. Her house was not as fancy as my grandma's — no one's house was that expensive — but my great grandma had a lovely home with a parlor filled with beautiful furniture made of oak. It was lovely and comfortable furniture that made everyone feel welcome. Her house was so warm, with heat, and the warmth you can only get from kindness.

Chapter 4

My father played favorites with us. I knew he was never going to beat me because he told me. It was our secret. It was part of me being his favorite, and the secret things we would do together. We had a special bond. He used to beat the shit out of everyone but me. One time, he had a strap and came out of the bedroom shouting, "I'm trying to take a nap!" All us kids were making noise, giggling and laughing. "Shut up!" he told us, but we couldn't stop laughing. Then, he started swinging his belt and accidentally hit me on my right ear so hard I thought I was going to be deaf for life. I was so shocked that I yelled at him, "You said you would never hit me!" Much to my surprise, he apologized to me.

His least favorite child was my one older sibling, Doris. He'd say that he'd hated her from the day she was born. Doris did not have a happy life with him. My father beat her. He would stand on the stairs holding a piece of wood. "You black crow!" he'd call her, "You're just as ugly as your mother!" And he'd beat her with the wood, and Doris would scream.

How could he hit her like that, as young as she was? He called her a "very difficult child." I think this was because she would talk back to him and defend herself. Because of her being "difficult," my sister was sent away to Grandma Smyde's. Doris was only with us at Christmas and some other times.

When she was with us, she took pleasure in beating me up. I was scratched and beaten more times than I could count. She was like a cat with all that scratching! I was smaller than her and so afraid. When I was standing on the stool at the basin, washing dishes, Doris would pinch me so hard. She would make me cry every time she visited.

Why did she beat me up, I wondered? Her life with the Smydes seemed so much better than mine. What threat could I possibly pose to her? Doris had pretty clothes, pretty shoes, and I had rags; rags and hunger. Doris had the most beautiful pair of figure skates from Grandma Smyde. Me and my younger brother Luc had learned to skate with mom's old white leather skates on the frozen pond in the back of the little red house. I had to wear three pairs of prickly woolen socks, so the skates would stay on my feet, even if they itched like crazy. And Luc had the tiniest feet in our mom's adult-sized skates. These skates had fur around the ankles and rounded blades - while Doris had the nicest figure skating blades with a toe-pick. Me and Luc would have such a great time skating, but Doris made fun of us in those big old skates that Luc and I shared.

Though she was mean, I wished that I had my sister's curly hair! My mother loved to play with my sister's hair, making "banana curls," but me – well, my mom just pulled my hair back as tight as it could go without pulling it right out of my head and braided it as if to hide it away. I had braids and very short bangs, and my sister had beautiful dark curls.

Sometimes, in those younger days, my mother would have a little extra money to buy us dresses. My sister got a pretty pink dress and I got a pretty blue dress; it was so pretty but I can still feel how rough the seersucker fabric felt against my sensitive skin. Along with the pink dress, my sister also got these beautiful white shoes with tiny straps and buckles so perfect for a little girl - while I got brown, lace-up, high-topped shoes that were practically short boots that a little boy could wear. I ended up crying because I wanted pretty, white shoes like my sister. "You can't have that kind because you're too much of a tomboy," my mother said. "You'd ruin them right away!" There was not enough money for that kind of foolishness.

I was a tomboy, and I must admit, as much as I wanted those girly shoes, my boots were perfect for climbing trees. I was full of scrapes and scabs from playing in the trees. Sometimes my clothes would get torn and they were often stained with something or other. My older sister Doris would never climb trees or get dirty. Instead, it was my younger brother Luc who was my playmate and constant companion.

Luc and I were only 15 months apart and were very close, practically like twins in that little red house. We were always together and protecting each other as best as we could. We were the siblings who were hungry together. We did so many chores together. We babysat together while my mother went to church meetings. We started school just one year apart and even studied together, helping each other with everything we did. We froze together in the wintertime; there was never enough warm clothing - except for lots of prickly wool. Luc's very light skin was like mine and we both had a tough time with the wool irritating our skin and scratching our skin raw. To this day, we both look for cashmere or very soft wool when we shop for warm clothing. The memory of the prickly stuff stays with both of us.

The winters are longer than the summers in Canada and, in those years, produced so much snow; we would be walking through tunnels in the streets that were higher than we were tall! Luc and I hated the itchy wool, but we loved the snow. We would go into the fields and build snow tunnels and play there all day.

My brother Luc was my partner in crime. I hated how my father would physically and verbally abuse Luc. And Luc and I felt so bad for my mother. We would sit on the stoop and spend hours planning how we would kill the old bastard, my father. But we were afraid of him and so was my mother with his guns and stories about how he got into fights and beat up men much bigger than him. Our fear was that we would try to kill him and not succeed. What would happen to us then; to our mother? It was enough to sober us right up and put an end to our plans.

One time, we babysat for little Jacques, who was our only other sibling at the time, after Doris was sent away. I threw a glass ashtray and hit Luc in the head. I didn't mean to hurt him; we were only playing. But Luc went after me and punched me in the chest. He punched the air right out of me and I lost my breath and dropped to the floor. I scared Luc so bad that day. Somehow, our mom found out and he got in trouble – and he never mentioned one word about how I had started it with throwing the ashtray.

In the autumn, Luc and I would gather apples that fell from the tree in a neighbor's yard. If our neighbor saw us, he'd chase us away, but we kept doing it because we needed to eat. Our neighbor was just letting those apples rot on the ground; why should he care if we took them? One time, he came out with a gun and fired it into the air to scare us. We were more careful after that.

Brother and sister growing up, loving each other, through so many tough times. We protected each other from hunger, deep poverty, and abuse. We had our first communion and confirmation together. Once we were in school, we were in school plays together; Luc once played baby Jesus.

He may have been younger than me, but I had so much respect for Luc. He got a job as an altar boy and would get up at the crack of dawn in the wintertime to help at mass. He made 25 cents a mass. The 25 cents were so important to him and he saved whatever he could - whatever my father didn't find and take away from him.

Luc was a small boy with blue eyes and curly blonde hair and big ears. When we weren't playing, he was very quiet and seemed to be deep in thought. That was his personality and his way of dealing with the abuse, the poverty, and hunger. His little savings was his way of looking to the future; of feeding himself; and preparing for tougher times, if such a thing was possible.

Luc could be so quiet, but he had a beautiful voice. My father's aunt was bedridden and very ill. Her bed was placed right in the landing so that when anyone went upstairs, she could see them and talk to them. She had a special fondness for my brother. She used to call Luc to come upstairs, calling him *mon petit merle*, my little blackbird, and she'd ask him to sing to her. Luc would sit on the landing - he never went up near her bed - and he'd sing to her and I liked to listen, too. In those days, a lot of people had Tuberculosis, which we called Consumption. It was highly contagious so that may have been the reason that Luc never went too near our aunt's bed.

My father would get a lung condition; pneumonia, called pleurisy at the time, that was not as serious as Consumption. Back in the day, when you had a chest cold or any ailment that had to do with your lungs, you'd put a mustard plaster mix on a clean white cotton cloth and place it on your chest. You'd stay in bed with the mustard plaster. Then you would get better.

One time, my mother had made this paste with dry mustard for my father and left it in a bowl on the kitchen counter. Well, Luc thought it was cake frosting because on the rare occasions that mom left the house and we had the ingredients, we would make the frosting. He took a spoon and started gobbling it down before I could stop him. It took a moment for him to realize that it wasn't frosting. It had gone down faster than he could taste it! Poor Luc's joy quickly turned to horror when he realized what he'd done! He spit it out, screaming, "It's burning me! Help, it's burning!" It was impossible not to laugh.

We both loved our sweets and we almost never had sweet treats. Just that bowl of old hard biscuits on the kitchen counter - a staple in our house - as if they could satisfy our hunger or our imagination! It was like eating wood.

Despite all of Luc's wonderful qualities, my father would abuse him. My father also abused our little brother, Jacques, despite liking him more than Luc. Jacques was my father's favorite son when he was little. Jacques' personality was not like the Smydes. Neither my brother nor my father was very proper with their sense of humor. One day, Jacques was sitting in Grandmother Smyde's kitchen, and he farted. She looked at him with "the eye" and asked, "What do you say when you do that?" Jacques looked at her with a mischievous smile and said, "Thank you." She threw him out.

Winter was the hardest because we were cold. When my sister Doris came to visit, she would have to sleep with us and she would pee in the bed. I would wake up wet and cold when she was there. Jacques also peed in bed sometimes. Because it was cold, we didn't manage to wash up all that much, so it was bad news when someone peed the bed.

Only in my bed with all my clothes on and heavy grey woolen blankets could I relax in the winter, and only when my sister Doris didn't pee in the bed. This became a normal part of our lives. This was our routine.

Chapter 5

Growing up poor, cold and hungry, with affluence as *part* of our family, and yet, not *in* our family, living with alcoholism and domestic violence, sometimes at gunpoint - these things were a way of life for us. Even so, we still managed to find the pleasures and treasures of childhood in the world around us.

For me, those pleasures and treasures increased when I made my first real friend in the world. I thought myself lucky when a little girl my age moved in with her family right next door to the little red house. Her name was Anne and she became my best friend. We were hardly two months apart in age, me being born in late September, and her in early December. Today, we still call each other on our birthdays. I was grateful that God placed Anne right next door to me. Before Anne's family moved next door, my father's aunt and uncle lived there, and their children, my cousins, were grown.

Anne and her family had moved into the village from her grandparents' farm in the hills. I saw Anne for the first time, coming out of her house from the side door. When she spotted me watching her, she stopped, and the first thing she said was, "Do you wanna play?" And then she added, "My name's Anne - what's yours?" I was so happy!

Maybe Luc felt the same way about his friend Gerard next door. All of us, together with Jacques, would all play bows and arrows, climb trees, pick hazelnuts, and throw rocks at each other. There were always rocks in my pockets! Occasionally, one of us would get hit in the head and be a bloody mess.

We loved to play in the big sandpit near our house. It was on government property and the sand helped with the snow on the road in the wintertime. We got caught lots of times but never got in serious trouble - we were just some poor kids playing in the sand piles, doing no harm.

Luc had a little pocket knife, and we would find pieces of wood to carve into arrows and pistols and play cowboys and Indians. We'd run around playing with trucks and tricycles. I can still hear the echoes of their laughter; so much laughter when we played.

Anne and I also played "Ladies" with our moms' high-heeled shoes and dresses. I was a tomboy, but also the designer and the decorator, loving fashion and make-up - especially red lipstick and nail polish. We had a sweet but tough relationship. Anne had grown up on a farm with brothers and was physically very strong. She was good at protecting me, as well as beating me up. She was taller than I was and when I did something that she didn't like, she would easily beat me. My only defense was to fall on the ground - which was all pebbles and hurt like heck – and hold my breath as if I was dead and not breathing anymore.

At this point, Anne would get so upset and yell, "Mom! Mom! Please come out, I think I killed Gaetane!" Her mom would come out, take one look and say, "She's not dead. Stop it, both of you." And that was the end of that - until next time. This is how I got back at Anne, time and time again. It never got old yet, somehow, she never anticipated it. I didn't have the physical strength to hit her back, so this holding-my-breath tactic would really scare her into not hitting me for a while.

We picked blueberries, strawberries, and raspberries during the summer, though we were very afraid of the wild bears that also foraged for these special fruits. We were more afraid of being hungry ourselves than being eaten by hungry bears.

One day, Anne decided that she wanted to go visit her grandparents on their farm. They lived miles from the village, somewhere in the mountains. I wasn't sure that this was a good idea, but there was no use in trying to tell Anne that. So, we set out on a journey down the road through the mountains to Anne's grandparents' farm. The worst part is, we knew we wouldn't have gotten permission, so we didn't tell anyone; we just took off. Even if we didn't say it out loud to each other, we knew it could be dangerous and that we were on an adventure. Anne said that she knew where she was going and even if that was true, we began to realize at some point that there were a lot of mountains and a variety of wildlife between us and that farm.

We walked for hours towards her grandparents' farm, singing *Frere Jacques, Au Clair de la Lune,* and all the church songs we knew. We picked violets for our mothers and everything seemed to be just fine until, suddenly, we got scared. Anne had grown up with fear; lots of it. It wasn't unusual for her to be afraid. Her mother was afraid of just about anything that moved: the wind, the rain, thunderstorms. She taught her children to be fearful as well. Most of all, she taught her children to be afraid of the police. Her mother made her children petrified of the police. I guess it was her way of keeping all those children in line, threatening them with the idea that the police would come if they were bad and would take them away forever. I don't think Anne ever knew where the police would take her, and it didn't matter. She was afraid of them, so it was a very effective parenting device on the part of her mother.

As we walked with our huge bouquets of wilting violets, neither of us sang anymore. We were walking along the road, but there were no houses or people in sight and hadn't been for quite some time. One car had passed us by with a woman driver, but that was the only car, and she had kept on driving and we had kept on walking. Anne was convinced that we would arrive at her grandparents any minute now and we would be safe, laughing at how silly we were to be so afraid.

That would have been the perfect ending, but that's not how it went. We were on this little road, but really, we were deep in the forest, and we both started to cry. We imagined big white bears behind every tree - big white bears that were going to eat us! Anne was crying that the police were going to come and that she would go to jail or somewhere else horrible. We knew that we were totally lost. We knew we were in trouble.

In the meantime, back in town, our absence had been noticed and our mothers were looking everywhere for us. They had the whole town looking, too. Somehow, the woman in the car who'd seen us earlier, had heard about our disappearance and told our mothers where she'd last seen us.

Back in the wilds, along the lonely road, Anne and I were still terrified, unaware that there was a rescue on its way, still crying, when suddenly a car appeared. Even if there would be police involved, we were determined to flag the car down and explain that we were lost and needed to get home - unnecessary, as it turned out, because who was in the car but our very own mothers! Although they were happy to find us, they were very unhappy with us and we were punished, of course.

"You're going to jail," Anne's mother told her, and smacked her right there on the old dusty road, not even waiting until she got Anne home. Anne screamed and carried on as her mother smacked her. For me, I received the usual punishment: not being able to play with friends or go outside. I was desolate because that's what I lived for. It was quite the day - one that we never forgot or repeated.

After our punishment ended, we decided to stay close to home. I didn't have many toys, so we would cut out large cardboard boxes and design houses, building a frame and cutting out windows and doors to create rooms inside for my old dolls. Shortly after Christmas, which was the only time we received any toys or gifts, the toys would break, and then we just played with cardboard.

Anne and I would also play dress-up and make lots of mud pies. To this day, Anne is the best person I know at making real pies. And we would play marbles together, though Anne was longer-fingered and would win. She would smile each time she won; smile because she was very mischievous and very good-hearted at the same time.

Anne had a little sister, Angelique, who was killed by a car while crossing the street in front of her house. Anne ran to my house, crying, "My sister! My little sister was killed by a car!" It was the only road, but it was often empty, so a child might not realize the danger. Little Angelique had seen her brother across the street and called his name. He yelled at her, "Don't cross the street!" but she had crossed it anyway.

Anne wanted me to stay at her house with her during this hard time, so I asked my mother if I could stay with Anne. My mother didn't seem to like the idea that the coffin would be in the house, but she allowed me to stay there. While the coffin was there, Anne would often go up to it and touch her sister. It was a very quiet, sad time. The body was laid out in their living room. It was the first time I had seen a dead person. Angelique had beautiful curls and lay so very still in that little white coffin. She looked pretty and clean, and at peace with the angels. If that was death - maybe it wasn't such a scary thing, after all.

Chapter 6

Because Anne and I were the same age, we started school together. In those days, there was no kindergarten, so we started first grade together with the nuns as our teachers. Anne was feisty and got into trouble. I became an honor student and did my best to never come under the scrutiny of the nuns. In fact, the nuns loved me because I was so eager to be a smart and obedient pupil.

Beginning school at age six was the most beautiful time of my childhood, aside from Christmas, of course. I started school though I didn't turn six until late September. My mom bought me a school bag, pencils, and a notebook. I was proud of my school bag! It was brown and real leather, which smelled wonderful. The bag had space on the front for my name, which was the first time I saw my name written anywhere besides the gift tags from Santa. What a delight that was! I also loved my pencil box because it had a cover that slid open and closed. I played with that pencil box a lot, sliding it open and then sliding it closed. It's a wonder that it didn't break! It never ceased to amaze me. I especially loved the touch and feel of the pencils inside.

I loved to write. I loved homework, which we did by candlelight. My favorite task was writing the alphabet in cursive. School was such a treat! My life was suddenly filled with erasers and wooden rulers and I was on top of the world. I felt like the most important person when I was at school. Somehow, I knew that I was going to have fun and be happy in school. I didn't feel poor when I was in school. I was a person, just like any other person; someone who God loved because He had bestowed this gift called school on me. Yes, I would be in my little dress that my mother had made, which I wished was cleaner than it was, but it was all I had, and it didn't really seem to matter when I was at school.

The school had nuns and secular teachers. The nuns were a delight to me. I still can see them in their outfits. They smelled so clean, and they had nice hands. I noticed these things because they were important to me. They were a sign of being educated and part of the clean people in the world.

One nun, Soeur Veronique, loved me and I loved her. She had a long navy-blue dress and a white headpiece. I wanted so much to see if she had any hair under that headpiece but was afraid that it might be a sin to ask. I would look closely at her to try and figure out how she put on her habit. It looked very complicated but then, she had dedicated herself to God and had to do many difficult things, so how difficult could it be to wear this habit for Him? Other kids said she was mean, but I didn't think so.

Oh my God, it was so easy and fun to learn! I soon discovered that I was a quick learner – maybe because I loved it so. That doesn't mean that it wasn't a challenge for me, but I welcomed the challenge; it was a positive force in my life. School became my refuge and because I was smart, I got noticed and received attention and acknowledgment. My hand was always up because I knew the answers, and I asked a lot of questions, too. I got the Medal of Honor time and time again. There was a large, medium, and small medal. I was in the top three categories every time. I was so proud!

I had friends in school and plays that I participated in. I was a very outgoing child and often had a crowd around me. I wanted to participate in everything! Being short, it was quite amazing that I even was good at playing basketball. We wore long navy-blue underwear under our short basketball skirts; the nuns made sure we wore our underwear.

Doris was in the next grade at the same school and, in contrast to me, she had a hard time with schoolwork. In fact, she'd beat me up on a regular basis because she was jealous of how well I did in school. I know I'm painting a dark picture of my sister. Doris was very intelligent and smart in her own way. We just had different gifts and one of mine was learning new things.

Along with writing, I also loved to read and pronounce new words. I first learned English in second grade. I loved learning English! The book that taught me English was called *Dick and Jane*. I loved the smell of the books and school supplies. You're probably imagining me going around school smelling everything from the pencils to the nuns, aren't you? Well, my senses were alive at school, so it's probably an accurate imagining. Even the little desks we sat at each day had their own texture and temperature. I loved everything about school.

When we started to learn about history and geography, I was excited and curious about how other people in the world lived. We learned that there were lots of other poor people besides us. And this was the part of school I didn't like so much; reading about the poor. *I* was poor. I didn't want to be reminded about being poor. School was a place where it didn't matter if I was poor. I was part of something that felt very rich to me. Even on my first day of school, I knew I never wanted leave.

Luc started school the year after me and did very well. We helped each other study and were even in school plays together. However, our little brother Jacques had the worst time learning to read and he struggled with math. He had a hard time remembering any of his studies. As a result, he was left back in every grade from first to fifth. My mother spent so much time with him, trying to teach him to read and write, and he just couldn't grasp it. I think my Mom was afraid that he would be illiterate like my father, no matter how she and the teachers tried to help him. In those days, there weren't any special programs for children with learning disabilities.

Despite Jacques' difficulty with reading and math, he had a talent for music. He could pick up any instrument and play it – a guitar, anything – he was like a musical genius with his natural ability. My mother had a soft spot in her heart for musicians because of my father's family. My father thought music was a waste of time, and Jacques was never allowed an opportunity to fulfill his gift. None of us were.

Snowstorms continued all winter and it would snow for days. In the morning, going to school, we breathed icicles on the scarves covering our mouths.

Going to school with a lunch packed for me made it even more special. I'd get up in the morning really looking forward to the day. But one of my first thoughts was, "How will I eat today?" There was never enough food at home and I was hungry. I was so hungry in the little red house, I even stole my brother Luc's baby bottle and drank it. I'd steal it, hide under the bed, and drink it as fast as I could. It was not easy to suck the milk out! We couldn't afford real baby bottles, so my mother used an old bottle that originally contained a sweet, brown liquid called Fletcher's Castoria, which was a remedy given to babies when they were constipated. My mother added a big, red rubber nipple to the bottle.

There I was, hiding under my mother's bed trying to suck the milk down as quickly as I could, with baby Luc crying because I'd stolen his bottle. Seeing my mother's feet coming into the room as I peered out from under the bed, I would swallow the milk as fast as I could because I knew she was looking for the bottle. The taste of the rich, sweet and warm Carnation milk formula is a sensory memory that remains with me.

Bringing lunch to school felt like we had all the food in the world, though we really didn't. The lunch my mother packed would just be a little sandwich of bananas, eggs, or canned meat. For dinner, my mother would bake biscuits with flour and water and cook the deer meat that my father had butchered. Deer meat smelled terrible to me and the biscuits were so hard we could hardly chew them. It was during this time that I decided to steal food. My stomach hurt often, but on this day, there was something about my hunger that I just couldn't ignore.

There were two grocery stores in town, but one belonged to my mother's relatives, so I wasn't going to steal food from there; I went to the other one. I walked right in. I could see the counter where the butcher was helping his customers with fresh cuts of meat for their lunches and dinners. I could see the aisles. I knew exactly where everything was; all lined up and stacked with so many delicious things.

To the left of the butcher was the cash register and counter where all the candy was - the peppermint candies were two for a penny, and the bubble gum, too. On the other side was the aisle with all the cakes and canned goods. I walked right down that aisle. Walking down that aisle, there was no thinking or choosing. When you're that hungry, the only thing you think about is food and it doesn't matter what it is. I grabbed a little yellow cake in a cellophane wrapper on one of the lower shelves and quickly hid it under my dress, tucked safely where I hoped it would stay until I could get out of the market. I did it quickly, glancing around me to be sure no one was watching. All would have been fine, but the grocer's wife spotted me. She just happened to be coming down the stairs from their upstairs apartment over the store; she must have had her eye on me. There was no doubt that she'd seen me take the little cake. I could feel the panic rising in me and I knew that I needed to get out of there as quickly as possible!

As I turned to go, she called out to me with a loud, "Hey!" Startled, I turned back to her and the cake, which I'd tucked away so discreetly, somehow managed to work its way out of my dress and land with a thud right on the floor in front of me. There was the cold, hard evidence staring me right in the face. I looked down at the cake and then up at the grocer's wife. I began to shake, and my stomach turned over; this time, from fear. I was petrified about what might happen to me. I couldn't move.

She came rushing over and yelled, "You little thief! Get out of here and don't ever come back!" Well, that got me moving. I was only too happy to escape her accusations and all those customers who were suddenly watching me. I escaped; I ran and didn't stop until I got home.

Once home, I thought and thought about what I'd done. I felt ashamed, but I realized that she called me a thief because I *was* a thief. Who would the storekeeper's wife tell? My mother? My grandmother? The police? I was a criminal and I would probably go to jail if she told on me. It didn't matter that I was hungry and yet, I wondered why she couldn't see that. Why couldn't she see that I only stole the cake because I was starving?

After some time went by and I was still home, still safe, I realized that she hadn't told anyone because the police hadn't come. No one was any the wiser about what I'd done. I knew I could never go back into that store again, but if I had money, maybe I could go back in and that storekeeper's wife wouldn't turn me away.

I went back to the store and sat down on the steps, like a little homeless child. I needed to figure out a way that I could buy food. I asked myself what I could do to buy some food, and how much money would I need? I was so young, but I was going to figure this out. It was then that I had the most wonderful idea. I can still feel the cold creeping up the back of my bare legs from the cement steps, as the idea came to me.

I decided that all I needed was 100 pennies. After all, that was a lot of money. *If I had 100 pennies, I would be rich and would be able to eat and buy new shoes.* I thought of the shoes because I had a lot of cardboard in my shoes at the time. I realized that, if I wasn't so shy, I could ask 100 hundred big people for 1 penny each, and then I would never be hungry again!

As I sat on those steps, I pictured the actress, Elizabeth Taylor. She was the richest person my little mind could conjure up. I wanted to be her, so I could buy something to eat. I never asked any of the big people for money as I sat on those steps that day. All I could do was dream. I left the store that day, not one penny richer and still painfully hungry.

I made myself a promise never to tell anyone about the day I tried to steal the cake. It was my secret; a secret that I was convinced was the only thing keeping me out of jail. I held that story within myself for years; believing I was a thief and unworthy. For the rest of my life, anytime anything was missing from anywhere, though I had nothing to do with it, I panicked because I was afraid that someone would point to me and say, "You! You're the thief!"

With this desperate hunger going on in my life, it was so strange that, in school, we were required to help feed poor children in Africa and India. The teachers gave us little empty paper banks with the picture of a hungry child on each one. They called them "the pagan babies." The pagan babies had no food because they were poor, and it was up to us to help them. We had to bring this little bank back to school in one week's time with money in it. This would mean that we had done our duty to help feed those children.

But I couldn't bring myself to ask anyone for a penny for these poor children. When I brought the little bank back to school with no pennies in it, it was clear that people thought I had no compassion for these poor children in faraway countries. In the meantime, four children in my family were starving and no one noticed; no one seemed to care. I wondered if it occurred to any of those teachers that *we* needed to be fed, too, that there were hungry children right in front of their eyes.

Where were our little paper banks with our pictures on it?

Chapter 7

Growing up with hunger, I was grateful for our neighbor, Laura, an angel who lived right next door to us. She was my mother's very good friend; my mother talked to Laura often and about things she never shared with anyone else. Laura would feed Luc and me from time to time. My brother and I would go to see her when we smelled her cooking. We never asked her for food; we just showed up and somehow, she knew why.

In Canada, lunch was more like dinner and at night we had supper, so there were two big meals. Laura's kitchen was ready for either one. She made *ployes*, traditional Acadian pancakes made with buckwheat, and served them with butter. How I loved butter! And she had meat and vegetables and homemade pork and baked beans.

There was a big rocking chair in Laura's kitchen, and Luc and I would sit in it together, or we'd sit on the steps that led upstairs, and we'd just wait. Laura would feed us before she ate with her family. We never told anyone. Even Laura never told her family that she fed us all those years. Her children were either out playing or watching TV. Yes, Laura's family even had a television!

Sometimes, we'd watch TV with them: *Gunsmoke, Route 66, Have Gun Will Travel,* and *the Lawrence Welk Show.* These were all American channels, and though we didn't understand much English, we watched. The first time we saw Elvis was on *The Ed Sullivan Show* at their house. The only entertainment we had at our house was a little radio from Grandma Smyde that we would gather around and listen to in the winter, and we could only use it when we had money for electricity, which was rare.

Laura's husband was a logger like my father and cursed a lot. But he was a good man who provided for his family. He was funny, too. Laura and her husband seemed to do well for themselves. I know this because they had plenty of food and they were able to buy soda when soda first came out. They were both smokers and even had a little machine that made cigarettes. Grandma Smyde told us that women weren't supposed to smoke, and my mother never smoked one cigarette. This little machine sat on the dining room table. Luc and I would make cigarettes for them when we were there.

The best part was knowing this woman loved and cared about us — she had a wonderful smile when she saw us coming into her kitchen. She was a kind and gentle soul. I believe that she was a part of our lives for a reason. Her love for us helped me believe in that other life, a better life.

I especially loved long summer days when Laura and my mother would bring us all to the river. It would be Laura, her two daughters, her son, my mother and my brothers, and sometimes an extra friend. We didn't have too many swimming days in Canada, so on the days that we could swim, we went to the river and had picnics.

Mom would bring the big brown baby carriage for the little ones, so they didn't have to walk, or for the ones who didn't even walk yet. That carriage went bumping along on the rocky path to the river with all of us walking beside it. It was a good long mile to the river. For us children, it felt like twenty miles, and though we were excited on the walk there, coming back was another story; it felt even longer then!

We often stayed the whole day by the river. Though this day was a glorious escape, I didn't really like the water. It was very cold and there were a lot of rocks that hurt my toes. I slipped on those rocks constantly. On the long walk home and after swimming all day, my feet hurt. The sun bothered my eyes and made me cry. My mother said it was because I had blue eyes. But, the best part about the river was playing games with my friends. I loved the trees and I loved climbing with the boys.

And mom seemed happy with her friend, Laura. She laughed, and they had long, deep conversations together. These were such happy times for her. She loved nature and there was something about her that was different by the river. For that reason alone, I loved being there with her and willingly suffered the cold water, rocks, the sun in my eyes, and the long walk home.

And then came Communion: The Age of Reason. I was only seven years old, but this was now a time that you no longer did childish things. It was also a time when you were aware that you'd committed sins. Mom told us about the three different kinds of sin: original, venial, and mortal. Original sin was the sin you were born with, and the only person spared this sin was Jesus' mother, Mary. I struggled with Mary, wondering how anyone could be that holy. Isn't there such a thing as being *too* holy? On the other extreme, venial sin was just a little sin that could be forgiven; I was okay with that one. Lastly, there was mortal sin - and that was the one that would take you straight to Hell. Oh, boy. Stories about those sins were scary and it was difficult to comprehend that there was no forgiveness, ever.

My very religious Grandmother Smyde was very involved in our lives as Luc and I were being prepared to make our first communion and confirmation. This was a serious time of life. My father was not involved at all – of course, he wasn't. He never went to church. My mother was raised to never curse, smoke or drink. Mom taught us to pray well before school began and now, she was teaching us prayers to get us ready to receive communion, and teaching us the meaning behind the prayers, too.

Everything was a mystery to me. The Trinity was a mystery, so I never questioned it. Well, I might have questioned it in my head. I mean, *how can one God be three people?* I was frustrated with what I called the "holy stuff." Mom told us that it took faith to believe. But what was faith? How did you get it?

I stopped questioning the mysteries after learning about sin and what happens to people when they sin. Still, as we learned about the Ten Commandments, "Honor your parents" was a big one for me that left me full of questions I couldn't answer and was afraid to ask. After all, all the "proper" people believed; they had "faith," and because they did, God loved them. So, that was it for me. I would honor my parents no matter what.

On the upside, I was very excited to wear a beautiful white communion dress! It felt like a wedding dress. Remember, I was such a tomboy; according to my mother, frilly things were wasted on me. But this was different because it was expected. It was a rite of passage and it was truly special.

My sister Doris had already received her first communion. To her, a frilly dress was nothing new. I was delighted to be wearing a dress in church because the church was a special place - it was where God loved me just like all those other people who were the educated and proper. It was around this Communion time that my mother told me to never let my brothers or the boys in the neighborhood touch me in "*that* way." I was curious about the things she said and yet, I was afraid to ask questions. Luc and I shared a bed with the rest of our siblings, and there was never any "touching" going on. Being "touched" in inappropriate ways by adults was an issue that was never brought up, and my young mind still did not question the things my father did with me privately; I was honoring him; wasn't that the right thing to do?

My relationships with my brother and the other young boys were truly innocent. I was still playing with boys and I loved to take my shirt off in the summer, just like the boys did. Why was it any different for me? But there came a time during the Holy Communion process that I was not allowed to take my shirt off anymore.

Chapter 8

The day came that we were evicted from the Little Red House because my parents couldn't pay the rent. I was eight years old when we moved into the gray house down the street. The walls of the gray house were made of cardboard; literally, cardboard. Like the little red house, the gray house had no running water or toilet inside, just a water pump and an outhouse. It was bigger, though, with an extra bedroom. All three bedrooms were upstairs.

My brother Luc and I became very close in those years living in the gray house. We were the oldest children ever since Doris was sent away, so we did all the chores together to help our mother. If my mother needed water to wash clothes, Luc and I got the water for her. We would pump water outside. In the winter, we'd stand on a block of ice to pump water for the house. We were so small that we carried the pail between the two of us, one on each side of the pail, and it would take so many trips to fill up what we called a large boiler. All winter, Luc and I chopped wood together for the wood stove.

We were very poor living in that house. Thankfully, people gave us boxes of used clothes, so my mother didn't have to make so many clothes anymore. And we were so excited when my Uncle George and Aunt Debbie gave us a refrigerator! It had one door and a little compartment for a freezer. For the first time in my life, we didn't have to put our food out in the winter to freeze.

But our little refrigerator was often empty. We were still poor, and the hunger was terrible. We didn't live next door to Laura anymore, and Luc and I missed her cooking. Though Luc and I would go for the summer to stay with my father's family, where there was plenty of food, we lived with hunger the rest of the year. We ate a lot of deer meat, or other wild game meat, not the real meat that I loved.

This is when Luc started looking in the garbage for food, and I would go with him. Mostly, all he found were frozen hot dogs and apple cores, but he'd share what he found with me. His fingers and toes would nearly get frostbitten. When we got home, he'd put his feet in the oven to warm them up. We both did, even as we cried through the burning and stinging of our cold feet coming back to life.

Meanwhile, my father hardly worked, and the babies kept coming. My poor mother was again pregnant. My sister Antoinette was born next. She was born on my birthday. It was a beautiful sunny day and I was outside when our neighbor came by. She had a daughter who was also named Gaetane and I thought that was a good omen because she was very pretty and kind.

This neighbor was always chewing on something. I finally had to ask my mother, "What is it that she's chewing?" My mother told me, "Rice. Raw rice." I tried chewing it once, and it was like chewing rocks! I don't know why, but she chewed it. So, there was our neighbor on that beautiful sunny day, chewing on her rice as usual, and she is the one who told me, "You have a new sister."

I was very excited! When my mom came home with her; I held her right away and changed her diaper. I was a little mother to her. She was the most beautiful little girl I'd ever seen with lots and lots of very dark hair. Her eyes were brown but her hair and coloring were like my father's. To this day, she looks just like him.

My brother Jacques didn't like this new baby at all. He would call her ugly. But she wasn't; she was beautiful. He would hide behind a chair and sulk about Antoinette. He was intent on believing that she interfered with his place in the family and how much affection he'd receive if she weren't around. And I had to admit, I felt much the same way. Jacques was no longer the baby of the family, and, suddenly, I was no longer my father's favorite.

My father fell in love with baby Antoinette. Without a word, I was replaced. My whole world turned upside down. I felt jealous and sick. My father had told me I was special; that I was the most beautiful, the smartest, and the nicest one in the family. He had brainwashed me into believing that. But now he was completely distracted by my sister. I felt so discarded. If I could be so easily replaced, there had to be something wrong with me. I truly believed that the change in my father was because I did something wrong. I spent a long time trying to figure out what I did, what was wrong with me, and how I could change things back to the way they had been.

In my child's mind, I felt tortured most of the time. I just couldn't understand any of it. I went on crying and getting headaches. As I look back on this time, I realize that I found a way to survive. Ironically, it was up to me to take care of my sister, this little girl, who had replaced me in my father's eyes and affections. It's a wonder she survived and that I was able to love her despite my jealousy.

Antoinette was still a little baby in diapers when my next sister, Grace, was born. She was born in July in the afternoon at my Grandmother Smyde's house. I was 10 and had no idea about babies or where they came from. For some reason, we thought the Indians would bring this baby. The Indians were part of the Iroquois tribe and they didn't live that far from us; just in the next town over on a reservation. But we never saw any Indians; instead, we saw the old doctor coming with his big black bag - Doctor Cyr.

We were afraid. We expected to hear mom screaming and dying any minute, but all that happened was Doctor Cyr left the house and Grandma Smyde came out and said that it was a little girl. We were so relieved and wanted to see the baby, but we were not allowed to go near her because we had germs.

My sister Grace was tiny and very cuddly; a quiet baby with dark hair and brown eyes shaped like our mom's eyes. I loved to rock baby Grace in the rocking chair. I took care of her like she was my own baby. But my father never fell in love with her the way he had fallen in love with me or Antoinette, and he was cruel to her.

As Grace grew, she was a happy little girl who would never hurt a fly. When my father wasn't around, she had a very easy-going personality. When he was around, I could tell she was scared because Grace would be like the wallpaper; she blended in. She had this little high-pitched voice and loved to sit in the rocking chair, rocking, and singing. My father would hit her just passing by. He was a cruel, cruel man. She eventually stopped singing and was quiet. Because of this, I never got to know her well.

My mother had my sister Jacqueline right after Grace. We called her Jackie. She was blond with blue eyes. I changed her diapers and held her when she cried. She was skinny and tall, with long arms Her little legs were so skinny that I was afraid I'd hurt her.

Right after Jackie was born, my mother was pregnant again. I hated to see her in maternity dresses by that time because it meant that there would be another child, another mouth to feed; that I would have to help her and not be able to play. If it was a girl, it also meant that I might have to compete for my father's love again, too. That was in the back of my mind, but it never stopped me from loving and caring for my sisters. Jackie was attached to me from a very young age.

After Jackie, arrived Eileen. She was a big baby, eight pounds, with curly brown hair, and brown eyes, and fat baby legs. Eileen was quiet and ate a lot, not that we had much to eat. Grace, Jackie, and Eileen were all born while living in the gray house.

School remained my favorite thing in the world. We had the same circle of friends that we'd had at the little red house, except by then I also had school friends, like Julie who lived on the other end of town, and the other kids who took the bus together. Sometimes, we played together, but most of the time I helped my mother take care of all the babies. There were at least two babies in diapers; cotton diapers in those days. I had to wash all those dirty diapers. I helped my mother wash all the clothes, too.

The gray house belonged to a man named Jock Meraux, an old man who lived like a recluse way in the back of the gray house in his own separate shack near a little shed. He had never married, but he'd had a son who he'd raised. His son had gone off to Montreal to become an educated man. Jock was tall, and it was easy to spot him riding his bicycle around town. He made his living from renting out the cardboard house to my family and he was a bootlegger, selling American cigarettes and alcohol. As a bootlegger, he had a place in his shed where he would hide his contraband; that is when he wasn't drinking it himself. He got drunk regularly.

My father smoked American cigarettes, so he would send me to Jock to buy them - Chesterfields, they were. I had to go, and I would ask Anne to come with me because I was afraid of being around Jock, and I knew Anne would protect me. Anne was still my dear and close friend and, as pre-teens, we had all sorts of ideas about how to get into trouble together.

Jock had an old wood stove and had a fire going in his shack. One day, Anne and I went there when my father hadn't sent us. We lied about my father wanting cigarettes, and while Jock was in the shed getting his illegal smokes for my father, we stirred up that fire, threw ashes on the floor, and ran away.

This happened a couple times until, one day, he was waiting for us. We sent him for cigarettes and he came out with a gun instead and started yelling and chasing us away. As we were running away in the fields of tall grass, Anne fell. I wasn't strong like Anne, but I was faster. I was running like hell, screaming, and then I heard her scream, "Please Mr. Jock, I won't do it again!"

I looked back, and he was standing over her, so tall with that big gun pointed right at her. I ran for help so fast and I told my mother, who told Anne's mother. Old Jock was probably just threatening us and wouldn't really shoot anyone, but it was better not to take that chance. Anne didn't get killed, thankfully - our mothers saw to that.

You'd think we'd learned our lesson, wouldn't you? Not us. Even after the gun scare, we didn't let up on the old man. Old Jock had a crab apple tree and he had it fenced in to protect it from people who might try to steal his apples. Everyone in town knew that no one was allowed take the apples, so of course, Anne and I had to try and often, we succeeded. Once again, Jock came out with a gun to scare off any kid who touched his apples.

But stealing apples turned out to be a short-lived adventure. We left poor Jock alone once we started smoking cigarettes, and Luc started smoking, too. When my father would get work as a lumberjack, Grandma Smyde would come every day to visit, checking on how we were all doing. I made sure she never saw any of us smoking. After Eileen was born, my parents fought about needing a bigger house with more of the necessities. We were so many people in our cardboard house.

Chapter 9

My father's family were known for their womanizing, bootlegging, drinking, and fighting. I thought Grandpa Martelle was the devil himself. But my Grandma Martelle had nothing to do with the goings-on that my grandpa was known for. My grandma was another angel in my life. My brother Luc and I, and sometimes our siblings, spent our summers at their little house from the time I was about 8, and Grandma Martelle became the love of my life during these early years. She was so different from my Grandma Smyde, and it was here that I was truly loved and nurtured.

"La belle Gaetane avec les beaux yeux claire," (The beautiful Gaetane with such clear eyes). *"Elle est vite et intelligente,"* she would say about me (She is quick and smart). It was wonderful to be seen and spoken of that way! She never noticed one single thing wrong about me. She was happy to see me. I could tell that, in her eyes, I could do no wrong.

I had other angels in my life, but it was from her most of all that I learned about unconditional love and this was a very important foundation for me; in fact, she is the reason I grew up with the strength and resilience that I had and the major reason I thrived. She bestowed her love on me and Luc so generously and to my dying day, she will be alive in my heart and deeply rooted in my spirit.

Her hair was permed and oh-so neat. Her hands were the softest and most gentle hands I'd ever seen or felt. She wore a black onyx ring on her middle right finger, its dark oval looking so dramatic on her delicate white hands. She was a musician. She played the violin; something she gave up, as a promise to God. I still don't know what the promise was or why

God would want her to give up her gift of music. I would have loved to hear her play.

My grandma was also literate and bilingual. I loved to listen to her read to me. We never had any books in our own house because "books were for lazy people," my father would say. My mother had nothing to read to us until we started coming home with school books. I also loved to hear my grandma speak this foreign language called "English." It sounded so different from our French language.

Grandma Martelle was a great cook. I looked forward to the doughnuts she made us, still hot with melting sugar on top. Her doughnuts were heaven to a hungry child! And she was so clever, making the doughnut holes with a bottle cap.

I can almost taste them, so fresh and hot, how the sugar was scratchy and coated my lips as I bit into them. The sugar melted almost immediately and in no time, I was a sticky mess – mouth, hands, and even my dress got covered in the melted sugar. I didn't care. There was nothing better than Grandma's doughnuts! Plus, you could get covered in the sticky, gooey sugar and Grandma Martelle didn't care. She'd wipe you down and clean you up and that was that.

She cooked amazing meals with pork, chicken, beef, and golden potatoes. She'd roast chicken in a roaster pan in the old wood stove oven and she made fresh vegetables. Everything smelled and tasted so good. She also had canned food; eating tomatoes from the can was a special treat. I was never hungry when my brother and I were there for the summers.

If that wasn't enough to make her my special Grandmother, Grandma Martelle was often a conspirator with us. Such adventures we had! She'd take some of Grandpa's Coca-Cola from its green glass bottle and give it to me and my brother. It was our little secret. My Grandfather liked his Coca-

Cola and never wanted to give us any. Those bubbles went right up our noses because we had to drink it quickly! Grandma also took change out of Grandpa's pockets, especially when he was drunk and sleeping, which was often. She'd give us the nickels and dimes and we'd buy candy, of course. She was priceless! My grandpa never seemed to notice that his pockets were any lighter; he wasn't as poor as my father because he was a bootlegger.

Despite all the fun we had at my grandfather's expense, Grandpa Martelle was not to be taken lightly. I was afraid of him. He was so different than our sweet Grandma and yet so like my father and the men I was familiar with in our little part of the world.

My Grandma had married him when she was young - only 15 - and I often thought she just didn't know any better, being so young, and alone. Her mother had died and her only living relative, her older sister, had moved away to America; She talked about her sister with such love and pride. I wonder if my grandmother knew what she was getting into when she married into the Martelle family.

Grandma would protect us from grandpa as best as she could; she wouldn't end up hiding or crying like my mother. She distracted grandpa, so we could hide. Grandpa Martelle was not just scary; he was mean to my grandmother. He'd yell at her and insult her, and she was like his servant. If he called, she'd better run, run, run, to see what he wanted. He treated her like a slave. I thought he was the devil, especially when he was drunk. I can still smell the stale beer and cigarette smoke that he carried around with him. I was so happy when he was passed out drunk, but he ran that house and all the different people who came around.

Bootlegging was this whole operation and way of life. First, there was a lookout for the police with him. Living with the constant fear of being discovered as a bootlegger, he kept the alcohol and American cigarettes in these tiny, cramped places that weren't easy for an adult to reach. A big, burly police officer would have had a terrible time trying to get to Grandpa's stash. As a result, Grandpa would often instruct my brother Luc to go into the hiding places where he kept all those cigarettes and alcohol. Being younger, Luc was a little smaller than me, and he could crawl into the smallest spaces.

Most of the bootlegged items were hidden behind a door that was above the porch. Another hiding place was in the shed out back, below the shed floor. Grandpa would take me out to the shed and remove some of the floor planks and tell me to climb down to retrieve the alcohol he'd hidden there. It terrified me to go down there. I cried, but he made me do it anyway. After that, I hid from him whenever he was around because I never wanted to be forced to go down into that dark and scary place.

The people who would come around my grandparents' house for the bootlegged alcohol and cigarettes were also scary, but I saw that this bootlegging money came in handy as it was used to support the family and there was plenty of food. My grandfather would also take in handicapped and homeless people, so there were constantly these strange people around. He was abusive to them, yelling at them and hitting them, but he loved their disability checks. He had these poor individuals working for him or doing something for him, like crawling into those hiding places where he hid his stash from the police.

The furnishings of the little house were sparse; just some rocking chairs around the pot-bellied stove that provided all the heat for the house. Mostly, there were a lot of big ashtrays with the push buttons that opened to reveal the smelly, smoky hiding place for all the butts that were extinguished. The ashtrays were everywhere because everyone who stopped by — the bootleggers, musicians, and loggers — all chain-smoked. It was a house that had a party going on, especially on Saturday nights.

At night, the men got drunk and there would be these women who would come and go. My grandfather was fond of these women and spent a lot of time with them. I didn't understand what was happening for years, but it hurt that he could be so mean and nasty to my beautiful grandmother and yet was very friendly towards these other women who were complete strangers.

Despite the drinking and bootlegging, Grandpa Martelle went to church every Sunday at nine in the morning and expected everyone else to go with him. He was brought up going to church by his mother. There was this contrast of religion and sin in that house, especially with my grandpa's devout mother living right there with him. My Great Grandmother Martelle would sit in her rocking chair, praying over her rosary beads. She prayed so much, she used to wear out the beads. She hung her rosaries on the mirror of her dresser, so they were only a prayer away. She was a like a saint as she sat in her rocking chair and prayed, no matter what was going on around her. She looked ancient to me, dressed in black, wearing white pearls that highlighted her beautiful white hair, holding her rosary with her right pointer finger sticking straight out. I never knew what happened to that finger that made it unable to bend.

Her mouth was moving in prayer. I often wondered, what was there to pray so much about? Had she committed some horrible sin that required an endless asking for forgiveness? Was she praying for those around her who were so sinful? Her one daughter was married to a nice man from an educated, professional family. One of her sons had gotten an education and worked in a convent and educated his family. All her other sons were musicians and lumberjacks and bootleggers. Maybe it was for their redemption she was praying nonstop? Maybe there was a lot to pray about, so better to be safe than sorry.

This importance of religion was something my grandfather was raised with. Going to church on Sundays was a strict part of the routine, and Sundays were different than any other day of the week. Grandpa Martelle would get dressed up in his only suit, and my grandma was expected to dress up as well. Before she did, though, she would have to clean up "the party mess" from the previous Saturday night. One Sunday morning as I went into the kitchen, all I could smell was the heavy odor of alcohol and cigarette smoke. There were lots of glasses that needed to be washed before we could go to church, and cigarette butts overflowing all the ashtrays.

When this mess was taken care of, grandma would get all dressed up, finishing off her outfit with one of the hats that Grandpa bought for her. Only then would we all go off to church with our great grandma and her rosary beads – and, of course, my cousins. How we loved spending time with our cousins all summer long!

My Aunt Dolly had nine children, and they all lived in a little shack on the property. Dolly was a musician - apparently, God hadn't asked her to give up her gift of music - so she was away and out of the house most of the time. Despite all her hard work, and though she had a TV show for a while, her family was still quite poor. There was little discipline when we visited there because my aunt was never home, so all of us kids were pretty much on our own and had a great time together.

When my older cousins were around, we heard things we'd never heard of before; what we called "dirty talk," because it was about sex. Luc and I would secretly call them "perverts," but we thought it was funny and learned a lot. We smoked cigarettes and played *Hide and Go Seek*. The girls had to watch out for the boy cousins when we played Hide and Go Seek, though, because they tried to touch us in places that were not allowed. But it was all very innocent and in my young mind, I still didn't realize that my father was the sickest pervert with how he would touch me.

My Aunt Dolly had nicknames for everyone she loved, and she loved us. Luc was *Souris*, or Mouse, because she said he was quick like a mouse and could move around quietly. Jacques was *Noir*, for his dark hair. For the life of me, I can't remember what she called me, which is odd because she had a nickname for everyone.

My sister Antoinette was nicknamed "doll face."

"You look just like your father, but you have such a doll face," she'd say. She'd also say, "He's so damned attractive, your father." Though my Aunt Dolly thought her brother, my father was handsome, there was no love lost between them. My father hated Dolly. I don't know why; maybe he was jealous. He would often say, "If I see her on the street, I'll run her over with my car and kill her." Killing was his solution for everything.

My father also hated his father, who had been abusive to him and taken all his money from a young age. The only contact he had with the Martelles is when grandma would steal money from grandpa and send it to my father by mail. The only time I saw my father with his family was during Christmas visits. My father would just drop us off for the summer and was never around, even when we went off to church on Sundays. My father never went to church. After church, we'd come back, and grandma would make the best Sunday roast with brown potatoes. Grandpa Martelle was kind of nice to us on Sundays. He'd sit quietly in his rocking chair, still wearing his church suspenders. It was so different because on any other day he was a violent drunk. I guess on Sundays, "he rested."

Grandpa worked for potato farmers right across the border in Maine each fall, managing the living space for the workers. He hired children and adults as migrant workers to pick potatoes. School would close for two weeks for the fall harvest, and sometimes my brother and I would be among those children he hired. It didn't matter if we were 10 years old; we were expected to work as hard as the adults. My grandfather was a merciless boss.

The farming was such hard work but, from a child's perspective, I can still smell the earth, and feel the potatoes. I liked picking the potatoes out of the dark soil; it was soothing and something about it felt so rich to me. I got completely absorbed in the process. I often forgot how hard I was working for a wage I never saw.

"*La Cabane,*" The Shack, was the place where we lived for the season when we were picking potatoes. Most of the migrant workers lived in the shack, too. We slept together in the shack because there was nowhere else for anyone to sleep. This shack could be a very scary place. A lot of the laborers got drunk after being paid, and so would my grandpa.

The most horrible day came one year when I was back home with my family on a nice early June day, looking forward to spending the summer with grandma. A neighbor came to me and said that my Grandmother Martelle had "gone crazy" and had been taken to the "nut house." I was angry and upset and just cried and cried. I didn't want my Grandma Martelle to go crazy - I *needed* her! I couldn't lose the love of my life, my brightest angel, my pride and joy who I looked forward to seeing all year!

Apparently, she'd had a mental breakdown. It was a tragedy that will forever remain a mystery to me. She was a smart woman. What could have happened to her that was so upsetting that she couldn't handle or process it? She'd seemed to handle everything so well, even her abusive husband. Later, I learned that my grandma was treated with electric shock therapy. When she eventually came home, she was never the same. For me she was an angel in my life; she was a Savior, whether she knew it or not. Soon after, we stopped going to the Martelle house for the summer. What was the point of going, if my grandma wasn't there? We were hungry again.

Chapter 10

Growing up with this huge contrast between my mother's family and my father's family, I knew from a young age that I wanted to live like my mother's family, and not the way my father's family lived. I was smart and could see that educated people lived beautiful lives. I knew that if I studied and paid attention in school, I could educate myself and rise above the poverty and hunger. I'd had a vision at a young age when I was hungry and counting imaginary pennies. But I knew I could never beg for pennies; I had never been able to ask anyone for one single penny. School was my new vision. I was going to become educated and have a beautiful life.

Because school was easy and exciting for me and the teachers believed in me, and because I had been earning all those Medals of Honor since the first year I started school, I knew this vision would become a reality. I was just about to go into fifth grade when I came home from school one day and I overheard my parents talking about me and my brother Luc. They weren't even fighting; they were having a serious conversation. My father was sober, sitting across from my mother at the kitchen table. I heard the word "school" and I froze, standing there, holding my school bag tight with my arms wrapped around it like a hug. I had the best teacher at school. I loved her, her words and language, and her clothes, too. She spoke just like the Smydes did. She encouraged me, too. I wanted to be just like her. What was happening in the kitchen?

As I listened to my parents talk, I heard the worst news of my life. My father said they were going to take me out of school and keep me home "to help." Then my father added that

my brother Luc was going to go into lumberjack camp to learn how to strip the bark off the trees, which would help with "the money situation."

Then I heard my mother say, "I was educated and what did it do for me? All I do is change diapers." It sounded like it was my father's idea, but my mother was agreeing with him. I was horrified. What struck me first was if they took me out of school, I would become just like them! I wanted to scream, cry, and run all at the same time. It was not only the end of my vision; it was the end of my being able to learn. I was devastated. My parents had no money; they never had any money because my father said that he was "burnt out." It was us - the little kids - who were going to help them with their life of poverty, and they were willing to destroy our chance at a better life by taking away our education.

After overhearing that conversation between my parents, it was as if my brain left me. I began to fail as a student. Over the next couple of years, I went from being an A student to an F student. I couldn't read anymore. I couldn't remember anything. I became convinced that I was truly stupid. My belief system changed from being smart and an honor student to being stupid. One of the teachers who knew me said, "I don't understand why a girl who is so intelligent can't learn anymore? Why would you come to school and just play around?" How could I tell her that I'd lost all hope?

Finally, the day came when my mother sat me down and told me, "Gaetane, I cannot take care of all these children by myself. I need your help at home. Otherwise, they will be sent to orphanages or sent to live with their godparents. I was 14 years old and I knew it was the truth. I loved my siblings and I had no choice but to leave school and help at home.

The priest from my school came to our house, to ask my mother why I was taken out of school. Secretly, I listened to them talking. The priest reminded my mother that it was the law for a child to stay in school until they were 16. "Why would you take her out of school so early?" he asked.

My mother responded, "She just fools around when she's at school." And it was true; fooling around at school was all I could do since I had become so heartbroken. Ironically, it was based on my own behavior that my parents had finally taken me out of school. But that wasn't the whole truth; mostly, I was being kept home because my mother "needed my help." I felt betrayed when she lied to the priest. There were no social services back then, so that was the end of that intervention.

Luc still went to school and I never told him he might be sent away to lumberjack camp any minute. But for me, being taken out of school, helping with the children, I saw that other world I had envisioned slipping away. The wealthy people who spoke well, dressed well and educated their children, the families who read books with fathers who went off to work in suits – these people all seemed happy. The other world that I knew only too well was a poor, hungry, uneducated world, in which mothers cried and dressed in old clothes with unkempt hair; the children went hungry, got beaten by their father, and worse.

I noticed that despite all the drinking, the craziness, and having no job, my father managed to stay well dressed and there was never any shortage of cigarettes. I understood at this point in my life that we would be poor and miserable. We would live in fear; fear of having no food or heat on very cold winter days, fear of no electricity, fear of my father's drunken rages and random violence, and living with mom's depression and all the crying.

I could see the path that I was being forced to go down. I got discouraged, sad, and very angry. My only way out of this poverty and abuse had been education; I'd had no doubt this would be my saving grace, and now it was gone. Though I lost hope, somehow, I knew that I was not going to live like them, even if I couldn't finish school. A new plot was hatching – I just didn't know what it was yet. This was a pivotal point for me.

The summer arrived. I was only 11 and it was during this time that I went through one of the most beautiful and most painful times of my life. I went to visit my Uncle George and his family for the summer since the days of going to Grandma Martelles were over. My Uncle George was married to my mom's sister, Aunt Debbie; they were the ones who had given us the refrigerator. Their house was bright and sunny, and filled with beautiful furniture. They had running water and indoor plumbing - it was a relief that there was no dark, smelly outhouse to face daily. They had plenty of food and were generous.

My Uncle George worked as a welder for a large company and he'd come home at night covered in black soot. But he got himself cleaned up right away and I thought he was so handsome. My Aunt Debbie was pretty. She had gorgeous clothes because she would often go out dancing. My Aunt Debbie was a great dancer. Uncle George was also a musician who played the clarinet. They *loved* music.

Aunt Debbie and my mother were sisters. A summer with my aunt and uncle was precious. It felt good for me to be with them, but it also felt awkward. In their family, no child ever did adult chores. I was never asked to help though I was very good with children and household chores. Why would anyone want me around, if not for cooking and cleaning, chopping wood and fetching water? Instead, they cleaned me up and nurtured me as every child deserves to be nurtured. When they took me for the summer, it was simply to care for and love me.

When I stayed with them, my aunt bought me beautiful clothes and brought me to the dentist for the first time. My uncle even bought me ice cream cones, which was an exceptional treat. And their daughter, my cousin Lydia - it was so easy to make her laugh! How lucky I thought she was. She had a *real* mom and dad. She had parents who took care of her, a father who worked hard to provide for his family with a great, giving heart. I loved my uncle, George. As young as I was, I could feel his compassion and kindness. He was a beautiful human being. I can still hear his laughter in my memories.

The most painful part of that summer, and why I consider it my summer of awakening, was that I noticed the relationship that Uncle George had with his daughter through different eyes. I noticed how he treated her; how he was with her. I noticed that he held her in his arms in a different way than my father held me. I noticed that when he kissed her, it was different than the way my father kissed me. Most of all, Uncle George had no secret place that he ever took my cousin Lydia. I quietly watched him tuck Lydia in bed for the night, saying prayers with her at her bedside. He came right back downstairs.

I would listen and watch them closely, and it was with such horror that I finally came to realize that what my father had been doing to me ever since I could remember was not what good fathers do with their little girls; that what my father did to me and to himself while he was with me - was *wrong*. Every day, my uncle's family showed me another way of life. As I look back, they were a gift from God because that is when I finally knew what a family should be like; what *true* love in a family really felt like, especially between a father and his daughter. There was pain in that gift, too; the pain of realization. A pivotal point.

I got scared. I never wanted to go back home. It was a dark and a hopeless feeling that I had never felt before because I hadn't known the awful truth. I had no words for incest, child molestation, or sexual abuse. All I had were feelings, and I could suddenly feel in my heart how it was *so* wrong what my father did to me. But now that I knew it was wrong, how was I going to make it stop?

Too soon, the day came that I had to go back home and when I did, I ran upstairs and hid in my bed. I thought I was going to die. I cried so hard, my father heard me crying. I could hear his heavy footsteps coming up the stairs, and I was so afraid as I cried under the covers. He told me he was there to "comfort" me. I knew better what he was really going to do. And for the first time, it was wrong; so terrifyingly wrong that, for the first time in my life, I dissociated. I completely left my body and my consciousness. I can't even remember what happened between us. All that was left afterward was a sickening feeling and fear.

I realized it was not the drunken nights I had to watch out for; my father was never drunk when he came to me. What I had to watch out for were the sober days and nights, especially since I'd been taken out of school and was home. Ironic, isn't it, that I was safer when he was drunk? I learned to fear the sound of his footsteps. That became the trigger for my dissociation, and I would never remember anything after the footsteps. The physical acts of sexual abuse were not part of my conscious experience.

I never spent another summer with my Uncle George's family. The next summer, it was my Aunt Betty and Uncle Bernard, my mom's brother and sister-in-law, who took me in.

They took me to their house on the lake where I met my cousins, Edward and Joseph. My cousin Edward was very active and playful. My cousin Joseph was serious and very close to his mom. They were the cleanest and most well-dressed boys I ever saw. They had lots of real toys, unlike the home I came from where we made toys out of sticks and cardboard.

I helped take care of my cousins that summer. Although I loved that, I knew that the reason my aunt and uncle took me to their house was to take care of the children and clean. It was not because of any great love. I felt strangely comfortable there and uncomfortable at the same time. There I was with my rags for clothes and smelly hair, taking care of their children and cleaning the house. I was like a maid in my own family. It was so different from my time with my Uncle George who didn't use anyone for anything.

Though this was a reprieve from my home life and I was fed, my Uncle Bernard was drunk most of the time. And he was a mean drunk. In some ways, they were living the same way my family lived; with the male head of a household having an ever-present alcohol addiction and a tendency towards meanness. I didn't recognize this very clearly at the time because, to me, it was just life and that was how I lived, too. I knew on some level that it was wrong, but it was so normal in my family.

That was my last summer away.

Chapter 11

We moved to Hell House when I was 14 years old. We might have lived in the cardboard house forever, except that it was right in the path of the new highway that was going to be built. All my life, I had lived on the back street, but this new house was on the main street. Our family moved to a place that had the reputation for all sorts of disreputable, despicable and wicked things going on, or so I heard. The last family that lived there had moved out quickly, saying it was a very evil place.

On the bright side of Hell, the house was bigger and finally had a toilet inside. The days of the outhouse and slop pots were over. There was running water for washing and the wood stove could be heated with oil. The house had a large living room, a big kitchen with a pantry, and a refrigerator. Downstairs was a bedroom, and upstairs there were three more bedrooms. All the bedrooms had curtains for doors; we just couldn't seem to ever manage any doors in our family. There was a bathtub, too, so you could take a bath once a week and not have to carry water from outside.

Despite all these luxuries, our lot in life really hadn't changed. We were still poor; still struggling though we were now bootlegging. Most of the bootlegging operations took place downstairs in the extra bedroom, but the customers would come upstairs to use our bathroom. There was no privacy anywhere.

We were bootleggers now, and I still couldn't understand why there was never any food. My father never worked, but he'd get a check from the government; a little bit of money for each child. Did we ever see it? No. He'd take the whole check and go drinking. Then he'd go hunting with a buddy, kill a deer and bring it home, and expect us to be grateful for his support.

It was while living in Hell House that my mother, who was sick by this time, told me that if I didn't help, my siblings would be sent away to orphanages or foster parents. I panicked at the idea of never seeing them again, so I decided that my siblings would never be hungry, the way Luc and I were. I stayed there and raised my siblings as my own children.

It was there at Hell House that I met Andrea, who became my best friend. She'd been living next to Hell House her whole childhood. I knew who she was from school, but she was one year younger than me and we hadn't been in the same grade, so we hadn't really spoken. Her mother was widowed and pregnant when Andrea's father died. Andrea's mother had six kids to take care of and struggled to make ends meet. Andrea's life was no easier than anyone else's and yet she loved to have fun just like I did. We became great friends.

Andrea was the one who told me the stories of Hell House, like how the last family that lived there had moved out so quickly because the "energy" was so bad from all the bootlegging and other evil things that had gone on before; that's why we started calling it *"Maison de l'Enfer,"* Hell House. Andrea also told me that her mother had warned all her children for years about the bad people next door as she grew up, but she had especially warned her daughters that if men tried to talk to them and offer them money, they should say no and tell her immediately.

Andrea and I had fun together. We smoked, which we didn't really need money for - not when we could steal cigarette butts from inside this one store. The owner of the store only smoked a bit of the cigarette, leaving the butt in the ashtray right inside the door; easy pickings. My mother hated that I smoked. But everyone was doing it and I wanted to be like everyone else. Soon after we moved into Hell House, the day came that my brother Luc was taken out of school and sent to work with the rest of the Lumberjacks. At 13, Luc was very smart, but his continued education wasn't as important to my parents as bringing more money into the household.

Luc was small in stature, weighing only 120 pounds. I was sad when he had to go to work at the lumberjack camp. I hated our parents for what they were doing to him. Over the years, he worked hard, and they took his money. We all worked like slaves and they took everything.

While he was away, I worried that Luc would become just like Grandpa Martelle. He was Luc's hero. He always had a pocket full of money, and that is what Luc liked about him. He thought Grandpa Martelle was generous because he'd give us five cents or sometimes twenty-five cents when he stopped by the house going to the city in his cab when he would drive people from town to Edmundston. Our grandfather made money any way he could and most of the time, it wasn't in any legal way.

For Luc, our grandfather was someone who he could look up to because he was someone who found a way to make money and had enough to share. When Luc could hide some money from my father, he was good at saving. Once, Luc saved up enough money to buy himself a bike - a red two-wheeler! Luc made me promise not to take his bike, ever. But I decided that I needed to learn to ride that bike and took it anyway. I almost killed myself when I went right into a ditch; a deep one and hurt myself. But the worst part was that I broke his bike. It was the first time that Luc got mad at me. The guilt I felt was intolerable. He had saved for so long for this bike! I was truly sorry because I knew it meant so much to him.

Meanwhile, my mother was pregnant again with my brother, Adam. He was born in a huge snow storm; so powerful that my mother was in a car following the snow plow on the way to the hospital. The house was freezing because we didn't have enough oil to heat the house. The money that came in from bootlegging and the government never bought us oil. Luckily, we were able to use wood, which was available for free if we could find it. So, of course, we did our best to find wood to keep from freezing to death.

When Adam was born, I was amazed at how small he was. He was just 5 pounds, 11 ounces. I took care of him, especially during the night because my mother was sick. He would wake up for feeding and being changed and I would get up and take him to a little corner by the chimney and take care of him there, where it was warm. At fifteen, it was like I had my own baby. He was the cutest thing with blond hair and blue eyes, and my girlfriends and I did wicked things to him. We made him smoke cigarettes when he was only two years old. It was horrible of us, but he was a great distraction from everything else. We'd dress him like a girl and put fake boobs on him. I would make him curse in French and English. He thought it was funny and so did we. It wasn't all torture. I loved to wash him and make him look clean and adorable. My mother celebrated his first five birthdays on the wrong date. She kept forgetting if it was January 26th or 27th and I would remind her.

During the early years with Adam, my mother was sick with high blood pressure. She would get nose bleeds and would go to the hospital to get her nose packed. I would take care of her and the others. I was afraid of losing her. So many children to care for and my father not lifting a finger except in anger.

Chapter 12

When I got my period for the first time, I knew nothing about menstruation. All I knew is what I heard and what I heard was that once you got this sickness; this *malade*, if a boy "touched" you, you could get pregnant. My body was quickly changing into a young woman's body, and I knew my father was "touching" me, even if I couldn't remember all the details. *What if I got pregnant?* Everyone would know the truth, or at least, a truth that was fabricated by my father because he'd never admit that *he* did this to me. No, he'd act surprised and lie, even asking, "Who did this to you?" No one would believe me.

I knew that for a fact because, one time, my fear turned to such hate and anger that I confronted my father.

That time, I told him, "If you don't stop, I'll tell on you!"

"No one will believe you," he told me; "I'll say you're a liar." Instead, I said, "I'll run away." My father laughed.

"I'll find you no matter where you run. Anywhere in the world, I'll find you and kill you."

The thought of being called a liar struck a nerve with me. I'd been called a liar once before. Years ago, at the red house, one of my older cousins had taken me to the outhouse and wanted me to kiss her. I managed to get away from her, and ran inside the house and told my mother, who got very upset. When my mother and I confronted my cousin, she said I lied; that I was lying about it all. I was so shocked and horrified that no one had believed me! They all believed her, even my own mother. It was a moment that I looked back on - a child telling the truth about something awful that happened to her and no one believing her. So, here I was again; threatened with being called a liar if I told the truth.

I had nothing left to say after that. All that was left was for me to continue dissociating when he touched me every day. Though I felt deep fear, I said nothing, not a word or even a hint to anyone and all the while, so fearful that his touching might result in a baby growing inside me.

Around this same time, I started noticing boys in a different way. Growing up, the company of boys was fun because I was a tomboy. Now, I was painfully aware and afraid of the way my body reacted when I was around them. I was ashamed and thought that somehow, I could stop the changes in my body. Grandma Smyde had been full of lectures about sinful urges. I didn't understand the sexual arousal I began to feel around boys; I didn't understand what it meant. What was right and what was wrong? It all was jumbled together in one chaotic mess.

This was a very confusing time for me. My mother never talked to me about sex and I was too afraid to ask. I was all alone at a time when a girl needs her mother; needs someone to put things in perspective. Feelings of powerlessness, sadness, and fear filled this time of my life, when, conversely, I was growing into a strong young woman. The little girl was literally bleeding.

It was in this chaotic state that I fell in love with, oh-my-god, the most beautiful boy in the world. His name was Matthieu, but we called him Matt. We met at my girlfriend Celine's house because he was friends with the boy Celine was dating at the time. Celine was Laura's daughter. I went into the house and saw Matt for the first time. He had black hair and looked like Elvis Presley. If I knew the word "sexy" back then, it would have applied to Matt. There was another girl who would come to visit at Celine's. Her name was Vera and, as we'd say, she had "experience" with boys, so I thought Matt would be more interested in her. But he chose me.

One of the times I was at Celine's, Matt and I were spending time together, sitting on the couch. After a while, sitting very close to him, the chemistry started to fire up. He kissed me, and I thought I was going to heaven! I wanted to keep on kissing him and staring into his dark brown eyes. His body felt warm and safe. There was something here that was different than anything I'd ever experienced. We were interrupted by a knock on the door. Usually, when my father wanted me home, he sent someone to get me. He was a coward, sending someone to bring me back home; my brother or sister would come to tell me that our mother "needed me home to help."

This time, it was my father at the door. I didn't remember this for a long time. It was told to me by friends and later, by Matt himself. My father stood in the doorway and looked at Matt; then he looked at me. It was the "I'm going to kill you" look. I don't remember anything after that.

Matt and I dated secretly over the next year. We loved to ice skate together. I would wear my sister Doris' old hand-me-down skates. We would hold hands and hold each other up and laugh as we skated and glided across the ice together. I wished that we could just skate away forever and I'd never have to go home again.

At some point, because it was so difficult for me to get out of the house, our meetings became few and far between, until we just stopped seeing each other altogether. There was never a real ending to our romance; it just faded away until it disappeared. It broke my heart to imagine that Matt had never really loved me; that there must have been something wrong with me; because I was poor, or not as interesting as other girls. I also blamed him because if he really cared, he wouldn't have disappeared.

Meanwhile, there were mouths to feed and never anything to eat. I finally realized that *I* would need to become the breadwinner in my family if I ever wanted any food in the house. I was determined that my siblings would never starve like Luc and I did.

My friend got me a job working at a nursing home that was part of the local convent, run by priests and nuns. I was hired at 25 cents a day to clean. I can sincerely say I never went hungry again, and neither did my siblings. I provided for the family, while all the while, the man who was supposed to be the provider for our family was hiding upstairs, unemployed and burnt out.

There was an all-girls private high school next door to the convent. I would see the girls and wish that I could go to school, too. They were my age, around 16 years old. Their uniforms were clean and starched; grey pleated skirts, white blouses, light gray cardigans, knee socks, and polished shoes. The girls wore wristwatches. Boy, did I want one of those! With the little money I earned, I scraped and saved so I could buy myself a wristwatch. It was so expensive, and I was proud of myself, but I also felt guilty. I was hiding my savings from my parents. I was supposed to help feed the family - but buying myself that watch gave me some strength and dignity that I couldn't find anywhere else.

These schoolgirls were another example of the clean people and how their lives were so different than mine. Their families had to be rich because it was a private school. They were fluent in English and French. I would hear them talking about boys and laughing; talking about their classes and teachers, too. They would sit on the big, beautiful lawn in front of the school with their books, laughing and talking. I also remember seeing some of them smoking cigarettes behind the school building, so maybe they weren't as goody-goody as they seemed.

One time, these schoolgirls spotted me and my friend; we were taking a quick break outside the convent, in our aprons. This was the one time that they took notice of us. Well, they started laughing and calling us "the little maids." I felt truly beneath them at that moment; worthless, in fact. All I could do was turn around and go back to the convent. I couldn't say anything to them. I couldn't defend myself because they were right. I *was* a little maid.

The saddest thing was seeing Matt one day while I was working at the convent. He never saw me; I made sure of that. One day, I saw him jump the fence at the school. A little later, I saw him walking hand in hand with a pretty girl. I was heartbroken and even more convinced that he stopped seeing me because something was wrong with me. Matt came from a good family; he'd had a privileged life. I'd think, "If they ever found out…" Compared to his family, my family was just a bunch of bootleggers; low-lifes; filthy, poor, and disgusting. I never wanted him to know how bad my life was; That's why I never brought him home; that and my father would have hurt him or, at the very least, threatened to. I imagined that if I were rich and went to that school, he would jump a fence for me; he would walk hand in hand with me if I were from a rich, clean family.

One day at the convent, this friend who had gotten me the job, said "Hey, Gaetane. There's a big refrigerator in the back filled with oranges and cookies. Let's get something. I'm hungry." Well, I was hungry, too. I knew that no one should go back there. The food was exclusively for the nuns and the priests. But we went anyway. We went in the back, imagining a cold, juicy orange or a buttery cookie. We went in the back to raid the refrigerator of just a few things. Who would even miss them?!

What happened next was almost more than I could bear. We got caught. But worse than that, my friend got off scot-free. She was told to go home and think about what she'd done with every expectation that she'd return in the morning. Maybe it was because her aunt was a nun there.
But for me? I had to follow that nun into her office.

She sat me down and then sat herself down in front of me. She was big and fat. Whatever happened to being servants of God and eating only bread and water? I wondered if she was ever hungry with nothing to eat. She looked me right in the eye, looked deep into my soul and said, "You are a thief and once a thief, you are a thief for the rest of your life. Now, get out of here and don't ever come back!"

I tried to say that my friend made me go with her into the kitchen, but it didn't matter. She didn't even listen to me. I was a liar again and I was out. Fired. Gone.

Chapter 13

After I got fired from the cleaning job, I realized I needed to get better-paying work if I was truly going to help my family and be a better provider. And, it would need to take me all the way out of the house, where I could control the money I earned and not have it taken away so easily.

Thanks to some family members in Edmundston, I got a job working as a nanny for a small family. I was delighted to be working in the city and getting the hell out of Hell House. Most of all, I found a way to "run away" from my father without running away or abandoning any of them. Everyone knew where I was, and I was sharing my money with my family. It felt like the beginning of my freedom, the beginning of a life of my very own - I was finally out of prison!

I took care of two children and cleaned and was paid about $15 a week. I was 16 years old and happy. Matt even came to meet me one night, although things were different with him. I could feel it. He was not very respectful, and he was arrogant; I wondered if he'd been drinking. I knew how it changed people. I was so disappointed!

My freedom turned out to be short-lived. After working as a nanny for less than a month, my mother and father came into the city to see me. My mother explained this plan to open a small canteen restaurant on the lower floor of our house, and that it was going to be such a good opportunity for our family. They had come to get me because they "needed my help." *That fucking word "need" again*, I thought, *and that fucking word "help."* They promised that I would be paid as a waitress; that I would make the same salary I was making as a nanny. This was my mother speaking for both; my father just standing by quietly, letting her do the talking.

"I don't believe you will pay me," I said to my mother. She promised me repeatedly that I would be paid. In the end, I gave in. I hoped that I wouldn't be deceived and hurt again; betrayed by my own mother. A part of me knew I should just say no, yet there was another part of me that just had to go back again. I knew what her promise meant, and I knew that somehow, I wouldn't see a dime of what she promised me. But I so desperately wanted to believe her that I gave in. I mean, what do you do when you're 16 years old and your siblings are babies and your mother is sick and your father threatens to kill everyone, and your mother is begging because she *needs* your *help*? Inside my heart, I knew it was a lie and I didn't want to go back with them, back into a life of slavery with no money or freedom, serving my family, and now everyone in town. At the very least, I knew there would be food if there was a restaurant. And I knew my family needed me. And I knew my pervert father needed me, though he remained silent the whole time. Our "little secret" was the worst part of going back. There was no choice for me.

Soon after, I left the job as a nanny and left my freedom behind. For years, I would say to myself, "I want to live those few weeks again when I was 16 and free…"

It was my father's idea to convert the downstairs of Hell House into a little canteen restaurant; he certainly had a built-in workforce in me and all my girlfriends who I had come to know through the years in our little village. According to my father, this little canteen was "going to be something big." I take a moment here to call him out as the bastard he was because, as I've said before, he never worked; everyone else worked for him and he took everything. As usual, the lazy bastard put my mother in charge, so he didn't have to do anything.

Our living room turned into the customer's dining area: a counter with stools, 3 tables with 4 chairs each, a jukebox and a Coca-Cola machine. Where the money came from to do this, I have no idea. Food was prepared in the large kitchen and stored in the pantry, and the bootlegging operations still ran out of the extra bedroom downstairs as they had been for years. So strange, I had been hungry my whole life and now our living room was a restaurant? There was never any more hunger. But there was so much work, and I was never paid.

For me, life became all about the canteen, being a mom to my siblings, caring for a sick mother, doing the chores, bootlegging, and waiting on customers. I ended up working there day and night - me, and my best friend, Andrea. We were now co-workers. My father had us wearing white aprons and little white dresses with white stockings and shoes. We looked like little nurses! There were many 18-hour days back then.

My body disappeared; it literally went away during this time. I only had a face. Mom often needed to take a nap in the afternoon. I never understood why she needed a nap when I could work 18 hours a day, seven days a week, with no rest at all. It was another reason I grew to hate her. Little did I know that she was in a constant state of abuse and fearful for all our lives, that she was exhausted, that my father blamed her, and she took the fall as "the bad guy." I wouldn't realize that for some time yet.

Even with all this work going on, I managed to live a double life; a secret life. How is it possible to live as I did and yet, have so much fun with my friends? I don't have the answer. All I know is that I loved life and people, and the time with my friends was the only time I felt alive; joyful. When my friends would come and visit the canteen, these were the hours in my day that kept me sane and looking forward to the next day. My friends had no idea what it did for me when they'd come and hang out with me. It was the one place I could see them and have fun.

We were all teenagers; all silly. Some of us were quite mischievous. My friends didn't drink alcohol and didn't do drugs, and we didn't have any cars. In fact, Marie would come to pick us up in a tractor covered in mud, and we would drive all over town in that tractor. Marie was very quiet, and she didn't smoke, although the rest of us smoked a lot of cigarettes riding around in that tractor. Because my mother saw Marie as a "good girl," I could go out with her on occasion.

My friend Kathy helped at the Canteen, too, and when she did, I could go out sometimes. Mom and Kathy really liked each other! Kathy said that my mother was fun to work with, and Mom must have felt comfortable with Kathy. I couldn't have fun with my mom because I didn't like her too much. This was another thing my father stole from me.

One of my canteen friends is a great artist now. Her name is Jodi. She was a big part of the canteen life and a very gifted artist even in her early teens. She'd draw our likenesses on napkins, and it looked just like whoever she chose to draw that night. One of my other friends, Celeste, was a very funny girl. Her mom was funny, too. Celeste's mother had grown up on a farm and the sayings she came up with were so funny. She said to my mother one time that one of the girls down the street was "so fat that her knees were as big as a cow's forehead." Another girl was so skinny that she said, "Celeste, she is so skinny, she's wearing a striped dress - and there's only one stripe!" She made me laugh.

Andrea and I would read cards to tell the girls about their futures. We did it so much that we began to believe that we really could! Andrea's mother had sent her out to work at 15 or 16 years old, and I could compare her life to mine in so many ways and yet, she was still allowed to be a teenager. She had the latest fashions and makeup. How I wished I had Andrea's life so that I could have the freedom to go out with my friends, date boys, and be allowed to just be a teenage girl, instead of saying goodbye at the canteen when they would all go out for the night. When Andrea would get ready to go out with our friends, she would sing while we were working because she was happy. Andrea would tell me all about her nights out, but never in a way that would make me jealous of her; it was entertaining because Andrea was a great storyteller and a great friend.

It was the 1960's and there was a lot going on in the world: music, drugs, and war. In our small town, we felt far removed from most of it. We were in our own little world — until the Americans started coming. Our canteen was right over the border from Maine, right over the bridge, and our little restaurant was the only place to get a meal or hang out in town.

American "Fly Boys" from U.S. Air Force bases started to show up at the canteen. They'd drive across the nearby border from Maine where they were stationed, looking for some time off and fun. They were from all over the United States, from places we'd never heard of. Wow, there were so many nice-looking, tall guys - that was really something! The French-Canadian men we knew were nowhere near as tall as the Americans.

Some of the Americans had dark skin. We had no idea about any other people besides white Catholic French Canadians and Indigenous Canadians who we never saw. As I see it today, these dark-skinned men were probably Spanish,

Puerto Rican, and maybe even Italian. Yet, dark-skinned or not, they were all *American*. We had to struggle to communicate with any of them; there was a big language barrier because in my area of Canada, everyone speaks French. It didn't seem to matter so much when we were dating, though.

The best part of it all was that jukebox in the canteen - a miracle! It only cost 25 cents for 4 songs. The jukebox filled the air with Roy Orbison and Beatles' tunes, rock and roll, and slow-dancing music. It was the end of the Elvis era and the beginning of the Beatles era. The Beatles were big and even bigger at our little canteen. Of all the music we listened to, the Platters were my favorite, and they take me back to the canteen every time I hear them.

My friends came to spend their allowance: 25 cents for the music and another 25 cents for a bag of potato chips and a glass bottle of Coke. We had one of those big red Coca-Cola coolers with the bottle opener attached to the side of it. When the guys bought Coca-Cola and peanuts, they would put the peanuts in the bottle and drink them with the Coke. We had lots of laughs and we all dreamt of leaving our little town someday; pumping each other up to really do it. I never talked about how abusive my father was; I didn't even want to think about him, especially when I was having fun with my friends. I would just say that I was going to leave because I hated my father so much. That was enough. We kept on wishing and dreaming and planning our escape.

It was especially a treasure to go dancing on a weekend night with all my friends and these handsome Fly Boys. My musical Aunt Dolly opened a catering hall in the next town called "The Jive Dancing Hall" and that's where we'd go. We would get dressed up in fishnet stockings, mini-skirts, dresses and go-go pants, and long boots with pointy toes. We would tease our hair and put on blue eyeshadow and peppermint twist lipstick – it was so pale pink that it was almost white and shiny.

We took taxis to The Jive; 25 cents each and we'd fit in as many of us as we could, although it usually took several taxis. With a dollar admission, we had a great night of dancing and Coca- Cola! We'd dance to Elvis Presley, Roy Orbison, Chubby Checker, and the Beatles. Dating these Fly Boys, we'd also get four couples in a car and go parking and kissing – or necking, as we called it then. The Americans had cars like a Ford Fairlane or an old Chevy or Desoto. Some of them even had convertibles. Andrea's Fly Boy had a beautiful Mustang.

I was rarely allowed to go dancing and yet, somehow, I managed to go parking with eight people in a car, all of us laughing and no sex going on; only necking. There was a lot of heat going on in those cars. Many of the girls in town became pregnant and got married to those Fly Boys and left for far away, for good.

I dated one boy for a while, and, though my mother never approved of me dating, I could date him. When this boy went to Vietnam, he wanted to marry me. I said no. I wasn't in love. I broke up with him sending a Dear John letter; it was cruel looking back on it now and yet I knew I had to. I don't think I ever dated anyone other than Matt with any serious intentions.

One time we were all hanging out at the canteen, and there was a young man who was visiting from another town near New Brunswick. This fellow showed up and said that he had a gift: he could hypnotize people. He had a great sense of humor, so we thought he was kidding and some of us decided to give him the opportunity to prove he was a hypnotist and he agreed. That night, this fellow hypnotized our friend. He talked to him and told him that he wanted to go to sleep, and while he was asleep, he would do everything he was told to do. Well, he told our hypnotized friend that he was drinking whiskey, though his glass was empty; that he was drinking *a lot* of whiskey. Soon, our friend got up and began to stumble around, drunk on an empty glass! We laughed as we watched him. We seemed to find the silliest things to laugh about.

Then, the hypnotist told him to "snap out of it" - that he wouldn't remember anything when he snapped his fingers - and it worked! Our friend truly didn't remember anything he had just done and denied it when we tried to tell him! But, there was this small chance that our friend just been acting, and my friends and I were still unconvinced about the hypnotist's authenticity. So, we needed someone else to see if it was true.

Andrea volunteered, and he did the same thing to her, counting backward from ten to one, with the suggestion that she would be hypnotized. We were all watching Andrea intently as he counted backward. The hypnotist told her that Elvis was sitting in the chair next to her – Elvis himself! Now, there was this guy sitting next to her in that chair who all my friends and I knew Andrea didn't like much. It was clear to all of us that he wasn't Elvis and yet, on cue, she got up and kissed him like he was the King of Rock and Roll himself! When Andrea snapped out of it and then denied what she had just done, we were all roaring with laughter!

Chapter 14

Over the years, working at the canteen, I got to know a lot of people - all the drunks in town, essentially. Never the young attractive guys who would come to buy beer. My father would lurk in the background as I worked, giving any handsome boy "the eye", which meant they better keep away from me. He could be very intimidating, without even saying a word. All the other men, I could know. I regularly played cards with two "mentally challenged" men in the town who came into the canteen. I really came to care about them and I respected them. We played cards for five cents a round and it was fun, I'll admit. Still, this was supposed to be my entertainment because it didn't threaten my father.

I felt much anger and sadness. I hated how my mother denied me my freedom and I hated the drunken kids who came into the canteen after a night of partying. I couldn't stand seeing them enjoying their freedom when I had virtually none. One day, when Andrea and I were working, my parents went to Edmundston to buy alcohol for the bootlegging business. Another canteen friend came in and the three of us hung out, talking about boys and talking about everybody else in town, too - just like teenagers do. We talked about fashion, makeup, and the Beatles. But it eventually came to the point that this other friend of ours decided to drink some Moosehead beer, and got really drunk - on just one beer! Well, Moosehead is very strong, so maybe that was it. At any rate, I found out something from her at that moment that I didn't want to know.

In her drunken state, she told us that my father had given her some beer once and she had gotten drunk then, too. We were standing there, and she was staggering and swaying, and giggling a lot. She disclosed to me and Andrea that she was in love with my father! I was shocked. I was also very ashamed because everybody in town knew his reputation.

As she chattered on, it became apparent that he had seduced her, and she was completely head over heels in love with him. Later, I learned that he'd approached some of my other friends, too; wanting to kiss them, and even offering money so they wouldn't tell anyone. All my friends, said no. This was the first time I'd heard anything like this; that someone had said yes.

Andrea was staring at me, waiting for a reaction, and all I could do was continue looking down at the floor. I will never forget the humiliation of that moment.

Later, I found out that my father had hit on two other friends of mine, including Andrea. She said that he'd offered her money. "I don't want your shit money," Andrea had told him, "and if you touch me, I'll tell everyone in town!" My other friend had told him, "If you touch me, my father will cut your balls off!" We didn't talk about it again after that. I'm not even sure my friend remembered that she'd told us.

Then came the night that I had a date with a Fly Boy, and he was very handsome. I didn't tell my mom that I wanted to go out on a date because she would have said no. I said I wanted to go out with my friends. For once, she said, "Yes, go out with your friends." I asked my mom's permission to do anything; I never asked my father. I was ecstatic! This Fly Boy and I were going for a sleigh ride in the moonlight. It was going to be a full moon. If you've never seen the moon shining on all that pristine, white snow, know that it would take your breath away. It was such a romantic setting at night.

Come the night of the sleigh ride date, Mom suddenly told me I couldn't go out with my friends. I'd done everything

I was supposed to do: the kids were all in bed, I'd done all I could to take care of my mother who was sick, and I'd done all my chores - and hers, too. My father was there in the background, quietly watching and listening; never saying anything, when she said, "No, I'm very sick. I need you here."

The hate I felt for my mother at that moment! She totally betrayed me, again. Scammed me, again. How could I tell this Fly Boy that I couldn't go for a sleigh ride with him? I knew that he'd driven from the States, from Maine - for this date. I had no phone to call him. He'd think I stood him up; that I was a liar. That word again.

After that, I continued asking my mom if I could "go out with my friends," and secretly went on dating. There were quite a few boys and they seemed to fall in love with me - but I never fell in love like I had with Matt. Many of them were these Fly Boys, the Air Force men, so far from home, and probably feeling a bit scared and lonely.

There finally came a night, after sneaking out with Andrea, that I slept over her house rather than go home. We got to her house at midnight. We'd met some American boys and had a great time; laughed a lot. A boy named Kevin had kissed me goodnight. I was so excited! He was nice looking - dark, tall and handsome.

Up in her bedroom, Andrea and I laughed and carried on, as teenagers do. For me, sleeping over anywhere was so rare. I loved it! Because Andrea's house was right next door to my house, we could see inside my house from her bedroom. As we carried on, I frequently looked over at my house seeing that there was a light in one of the windows. Someone was up. I kept glancing over as Andrea as we talked, and finally, I saw him. It was not my mother, who you might think would be up waiting for me to come home. It was my father, looking like a man waiting for his girlfriend or wife, thinking that she was out and cheating on him. He looked anxious and angry. He also looked like a coward to me. Without his guns, he was weak. Make no mistake, he was dangerous, and I had to be very careful around him. But something made me feel brave that night.

Andrea and I finally fell asleep and didn't wake up until dawn, not until Andrea's brother was going to work. We woke up and my first instinct was to look out the window and into my house. What I saw frightened me. I saw my father just going to bed. He'd been up all night. Now, I was petrified to go home. He'd been up all night, imagining that I'd spent the night with some Fly Boy. I figured he would probably try to kill me when I went home. The fun and bravery of the evening went out the window as I wondered how I would survive the day without getting killed. I knew for certain that I'd be punished, and I knew without a doubt that it was *him* in absolute control; it had *always* been him.

I finally got up enough courage to go home, still not knowing what he might do. I told Andrea, "I'm dead. He thinks that I spent the night with a boy." At that moment, I noticed a rip in the fabric of the lower back of my dress. "Oh my God," I said, "This doesn't look good. He will kill me or beat me up." I was petrified. I had a sweater, which I wrapped around my waist to hide the tear. As I entered the house with a sweater wrapped around my waist to hide the alleged evidence against me, I could see my mother in the kitchen, making breakfast and my father standing there, too. Though I had a rebellious heart and nature, I knew that breaking any of the rules came at a cost.

I thought my father had gone to bed, but he was still awake and waiting for me! He looked much like a jealous husband waiting at the door. I thought I was going to faint. "Why do you have a sweater around your waist?" he demanded.

I didn't answer him; I just stood there. "*Putin*," he said, calling me a whore. "Where were you all night? You had your belly filled, didn't you?" he accused me. That accusation was so sickening.

All I could do was run upstairs and as I did, I screamed back at him, "I hate you! I *hate* you!" This is something I'd never said to my father, and I was expecting the worst and challenging him at the same time. For the first time in my life, I'd had the courage to yell at him. I guess I got to a point that I'd rather be dead; I could no longer live like this. My life of fear was nothing compared to the hate and rage I felt. To my surprise, I saw fear in my father's eyes. I was shocked that he didn't follow me up the stairs. He just shut up. My mother was petrified and shocked that he shut up. But I'd had enough.

A few hours after I yelled at him, the son of a bitch came to me and told me he was "worried" about me. What a *scammer* he was!

Chapter 15

After this incident, I knew deep inside that my father was a jealous coward. It was a clear thought that came into my mind as if from a higher realm and I knew it was the truth. I realized that a jealous person is a weak person. My father was only courageous when he had his guns. He was nothing but a weak piece of shit! Still, he was a dangerous piece of shit.

There was a way out of this hell I was living in; It was all crystal clear to me then. I finally knew how I would save myself. I felt a spiritual connection to this clarity, a grounded truth. I knew I was going to leave. I didn't know where in the world I would go; I knew that I was going to speak another language, the country I didn't know. All I knew for sure was that I would be leaving this hell and never living in it again.

From that day on, I schemed between myself and God. I prayed a lot, believing that there was another world and that I would find it. I had a lot of friends who loved me, and we had all talked about leaving and yet, no one knew what I was about to do. Not even my closest friends knew what I was planning. I had faith, courage and the hope that I would leave it all behind me soon. I knew in my heart and soul that my days in Hell were numbered.

I had one chance . . . and I blew it. This also was a pivotal moment for me.

Drunk and asleep on a beautiful summer afternoon, my father had managed to make it to one of the beds upstairs, a lit cigarette still dangling from his lips. I was hanging out with my cousin, one of my Aunt Dolly's daughters. As we entered Hell House, it was quiet, which was unusual for that time of day since there were usually people around. I don't remember where my mother was; the kids were probably in school. As we entered through the kitchen door, I saw and smelled smoke.

Everything downstairs seemed to be okay, so I ran upstairs. In one of the kid's bedrooms, there was so much smoke! The bed was on fire and I could barely make out an image on the bed, but someone was laying there. I ran right inside the burning room and I saw it was my father on the burning bed, still in a drunken stupor, coughing like crazy.

He was half naked; he must have fallen asleep smoking a cigarette. He had set himself on fire! There was a huge hole in the mattress, burning flames and so much smoke everywhere.

I screamed, and my cousin came running. It took both of us to pull him out of the burning bed, drag him downstairs, and prop him up in one of the kitchen chairs. All the while, he was yelling and cursing at us!

Once we had him securely in a chair, we began filling pails with water and carrying pail by pail up the stairs to extinguish the fire. We must have thrown a dozen or more pails of water on that mattress before it was a smoldering mess. We were coughing, and our eyes were tearing. Everything smelled of smoke, including us.

My mother didn't come home until after all this was done. She didn't seem at all surprised when we told her the story. She was the one who took the lit cigarettes out of his mouth or hands when he'd fall asleep drunk. So, she knew.

Just as I was thinking how great it was that we got there just in time to save my father's life - he starts cursing at me again, calling me crazy and a fool; chasing me like he wanted to kill me. "Why didn't you let me burn to death?" he yelled.

Don't think that it didn't cross my mind to let him burn, the old violent bastard. But instead, I saved him, despite everything he did to me and my brothers and sisters. And this was my thanks.

Another time, my brother Luc was home from lumberjack camp. I was 16 and it was winter. My father chased my mother outside to beat her, and Luc ran to defend her. I ran out after them and saw the whole thing. When Luc tried to stop him from beating mother, father turned on Luc and went after him with a shovel, chasing him towards a huge snow bank. Luc managed to leap over it and get away, the quick mouse that he was.

"I'll cut your balls off if you come back here!" my father shouted over the snowbank, also calling my brother a piece of shit. I was there. I saw it. I heard him threaten to castrate his own son like an absolute psychopath. There was never any remorse for what he said or did. Luc had no choice but to come back inside or freeze to death. It was then that my mother told him he would have to leave for good; Luc, not my father. "You have to go, or he'll hurt you." My brother had no choice but to go to Ontario where he had a couple friends who had managed to find some work.

My heart was broken. With Luc gone, I would be alone in Hell House with my father. I cried and cried when my brother left. I cried because he was leaving me behind, alone. *Good for him*, I thought through my tears, *but what's going to happen to me now?* It was only my faith in God and my dream of a better life that kept me sane as the closest family relationship I had was stolen from me.

Chapter 16

My Grandmother Smyde told me that I was a very intelligent girl and that I could 'be' somebody. We were standing on the wraparound porch, looking at her beautiful flower garden, the intoxicating scent of the pale pink peonies wafting over us; tall, beautiful trees all around. She was wearing a big old cotton dress with a clean scent and a rag sticking out of her apron pocket. She wouldn't use fancy handkerchiefs or buy tissues because she was very frugal. It was ironic because her husband owned everything!

My grandmother sent most of her children to University. After coming from a very large, poor family, education was important to her.

"You're intelligent enough to study nursing," she told me that day. "You'd make a great nurse." She said everything with such a strong conviction. What a boost this was to hear! Then she added, "You need to become a nun so that you get an education."

What? A *nun?!* My heart sank. There was absolutely no way I could become a nun. They would have to know my secret that I was not a clean person. I would have to confess everything. Then, my father would come to kill me for telling, if I didn't first die of shame.

I was so hungry to learn and hungry for an education and I would have entered the convent in a minute just to make that happen. I felt sad that I could not even consider the opportunity to be a nun, so I could become a nurse. This was yet another opportunity that my father stole from me.

During my childhood, grandma came to the house regularly. She would come and check to see if my father was abusing us. Not your typical grandmotherly visit for most people. For us, it was routine. She recognized the signs of abuse quickly - which made me wonder if she was familiar with it, too.

Where was the Devil when grandmother visited, you might ask? My father hid upstairs. Everyone thought it was because he hated my grandma but really, he was afraid of her. The thought of him being afraid of grandmother makes me laugh even today. She would have twisted his neck like a screaming chicken if she could. She used to kill chickens in the driveway, so believe me it's true. I know now that he was afraid of her because she knew what he was about; she knew that he and his family were all sick and both grandmother and grandfather had forbidden mother to marry him. *Why, oh why, hadn't my mother listened?*

One particular evening, as my grandma watched me from the rocking chair in the kitchen as I put on makeup at the mirror, getting ready to go out with my friends on a rare occasion that my mother said yes, my grandma said to my mother, "Loreen, you cannot do this to Gaetane. She is a young girl. You are stealing her adolescence. She will never be able to have that again. It's not okay - it's cruel!" She said that as angry as I'd ever heard her, and I'd heard her angry before.

My grandmother somehow saw all of this and yet was powerless over our situation. She felt powerless over the fact that she couldn't change anything. All she could do was show up at the house and make him aware that she knew his scheme. She had his number, so to speak, and she made it clear that he had *no* power over *her* mind. He was on the watch for her and he would hide every time!

After confronting my mother about stealing my adolescence and getting no response, my Grandmother looked at me and said to me, "Gaetane, I'm sorry this is happening to you. I want you to know that you will never be able to have this part of your life again. Each stage of life needs to be lived and experienced."

I felt very sad and angry hearing her words as she explained the reality of my life to me. I couldn't reveal the intensity of my feelings of powerlessness, hopelessness; I couldn't allow those feelings to surface because I knew I would not survive emotionally. I didn't want to think about my reality in those days. I didn't want to see the truth or ever think about it. I'd think only about things I loved – my friends, my plans, my faith – and try to feel happy and relieved from the sorrow that I felt losing my young life. The hatred that I felt that moment could have been very destructive. Today, I understand why victims of sexual abuse can become killers. The hate that went through me was so intense. It was so unbearable that I had to make it go away. She then said to me, "Gaetane, I promise one day that God will reward you for all you do here – for taking care of all your sisters and brothers."

I considered what the word "reward" meant to me at that time of my life. *Okay*, I thought, *she doesn't know this, but I will leave this hell one day soon. Maybe that will be my reward.* Even my grandmother who cared so much about my well-being and my future didn't know about my dream of leaving. I kept my dream between me and God because I did not want it stolen along with everything else. It was painful to keep this from her, just as I kept the abuse I endured every day a secret.

"Does he touch you?" she would ask me directly, privately, when no one could hear.

"No," I'd lie, though I wanted to shout: "Yes, he does, every day, and sometimes, throughout the day."

I thought of telling her. She was the one person who I knew would believe me if I told her the truth. But she hated him so much that I was sure that she would kill him if she knew the truth - and then she would go to jail, and it would be entirely my fault.

I wanted to tell her that I also had a secret escape plan and that plan was marriage. I didn't need to become a nun or a nurse. I was going to get married and leave here forever.

Funny, up until God gave me this plan, I was never going to get married. I was terrified to end up like my mother. And yet, I knew that when I got married, my father would leave me alone because my father was a coward and he'd never challenge my husband. I would marry a man who was much stronger physically than my father, someone of whom my father would be afraid. It would be the only safe way to go for me. Otherwise, he'd just send someone to get me back, with those fucking words "help" and "need."

I also knew that I was going to marry a smart man, an educated man. I was going to marry a man who lived far away, and we were going to live a nice life; I knew that I would learn to speak another language. Don't ask me how I knew. This was the message that came to me through my awareness. It was all so very crystal clear to me.

I wanted to tell her how it took all my energy to design my escape to save my life while taking care of my family and feeding them, working 18-hour days and more. I wanted to tell her that I even planned it in my sleep. But I didn't.

Chapter 17

Soon after that incident with my grandmother, God sent me the means to see my plan through. His name was John. "I'm going to marry him!" I happily and loudly proclaimed to my family, especially my father: "He's a marine! He's a black belt in karate! We're going to get married! I'm going to move to New York!" I felt all my dreams coming true. I watched for my father's reaction. He said and did nothing. I knew that I'd let him know he was done. We were done. It was over.

I met John at my sister Doris' June wedding when I was 18. John was Doris' new husband's cousin, and he lived all the way in New York. He liked me immediately. He drove all the way up to Canada to see me every month. He even took me to New York for a few weeks, and there were so many sights to see of this very different world I'd soon be living in. I was thrilled! He was older, and I saw that as a good thing.

When I told my friends I was getting married, they were shocked.

It was right around Christmas that we got engaged. John bought the most beautiful engagement ring for me. Our engagement party was at my Grandmother Smyde's house. I wore a beautiful black mini-dress and gorgeous black suede T-strap pointy shoes, and I had never seen my grandma so happy because she knew I was getting away and going to a better life, too. My father was there at the engagement party. My fiancé was a strong man, but I was still afraid of my father and what he might do. But he just stayed in the background, probably afraid of my grandmother and my new fiancé, and probably terrified of Doris' new husband, because he was a police officer in a special unit that worked with domestic violence and bootlegging. He was part of the Smyde family now – how ironic was that? - and must have known my father was a real piece of shit. He heard my father talking to my mother in an abusive way once and he told him that if he ever heard him talk that way to her again, he'd beat him senseless, throw him in jail and keep him there.

My mother seemed happy for me because she knew that I liked John, even if I was not in love with him. I told her that we planned to get married in April. She took the news quietly; she never lifted her eyes to meet mine. A few days later, my mother came back to me and asked if we would wait to get married. I was beginning to suspect that she was my father's puppet; that this was his request, not hers. What was another month to wait, when I was leaving?

I said, "Sure, we'll wait. We'll do it in May." My mother agreed, sadly, saying, "It's time." I'm sure she meant that it was time I got away from this hell we were all living in, no matter the cost to her and my siblings.

John and I got married in May 1967. I was 19 years old. My vision had come true; my plan was working, thank God. I will never forget that day that I ran to Andrea's house, slamming open her door and running up the stairs to her bedroom; there were never any locks or knocking in those days. "Andrea! Andrea! I'm all packed up and I'm finally leaving!" I was so happy, but she was heartbroken. Later, I learned that she had gone to her mother and told her how sad she felt. "Why is she leaving?" she asked her mother. Her mother said, "Andrea, don't feel sad for her. It is the best thing that can happen for Gaetane." Somehow, her mother must have known what a horrible life I had – possibly, she had even known about the terrible secret I'd been hiding.

My siblings' reaction to their caregiver getting married and leaving was nothing short of devastation. I didn't realize the depth of its impact at the time. They didn't say anything to me. No feelings were discussed. It was the best and hardest day of my life when I left Canada that June. I could feel all the sadness and fears tucked so deep inside of me. Yes, I would miss my family, my friends, my town, my country, and even my language but I had hope. I knew I was going to make it!

My mother gave us a beautiful blanket as a wedding gift. I'm sure it was all she could give, and that it was very difficult for her to lose me, but she never made me feel guilty at all. As for my father, he never said anything; he just retreated into the shadows.

Chapter 18

I'd been a hostage for so long, virtually enslaved and kept between four walls and now, here I was in *New York*! I moved from a village of fewer than 2,000 people to a place with millions of people. I prayed and hoped and endured for so long. I was finally free!

John and I planned to move into the basement of his mother's house in an area of Long Island called Floral Park until we could find a place of our own. When we arrived, the basement wasn't ready to move in, so we lived in an extra bedroom on the main floor with his mother and stepfather. I believed that I was beginning a beautiful new life. And yet, stories don't go the way you expect. The joy of my newfound freedom was short-lived.

John's stepbrother lived upstairs with his wife and four children in a cluttered cramped place. I met their little 4-year-old girl soon after arriving. She was born with a defective heart and had these watery fawn eyes and a loving smile. Her arms would open, reaching out to me, wanting to be held. Meanwhile, her nose would be runny, and her long blonde hair was dirty and tangled. Of course, my heart went out to her! This little girl needed love, needed to be taken care of along with her siblings, just like the siblings I'd left behind. I cleaned her hair, combed it, and cut it. Soon, I found myself taking care of little children again.

But worst of all is that some of the old feelings were rushing back at me; the feelings of not being safe. Specifically, there was something about John's mother that made me uncomfortable. I couldn't put my finger on it, but one day it became clear.

I took showers in the main bathroom of the house. I couldn't lock the door because the lock was broken. One day, I was in the shower when I realized that someone else was in the bathroom with me. When I pushed the shower curtain aside, there was John's mother with a sickening smile on her face. She looked my naked body up and down and said, "What a sweet girl you are. Gaetane, don't be afraid. I'm so glad you're part of our family now."

I knew that look and I understood her intention.

"Stay away from me!" I shouted, jumping out of the shower and pushing past her without even grabbing a towel. I ran to the room that John and I used as our bedroom and locked the door as fast as I could. Soaking wet and terrified, I knew I couldn't live in this house with her. I'd had no trouble screaming at her because she wasn't my mother or father, but how could I get away from her? There was nowhere to go.

I knew I had to tell John. As soon as he got home, I told him happened and said, "If we don't move out right away, I am going back to Canada." That was a bluff, of course, because I could never go back there.

We moved just as quickly as we could. We chose a weekend that his mother and step-father were out of town. John had friends in Brooklyn we could stay with until we found our own place. It was such a relief that he believed me and acted so swiftly to protect me.

When John's mother discovered we'd left, I heard she went crazy, calling us ungrateful thieves in the night. I still don't know what John said to her and I didn't care. I told him I never wanted to see her again and he never argued about it, though he continued to visit her himself. I never asked John if he had been sexually abused, and I didn't tell him that I had been. I also worried about those children upstairs, but I didn't know what I could do about it.

It wasn't easy living with John's friends. We were sleeping on their couch for starters. I knew very few English words, so I couldn't participate in their conversations. John grew up in Canada until he was seven, so he understood French and even spoke a little. That helped.

I was glad when we finally found our own place after just a couple months. It was in the upstairs of a two-family house. The entrance was through the front door and up the stairs. Funny, there still was no door separating our upstairs from the downstairs. I wonder about that sometimes. What was it about no doors? This made John uncomfortable because he was convinced that the landlady snooped around when we weren't home. Despite his concerns, I felt safe there, especially because I liked the landlady and her family. They were young parents. Her husband worked, and she raised the children and took good care of them and the house. I was never put in the position of having to help her with the house or her children and I never felt unsafe around her. She was welcoming!

By then, it was September and John arranged my very first birthday party. He invited some of his friends and even gave me a gift - a blue topaz ring that was beautiful! Yet, I didn't feel that I deserved it. Instead, I felt embarrassed and ashamed because I had no idea what to do. What *does* one do at a birthday party, especially as the guest of honor?

I began to settle in and I found this little Italian neighborhood in Brooklyn that I loved! It felt like we were living in the heart of it all. Our landlady even taught me how to cook Italian food. I became a good Italian cook and gained weight for the first time in my life.

I also needed to rest a lot during this time. I'd been burnt out for so long; my body was aching for rest. Meanwhile, John loved his job and would leave very early in the morning. When he got home in the evening, I'd make him dinner and he'd drink a few beers and go to bed. I'd go to bed later. That was our life. There was a lack of emotional and physical intimacy from the beginning and we never did anything for fun.

I found myself deeply homesick for my siblings and friends, knowing I could never go back and live in Canada again. I cried a lot, missing my friends. On Saturday nights, I wondered what they were doing. Were they out dancing while I was with a non-social old man? John being older than me didn't look so inviting anymore.

I needed other people in my life and I wanted to get a job, so I knew I needed to learn English quickly. I felt alone with no one to talk to. I decided to get a job in a super market as a cashier so that I could learn to have conversations with people. Reading the newspapers, I realized right away that I was not up to reading the NY Times, so I stuck to the Daily News and The Post. I had my French/English Dictionary close by, especially when I was reading. Some words were very similar to the French words, and I slowly started to understand a little more English.

During this time, I learned that my mother had suffered a major heart attack. She might have died except that my aunt found her on the floor and called for an ambulance. Despite the protestations that came from John, who didn't want me to go back to Canada, who didn't even want me to be around other people, I defended my decision to go back to Canada to take care of my mother and my siblings. It was only going to be temporary until my mother recovered.

For the first time in my life, I flew on an airplane. When I got back to Hell House, my siblings were happy to see me. Sadly, I found them all in a state of neglect: cold, hungry, infested with lice, sick, and dirty. I couldn't believe my eyes. I'd been gone for less than a year! It was as if nothing I'd done before mattered; it was all undone. Adam was sick, he needed to be hospitalized and wound up in an oxygen tent at only four years old with pneumonia. Adam and mother were in the hospital the whole time I was there. As I cared for mother, I was overcome with fear of her dying and leaving all the children behind with my father. My mother even asked me to take my brother Adam and raise him if she didn't make it. I agreed. While I was at Hell House, I helped as much as I could, cleaning up my siblings and the house, making sure they had meals, getting rid of the lice. Meanwhile, my husband was calling me every day to come back home! I was very sad and angry with him; I couldn't leave these kids alone and mom in the hospital dying. His constant calling tore me to pieces.

My father was his typical drunk self. Nothing ever changed with him. I avoided him, and he stayed away from me because he was afraid of my husband. I visited a couple friends, but this trip was about helping my family because they needed me. I stayed only a couple of weeks because I had another life waiting for me, as my husband constantly reminded me. My oldest sister Doris came and took care of everyone for the next two months; she left her husband behind to do so. It gave her a chance to get to know our siblings since she barely lived with us and they got to know her as well. But God didn't want me back in that hellhole for more than two weeks. God did for me what I could not do for myself.

Before I left, I promised my brothers and sisters that I would return and bring them all new ice skates – real figure skates! I knew then that I needed to make it a practice to return once a year. Whenever I returned, they were excited that they would go out into the street to wait and watch for the car that brought me back to them. Thankfully, both Adam and mother recovered, although mother was never the same again. Her heart was damaged, yet after she got out of the hospital, she went right back to work at the Canteen; there was no reprieve for any of them.

Back in New York, summer was coming, and I was so happy when my landlady introduced me to a group of people on the block who sat together on the stoop at night to stay cool. New York summers are so hot and almost no one had air conditioners, so the stoop was the place to be. We had lots of laughs on the stoop! It all started with my name; what a challenge that was to explain because my English was very limited.

"Wait, *how* do you pronounce it?"

"Gay-*tahn*," I repeated.

"What does it mean?"

"It's Italian for Tom," one of them said.

"Can we just call you Gae?" another asked.

"Or Frenchy?"

"No," I said. Me saying no was a big hit with them, though it was embarrassing to me. They ended up calling me "Frenchy" anyway because they had such a difficult time with my name.

From then on it was, "Hey, Frenchy, where ya goin'?" or "Frenchy, whattaya doin'?" in their Brooklyn, Italian-American accents. My face would turn so red!

I loved people, but I was shy, and they kept on asking me questions that I couldn't answer in English. Still, I loved spending time with them, trying to get to know each other and laughing as we drank lots of iced tea; no one drank alcohol. I'd "hang out on the stoop" with Frankie, Mickey, Angelo, Carmine, and Josephine. Learning English with them, I thought that all New Yorkers spoke this way with phrases like "forget about it," pronounced "fuhggedaboudit." I lived the way my friends on the stoop talked and lived, and for the longest time, I spoke English with an Italian and French accent.

One of my stoop stories is about the F word. Whenever we were sitting on the stoop, everything was "F this!" and "F that!" and sometimes, "F you!" It was a word that was used repeatedly in conversation. It was used so many times; I knew it had to be a very important word! I asked what it meant and the answer, even from John, was "It's an expression." But they said it too many times for me to be satisfied with those answers. This important F-word was not in my dictionary. Determined to figure it out, I realized there was a word in French with the exact same sound - *phoque* – which meant seal, the sea animal. Armed with this knowledge, I decided that at the next stoop sitting, I was going to participate in the conversation.

"I got it. I know what fuck means!" Everyone stopped talking and looked at me. I continued.

"My grandfather bought my grandmother beautiful *phoque* coats."

They all lost it. They were laughing so hard and I couldn't understand why. I tried spelling it and explaining that it meant seal.

Now, they were roaring with laughter. Finally, they said, "No, Frenchy, no. It's a *curse* word."

Well, then I needed to find out what a curse was. When I looked up "curse" in my French/English dictionary, I was embarrassed about how I had used this word! But at least, now I knew what the fuck meant. Being an immigrant is no joke.

Every word can be a challenge. I continued hanging out on the stoop and working on my English, but I found my husband didn't like it that I loved people so much and made friends so easily. He'd come and get me from the stoop. He wasn't nasty about it, but he wasn't nice, and we all knew he had an attitude. He did nothing but work, drink beer, and seem to hate everyone. I found out that he had a shitty attitude, grumbling about everything except his work.

Chapter 19

I was still an immigrant with much to learn. There was this whole culture of womanhood on the stoop. I learned that the married women planned to have children, stay home and take care of the kids. It was the younger unmarried women who would talk about going to work. I never met any women who had a career and children.

The most confusing thing was when people would say that they worked in New York as if it was some faraway place. The first time I heard that I said, "Oh my God, I'm not living in New York?" They just laughed. Learning about the layout of New York was a huge challenge. Later, I asked John, "Why aren't we living in New York?" He explained to me that there were several parts to New York. There was a big rural area called "upstate," plus another five parts; he didn't use the word "boroughs", or I would have been more confused. It went like this: there was Queens, Brooklyn, Staten Island, the Bronx, and Manhattan. And Manhattan was the biggest city of all. It was the heart of New York, so people would say they work in the city or work in New York, and it meant that they worked in Manhattan. Even the mailing address for Manhattan isn't Manhattan, N.Y. – it's New York City, N.Y. Oh boy, that was confusing! But it made me decide that my goal was to get a job in Manhattan; in the *real* New York.

One year after learning some English I went into Manhattan to get a job. I figured that I knew enough English words to have some conversation. I had lots of knowledge from my stoop friends! First, I knew that I needed to take the subway to get to Manhattan, and the subway was right down the block. They would talk about "the L train at the New Utrecht station."

What the heck was an L? Even if I had asked, I don't think that I would have understood their answer; that it was called that because it's an elevated train running high above the streets. Most of all, I didn't want to ask anyone I knew for help. I could ask for help at the subway.

I'd read enough newspaper ads that one agency had stuck in my mind because they had lots of ads in different areas of the classifieds. I got dressed up in a beautiful yellow and black skirt-suit with a matching scarf. I looked very professional, which gave me confidence. I walked down the block with my newspaper under my arm, right down the stairs to the subway station for the first time. It was midday, and no one was around except a clerk at a central booth near the turnstile entry. I showed her the newspaper ad hoping she would tell me how to get to the agency.

"It's fifteen cents one way for a token," she said. "You're going downtown. Take the RR to Atlantic Avenue, change trains across the platform to the E. Make sure it says local and not express. Get off at Water Street, go up and make a left. The agency's right there."

I was suddenly scared. Change trains? Platform? Downtown? What did I know about local or express? I just knew that I needed to pay attention to everything she told me. She pointed to the large subway map and told me how many stops the train would make before I had to get off and even wrote it down for me. "Just look for signs," she said.

So, I put my token in the turnstile and walked up the stairs to the *platform*. Soon, the train came with a big rush of wind, and off I went! Not speaking the language in a new country can be very challenging, especially alone. I couldn't believe that I was doing this alone, but I was not afraid. I was curious, I was excited! I followed the instructions and got to Water Street without getting lost.

The underground station was hot and humid, and I can't say that it smelled all that great. But when I got up onto the street, wow! So, *this* was New York City. Huge buildings with old architecture. Everything was moving around me; wide streets full of cars and sidewalks full of people of every kind. Here I was from a small village, seeing all these other people besides the little *Riviere-Verte* town colors, cultures, and religions. It felt rich and alive! I loved the energy of the city instantly; I knew it was for me.

I walked to the agency. It was a small office with a fan whirring around, trying to keep everyone cool. A gentleman greeted me by the door and asked me some basic questions - my name, my accent, where was I from, where I lived. I was so thankful I knew how to answer these conversational questions in English. But when he gave me an application to fill out, I needed help; I hardly understood any of it.

"Do you speak French fluently?" he asked me.

"*Oui.*"

Well, he scheduled me for an interview at an international bank and gave me the address and that was that!

Because I knew about the subway now, I was feeling more confident, but I still needed some help getting to this new address. People were friendly and helpful and got me there. It turned out, the international bank was on the 9th floor. I'd never been in an elevator before and I thought the 9th floor was so high up! The interview was for a job as an investigation clerk in the French department of the bank, researching banking errors in French documents. There was no computer; back then, it was all microfiche. Reading French was easy for me, and I got the job! It paid a whopping $130 per week plus medical benefits.

On the way home, I thought I was going to pass out with excitement. I couldn't wait to get home and tell my stoop friends and my husband. I hadn't told anyone I was going to do this. John was shocked that I had done this by myself. He said to me, "When you put your mind to something, you make it happen."

That's right, I do. Looking back at how courageous I was to just pick a classified ad from the Daily News and away I went to the city of opportunity, I'm still so proud of myself. It feels like one of my greatest accomplishments. I'm still excited every time I go to Manhattan - to New York, I mean.

It turned out that I loved working in the city, but I didn't really love the job itself. I knew I needed to finish my education if I wanted a real career. I wanted to go back to school and sit in a classroom; I wanted to be a student again, so I could learn and become somebody. I'd been working as a professional in Manhattan for a few months, but I felt like a little kid walking into the local high school in Brooklyn. It took a lot of courage to tell the principal I wanted to go to school there.

Remember, I only had an eighth-grade education. But it was more like a fifth-grade education because I failed in school after I knew I was going to be taken out. The principal realized my English was limited so he spoke slowly as he explained that I what I needed was a GED; that I could not be a student there because I was too old for high school. He was very polite, but I walked out of there feeling stupid!

Eventually, I saw an ad in one of my newspapers for a correspondence course that would allow me to get my GED as well as a career certificate. The career option that really caught my interest was the medical receptionist/assistant certification. Grandma Smyde told me that I would make a great nurse. I knew I was smart enough to work in a medical office and be an assistant. Plus, the Latin-based medical words were like my French language. The school even offered private English as a second language tutors to help with the course. I knew that I needed this extra assistance. It was expensive, but John offered to pay for it. He even helped me study sometimes, although I hated that I needed help.

When I was studying, feelings would come up. There were times I was in tears, in a rage, and full of hopelessness, still stuck believing that I was stupid, that I couldn't learn. Throughout my life, this wound, this belief, reappeared though it was not how I started out. These emotions were so difficult to experience, but I was determined to do this. The course would take at least two years to complete.

I decided it was a good time to get pregnant, quit my job, stay home and study. Having a baby seemed like the normal thing to do; it was expected of a married woman. But I needed to fix something first. My period had been irregular for years. When I made my first gynecological appointment, I had to take my mind somewhere else while the doctor inspected me under the white paper sheet. Everything about getting pregnant was very scientific. I was given medicine that regulated my period and a thermometer to test when I was ovulating, and then I would tell John. There was no passion there or emotional connection; it was just a physical act to create life.

In the spring of 1969, I was pregnant. It was an emotionally difficult pregnancy. The long years of molestation had left a residual feeling of being dirty inside. My baby would have to pass through all that dirt and filth to be born. I couldn't even tell the doctor how I felt. It was another secret suffered alone. I couldn't even tell my old friend Andrea how I felt when I saw her that summer. She was pregnant, too! She had moved to upstate New York with her new husband and I visited her, then we flew to Canada, and returned to Brooklyn where we were pregnant and suffered in the heat together. Especially compared to Canada, New York summers are so hot and muggy, even at night.

My baby was due 11/19/1969, and that's when my sister Doris arrived with her husband. After our relationship growing up, I knew how Doris could be so nice, and then become so abusive very quickly. I had mixed feelings about her coming because I never knew what to expect, but she was kind to me the entire visit. Our husbands were relatives and old friends, and they would drink their beer and talk, and my sister and I would spend time together and wait for the baby and talk. I told her how Andrea's baby boy had been born a month earlier.

On 11/30/1969, I gave birth to the most beautiful little girl in the world - my daughter, Elizabeth. I was only 22. After the birth of Elizabeth, I became anemic. My sister Doris was a nurse's aide and she loved her job. She was helpful to me and little Elizabeth.

My brother Luc came to the United States the year after Elizabeth was born. We were so happy to see each other! He stopped to visit me in Brooklyn on his way to Massachusetts where he had some friends and planned to start a business. Coming from the poor economy of our little town, America was the land of opportunity.

I proudly showed him my little girl, his niece. It was then that I learned that Luc had a son born just a few days before my daughter. He'd had this child with a woman in Alberta, and he showed me a photo of this woman. When he told me they were not married, the smile left my face. I was disappointed and disgusted with my brother for having a child out of wedlock; it just reminded me of our grandfather who he admired so much. Now my brother Luc was doing the same thing. As disappointed and disgusted as I was, I didn't say anything.

Luc didn't know where his child was. He said, "I will find him one day."

Frankly, it didn't matter to me what he did about it. In hindsight, I wish that I'd been more compassionate. My grandfather had never once cared about finding any child he had fathered out of wedlock.

Over the next couple of years, I worked at different jobs as we raised our baby and I continued my studies. My favorite times were when we would take off in summer and drive across the country in a Volkswagen with a pop-up tent. It was our version of camping and sight-seeing and we were finally doing something fun together as a family. John seemed happiest when he was driving, and I loved seeing all the different places and people and feeling this sense of movement and adventure in my life. And little Elizabeth would sleep so peacefully in the little loft bed.

It felt blissful.

Chapter 20

In 1972, John bought us an 'attached' house in Valley Stream, Long Island. I hated that it was right next door to a parking lot but, mostly, I hated that it was in a suburb full of retired older people and none of the neighbors talked to each other. I really missed Brooklyn! Long Island had a different energy.

I said earlier that I thought I'd escaped hell and often the story doesn't turn out as you intend. Another piece of this new story was realizing that John drank. I knew from our time in Brooklyn that he liked a few beers in the evening. Now that we had our own living room, my husband took up residence in the large recliner where he would smoke his cigarettes and drink his beer every night after work. Lots of beer. Now that I knew, I was angry with him and angry with myself, too.

I had no friends and I had a small child to take care of, in addition to cooking and cleaning for my husband. Living with John was emotionally lonely, and he had a negative attitude about many things, muttering under his breath words I couldn't understand. I had to ask him for money for food. This was not my dream of a better life. I finally got my GED and medical receptionist certification I studied hard for. I also learned to drive.

I wasn't happily married anymore. I was alone, raising Elizabeth and restless. My husband wasn't happy with his life either, and there didn't seem to be anything I could do about that. I knew in my heart that there still was another life for me. I was young and pretty. I was smart. I learned that working could be fun. At 25, I knew this and all I wanted was a divorce.

When I was 26, I made a decision. John was upset, but I didn't give him a choice when I took my daughter and moved back to Brooklyn and left him in his recliner in the suburbs. I got my own apartment and John paid child support, which was my only income. Back then, it was enough.

But there I was, along with a 3-year-old who missed her father. I realized that I hadn't given her a choice, either. What was I doing to this poor child, dragging her into my confusion like this? It broke my heart. I felt a mother's guilt, and I felt a Catholic's guilt on top of that. Marriage was a sacred vow; was I meant to stay with John? There was some part of me that felt the need to depend on a man.

I only stayed in Brooklyn for a few months. John welcomed me back to the suburbs, but he and I had no emotional connection. It was another year before I made a firm decision to get a divorce. We sold the house and I took my part of the money and left for Brooklyn. I got a job at a bank – again in the international department. It was a happy day when my sister Grace moved in with us when she was only 16. I honestly loved those few months of my life and I felt normal for the first time. But there was to be another long battle with confusion and pain.

It started when my sister went to the telephone company and put in an order for service; that's what you did back then. At the phone company, Grace met a man named Gerald. She liked him and asked me if she could invite him over and I agreed. Unexpectedly, Gerald showed up with his friend, Freddie. They were both educated beatnik types, but what I liked so much about Freddie was that he was from Manhattan. He had an air of confidence and worldliness and he was witty, social and adventurous.

Freddie became my boyfriend, and, for the first time, I had a real social life. I felt as if I got to *live* for the first time! He was a chef and he took me everywhere, even to a chef's ball at the Waldorf Astoria. He was smart. He had been a cab driver and knew all the people and places and was a great tour guide. I loved his mom and they loved my daughter, who was starting kindergarten.

At the same time, Gerald became Grace's boyfriend. They were both amazing artists and had that bond. However, Gerald smoked marijuana. So much for the educated artistic beatnik culture; after a few months, he just seemed like a stoned hippie to me. I had to tell Grace that Gerald needed to leave. I had a little girl to raise and did not want drugs around my daughter. They left together, and my sister moved in with him.

As for me and Freddie, we were now living together and fighting together. If his confidence had once attracted me, now he seemed too loud whenever we walked into a place. It was embarrassing! And though he loved Manhattan, he hated Brooklyn. He was arrogant and a know-it-all with a sarcastic sense of humor. I knew I didn't love him, but I didn't ask him to leave.

Along the way, I got a promotion at the bank where I loved my job and felt valued. My daughter was in school and Freddie had been very helpful to her. By then, Freddie had proposed to me several times, and I said no each time. Finally, I gave in and married him on January 7th of 1977.

Even walking towards Freddie in that courtroom, all that kept going through my head was, *I'm fucked.* Seriously. I said, "I do," knowing that it was not the right choice.

The next morning, I told Freddie I knew it was a mistake. He really flipped out! He got angry with my daughter and went to hit her, and that was the end. I took her hand and we walked out of that apartment and got on the train. Where did we go? Straight to my ex-husband John, my daughter's father. She was so happy!

Freddie and I had been together for almost two years, but it was a one-day marriage with the ink barely dry on the marriage certificate when we divorced. And that was the end of that adventure!

Once again, John welcomed us back. He was now living in an apartment in Kew Gardens, Queens. Soon after we moved back in, I was pregnant again.

When I told my boss I was pregnant, I don't know what I thought would happen, but I certainly didn't expect to get demoted! I'd had such a big position at the bank, working with the vice presidents doing public relations work. In those days, pregnant women were not to be seen in those visible positions. Soon after, I quit that job. I knew my baby was more important than my job. I felt humiliated that I'd been demoted. That humiliation stayed with me even after I chose to leave.

John and I remarried so that our new child would have his name and I could keep peace within myself and God. It felt like a religious obligation to be married. It seemed perfectly reasonable that God wanted me to marry John and stay married to him. The underlying message, however, was that I didn't trust that I could be on my own.

With two adults, a child, and a baby on the way, there was no way our family could stay in the little apartment John was renting. I knew I couldn't live in the suburbs again, so we bought a Victorian house in Richmond Hill, Queens. It looked like a beautiful place to live! The entire block was made up of Victorian homes. There were large trees on the block. I loved our house.

It was July when we moved there. I was 6 months pregnant. When we first moved in, there was a block party going on. It was a great opportunity to meet our new neighbors. Of course, I attended and, when I introduced myself and gave people my name, they had lots of questions. The block was made up of a diverse group of people, which was something I enjoyed. As I walked around, I saw Belle for the first time. She was bigger than life - a beautiful blond-haired woman with turquoise eyes, the biggest smile and the whitest teeth. Her hair was wild and beautiful and when she smiled at me, I could tell that she was going to be a lot of fun. Of course, she asked about my name. "What is this name, Gaetane? Is it Canadian?" Over the years, she called me "The Canadian."

It was October 7th, 1978 when I gave birth to our son, Jonathan. He was an adorable blond baby; the very picture of his sister! Elizabeth was now almost 9 years old. While I felt that going back to John was the right thing to do, it also took me right back to unhappiness. Nothing had changed except our location and that there was now another mouth to feed. John drank and worked incessantly while I took care of the children, kept everything clean, and still, I had no money. We were renting out the top floor of our house for extra income, so there was no reason I should be counting pennies to buy our baby's formula when John could afford all the beer he could possibly drink, and cigarettes, too. The baby formula cost a dollar, and I cried one day as I counted out 98 pennies; pennies that reminded me of when I was hungry as a child.

I decided I needed to go back to work, but I was done with banks. For the first time, I used my medical receptionist certification and got a job in a medical office. While the doctor was very happy with my work, his attention seemed to create animosity among my coworkers. There was one manager who made up a story about me stealing money as if this was a plausible way to take her jealousy out on me. I hadn't stolen anything, of course, and it brings up awful feelings to this day. If she only knew how I lived when I was little - working hard for everything, never taking a penny - she would know how absurd her story was. It tainted everything, of course, and my time there was short-lived.

It was a time in my life that I needed some fun. I gravitated towards Belle. To me, she was exciting and wild, and that meant fun. I found out that we had a lot in common, like having grown up in 'imperfect' families of 9 children. Like me, she worried about her siblings; and had high anxiety. She had brothers who had issues with the law, others with drugs. She had a heart of gold and was the most giving person I'd ever met. She offered her home to those who needed her. One of her friends was married and very poor, so Belle offered her house to come and take a hot bath when she had no running water. Any woman who needed a place for the night was welcome, kids and all. She was a savior. She wanted everything to be okay with everyone.

Most of all, I admired that she could be divorced with a child and still make ends meet. She lived with her daughter who she loved more than life itself. She adored that girl and was very protective of her. And Belle made her own money. She was a professional florist; she did upholstery; she worked with famous people in Manhattan, like John Lennon; and she even dated celebrities from time to time.

Belle adored the flowers she worked with. She loved nature and was not afraid to get her hands dirty. Her fingernails were broken because of her work and she had big, strong hands. She was the first person I knew who talked about organic gardening and farming. She would buy natural vegetables and herbal teas that you couldn't find in a regular supermarket. She had fresh ginger and herbs in her kitchen for the teas she made. She was ahead of her time in many ways.

One day, Belle asked me to go to the beach. All I could think of was the river in Canada where we'd go on a summer day, with the sun that hurt my eyes and rough rocks on my feet. I said, "No, I don't like the beach."

"How the fuck can you not like the beach?" She asked me. "Let's go!" Finally, I gave in. I marveled at the power of the ocean; it seemed like the most powerful thing in the world. And in New York, the ocean is warm, and the sand is soft. We'd pack up the kids and off we'd go with Belle driving her old car with one hand on the wheel and the other putting on mascara. And a cup of tea that she could balance under one arm.

My daughter loved Belle; I think Belle was her idol for a time. Elizabeth would say, "Mom, did you see Belle's shoes? Did you see her clothes or jewelry or new haircut?" Elizabeth loved everything about Belle, and they laughed together. Poor Elizabeth. At the time, she certainly didn't have a mom who was very funny, like Belle was. I didn't have that kind of lightness in my heart. I was still very angry and confused. Belle just brought out the best in me; she brought out the best in everyone; she brought out the laughter in everything.

One thing that I loved about her was that she never bashed anyone, ever. She was not a gossip; she truly cared about everyone and all our problems. On the block, there were a few of us women who were not happily married. We hung out at Belle's house at night, telling funny stories, talking about serious relationship issues, who we were and what we stood for. We could go there to laugh, cry, scream, and talk, all while bleaching our hair or polishing our nails. It was the "beauty" place to be. We were all loved by Belle and had a feeling that we were protected and could be ourselves. What a loving time and so much fun!

Come Friday night, Belle would go off to the city with her friends. As I said, Belle dated celebrities from time to time, and she liked to hang out in Manhattan at all the famous places she knew. She was aware that I was unhappy in my marriage so one day she asked me to go with her and her friends to dance and listen to some music in Manhattan. I said yes. My husband wasn't happy about it, but he didn't stop me, either.

When we got to the place, it was mobbed with standing room only. You could hardly hear anything but the music. Someone next to me asked me to dance. I turned to look at the person and nearly fell over - it was James Brown himself! All I could think was, *Oh my God, James Brown!* How was it possible that I was standing next to *James Brown?* He didn't have a pretty face, but he had a huge smile and to watch him dance was something else! After we danced, he asked me to go to a party uptown. I got scared and said, "No, thank you." When I told Belle, her first response was exactly what I expected: "What the fuck? Go! Are you nuts?"

I couldn't. I was too afraid. Besides, however unhappily, I was married with children under God. But that night was an incredible experience that I'll never forget.

Chapter 21

Aside from the slice of heaven that was having Belle as my friend, I was completely lost when it came to my home life. I was living with secrets again and alcoholism surrounded me. I was in a state of deep emotional pain and full of anger and fear. It was an especially scary place with two children who depended on me for everything.

I went back to work again for extra money until, one day when I was working, little Jonathan hurt his finger. He had fallen out of the stroller in our driveway when my husband was watching him. Jonathan had hurt his finger badly that his fingernail was completely torn off! I decided then that I needed to quit my part-time job so that I would be the one to watch over the children. I couldn't trust my husband to be responsible for their well-being if he was drinking.

My pent-up emotional baggage showed up with me dressing my daughter all in white. Both of my children looked like photos from a magazine. My son wore saddle shoes, for which he was teased unmercifully. They both were washed, starched and ironed; pristine and perfect; the very model of cleanliness. Neither was ever dressed to play. Dirt wasn't allowed anywhere near them. The only time they really got to play was when we went to the beach with Belle or went camping for the summer as a family.

My need to clean was compulsive. It went as far as continually painting the inside and outside of the house to keep it looking fresh. One day, I walked outside with a new can of paint. I was going to paint the house again. It didn't even need any paint, but I was going to paint it anyway. And that's when it hit me that something was terribly wrong with me. I could not stop the tears as I stood there holding the paint can. I rarely cried; I preferred to be angry. But at that moment, I had a complete breakdown, because *I* was the one who was dirty inside in a place I could not reach.

I was now babysitting five children in addition to caring for my own children and still stuck in a loveless marriage. All of this was familiar. But my newest and biggest concern was that my daughter had started acting out, cutting school when she was only twelve years old and hanging out with people who smoked cigarettes. We argued constantly.

I knew that I needed to do something more; that I needed an anchor in my life other than my children. My husband felt like an anchor in all the wrong ways, like a dead weight slowly drowning the life out of me. I attended church and prayed, but it wasn't enough. In my desperation, I joined a group in my church that met on Tuesday nights. These meetings were all about revival, renewal, being born again, focusing on a personal relationship with God, and expressing the gifts of the spirit.

Now, my faith runs deep, but some of these people were screwball fanatics. Take Peachy. One day, Peachy says to me, "Gaetane, I'm a virgin again." Peachy said strange things, but this was so strange. This was a woman who ran around town with every man she met! In all seriousness, I asked her, "Peachy, how can you be a virgin again?" She replied, "When you're born again, God forgives all your sins and you're clean. So, I'm a virgin again." I had serious doubts that what she suggested was possible; I'd had a relationship with God for years and I didn't feel clean.

At one of the renewal meetings, I met another woman named Rita. For some reason, I shared with her that my husband drank a lot of beer; that I'd grown up in an alcoholic home and that my father was crazy. I shared my opinion that all alcoholics were evil and violent because my father certainly was. At the time, I didn't believe that John was an alcoholic because he only drank beer.

She looked at me and said, "Gaetane, beer *is* alcohol." She told me that her husband was an alcoholic and had been in a program for many years. She herself regularly attended a program for family members of alcoholics, which had helped her a lot. She suggested that I should try going to one of those meetings. I'd heard about these "meetings" before and I politely declined because I didn't want to sit in a meeting and listen to people talk about alcohol. After talking about alcohol for just five minutes with her, I'd heard enough to last me a lifetime! And that was the end of that conversation.

Some time went by. My situation wasn't getting better and neither was I. Still, I went to church and prayed. At some point, I talked to Rita again. This time, she tried a different approach. She told me that she knew a very special couple named Tony and Joyce. "They pray with people. I think they may be able to help you." Well, that was more like it! I knew I needed to try something new and I made an appointment with them as soon as I could.

When I met with Tony and Joyce, I told them that I was concerned that my twelve-year-old daughter was acting out. I knew my daughter was suffering because of the life we had lived, moving so many times and changing schools. I told them that she was my main concern; that I feared for her future. I also told them that my husband drank lots of beer and that I was angry and sad, distraught and confused.

I confessed to this couple, "I don't know how much more I can handle."

I agreed to let them do what they were known for among the renewal group because I could no longer live full of rage and hate and despair. I let these people pray on me – or, I should say, *prey* on me, because that is not so far off from what I experienced.

In the middle of praying, Joyce asked me, "How many siblings do you have?"

"Eight," I replied.

"Well, God chose you," Joyce told me, "God called on you to break a curse or a chain of something that's generational and full of darkness."

I had been open to her perspective, but when she said this, my whole body stiffened. She continued.

"Out of your whole family, God chose you to break this very dark curse in your life." She went on to say that God wanted me to "go to meetings."

Meetings, again? I thought. *This time, a recommendation from God, Himself?* The whole thing suddenly felt like such a scam, and I went into a crazy rage.

"Oh really?" I replied, getting up and grabbing my things. "God wants me to suffer some more? Well, thank you - and fuck you! I will not go to some meeting or any place where they meet to talk about alcohol. Alcohol destroyed my life!"

I stormed out and never went back to them again.

It took another year of constant suffering before I met another woman at church who managed to tell me more about these meetings for people affected by the alcoholism of others before I could shut her down as well.

I write about it here as if everyone understands what "going to meetings" involves. I certainly didn't. I didn't think anyone could help me with the struggle of dealing with a husband who abused alcohol every day, let alone help me with the abuse I had suffered from my alcoholic father who I didn't even want to think about. It was easy for me to say no to these meetings because I had no idea that sharing my burden could be helpful, that listening to others' stories and insights could be helpful.

But I'd tried everything, and I was exhausted from trying things that didn't work. I was so desperate that when this woman brought up going to meetings that, for the first time, I listened. I didn't see myself as someone who could change anything. All I wanted was some relief from my suffering, and this woman was encouraging! By the end of our conversation, I was practically begging to find a meeting.

So, there I was on a cold night in March, heading to a meeting in my neighborhood. It was in the basement of a church; one of those common areas for coffee and conversation. There was a group of people there, setting up chairs in a circle. As I looked around, I was spotted by a gentleman who must have quickly surmised that I was a first-timer. He introduced himself by saying his name and then he added, "I'm an alcoholic."

I swear if I'd had a weapon, I would have hurt him. *An alcoholic? Great.* I realized I had ended up at an Alcoholics Anonymous meeting by accident, instead of a support group for family members of alcoholics, and I wanted no part of it. I just knew that everyone in that basement was an alcoholic; evil and violent; there could be nothing nice about them.

I told him that I was looking for an Al-Anon meeting, and he said there was one planned on Sunday night nearby. I thanked him and left as quickly as I could. I wish I had responded with more respect and grace but at the time, I had none to give.

That Sunday evening, I attended my first Al-Anon meeting. It was located at another local church, and I had my first experience with a group that would be a huge support system for me in the future. It was 1982, I was 35 years old, and my journey of "recovery" was just beginning.

During the next year, I was at that meeting every Sunday. It was a different kind of church for me because there was still a belief in a "higher power," but now the spiritual lessons were focused on the "disease of alcoholism." I learned how it had affected me as a child, and how it was affecting me now as an adult, a wife, and a mother. For the first time, I was able to get some perspective on what I had gone through and what I was going through. I never missed one meeting; in those days, it was the only thing that kept me sane.

I learned about myself as I interacted in this group setting. I had a lot to express; I was very opinionated. They called me "Firecracker" because I was so hot-tempered. I would react to things quickly, and not in a good way. I surprised myself with the mouth I had on me! Maybe it was from all the years of pent-up anger. I had thought that my anger kept me strong, but I came to learn that there was something underneath all that powerful anger: a deep sadness. I hadn't been able to feel the sadness before because it was too scary to feel. I learned that feelings weren't right or wrong; they just *were*.

As I began to recover, I realized that Tony and Joyce hadn't been all that far off when they said God wanted me to go to meetings - I just hadn't been ready to hear it at that time in my life. Going to these meetings, I became able to identify the roles I had taken on in my family, and I started to understand what Tony and Joyce had been trying to say about generational family patterns.

I still didn't think I could change anything in my life. I never expected my father to come to his senses and cure his disease of alcoholism and embrace any of the principles I was learning in these meetings. I didn't expect John to be open to the possibility either. *I* was the one who needed to be impeccable with my own integrity and truth.

I stopped trying to manage my husband's alcoholism. I was done nagging and arguing and being "codependent"; I began working on myself. Out of the blue, John came to me one day and said, "I think I have a problem with alcohol." He was especially concerned that he would drink before he went to work at five in the morning.

Of course, John knew I was attending Al-Anon. He wanted my help. I got him the number for an Alcoholics Anonymous sponsor. The next thing I knew, John started going to meetings and he stopped drinking - just like that.

I don't know what I expected from my husband getting sober; he was still a workaholic and a grouch. Drinking had never changed him that much, and sobriety didn't seem to, either. My next breakthrough came one Sunday at an Al-Anon meeting when a woman in our group shared her personal recovery story. She was beautiful and very well-spoken, but what really caught my attention was when she started talking about her therapist who had helped her. This therapist was a social worker skilled in the disease of alcoholism and even attended meetings herself. I was impressed with this speaker and the way she told her story that I decided to make an appointment with this therapist.

It was the spring of 1983, only a year into my recovery. Support groups had helped me personally, but I was still confused about how my life with John still wasn't working though he was sober. My daughter was still acting out. Going to see this private therapist was a special trip for me and a challenge. I could feel the excitement of what was about to happen and at the same time, I felt a sense of absolute terror.

I wore a navy-blue dress with a white collar, navy shoes, and a navy handbag. I took my proper, clean self on the train to her Manhattan office. I was early and not a hair was out place. From my new therapist, I would learn that these things didn't matter. "The world will not end," Ramona would tell me. In fact, she had traveled the world about sixty times, perhaps to prove just that.

Meeting her for the first time, I was astonished! She was tall and beautiful with a gentle spirit and smile. Her appearance wasn't perfect; she looked *real.* This was exactly what I needed; I needed a real person in my life. I loved her instantly! I still do.

At our first session, Ramona took out her legal pad and took notes as I answered questions about myself, my family, and history. I found myself sharing the intimate details of my life with this stranger. It was such a relief that I had someone to talk to; someone I felt comfortable with right away. Early on in our therapy, I told Ramona about grandma, my angel who had made the most delicious donuts; the love of my life who went crazy.

Ramona told me, "Because of your experience with your grandma's unconditional love, you will be alright." She explained that when someone is abused to the degree that I had been, the only chance of coming out of it okay is if they have someone in their life who loves them unconditionally; that many abuse victims don't have anyone, and their life becomes a struggle with self-esteem and finding a way to survive. Thriving isn't even an option without that love.

Hearing this gave me hope. Once again, because of grandma, I was going to survive.

After that, in memory of grandma, I started buying a donut every time I went to see Ramona. It became part of my therapy. I still feel her love even today, the unconditional love of my gracious, sweet grandma. I must have eaten at least three-hundred donuts as I went through my therapy!

I became so grateful for my grandma, and all the other loving angels throughout my life. And Ramona became another angel to me. From her, I learned so much about my creative self. I had no idea that I was so creative. I knew that my mother was creative, especially at Christmas time, and I knew that Belle was creative. I knew about creativity because I had seen it, but I knew nothing about myself when it came to my own creativity. Other people were the creative ones - not me.

"I'm not creative," I told her.

Ramona said right away, "You've been brainwashed." She said that with that big sigh of hers.

The word 'brainwashed' scared me. I knew nothing of brainwashing; only that it was someone else controlling your thoughts and your mind. Maybe it was like being hypnotized. One time a friend got stuck after being hypnotized and we were all afraid he'd never come out of it. She assured me that she and her team would help me to "deprogram" the brainwashing I'd received growing up. This was all about breaking generational patterns.

Chapter 22

In the first year of my therapy, I dreamt a lot. I got to know myself through my dreams, with Ramona's help. There were times that I didn't understand the dreams; I had no idea what they meant. Ramona would tell me, "When you dream, it's your subconscious. It's your truth. You'll know what it means, but only when you're ready."

One night during that first year, I had the worst nightmare of my life. I dreamt that I was trapped and buried under piles of dirt. The dirt looked like large dark triangles, piled very high – there were piles and piles of them. The feeling they gave me was one of disgust. As in many nightmares, there seemed to be no way out of this hellish situation. I kept looking for a way out, digging through the piles of dirty triangles, and finally, I found a hole. I dug at the hole; digging frantically to escape and what revealed itself was the face of a monster. I woke up in terror. The dream was so frightening that I was afraid to fall asleep for fear that I might dream about it again.

When I saw Ramona again and told her about this nightmare, she suggested I draw the face I had seen. She told me that art therapy was the best form of therapy for survivors of abuse. I was willing to explore my dream through drawing without any fear or judgment about being 'creative'. The work on these conscious and subconscious levels was a huge part of my deprogramming.

I went home determined to draw this nightmare. I had never been able to draw anything, but that night I started with what I had seen in my dream and only focused on drawing it and I did not stop. I still cannot believe what happened. As I drew, I realized that what I was drawing was not piles of dirt triangles like in the nightmare; it was feces. Piles and piles of shit.

It was the outhouse.

I saw that I was drawing one of the places — the *worst* place - where my father took me to molest me. I started sobbing when I realized it was the outhouse from my childhood. The "hole" was the toilet seat, covered in shit. In the hole was the monster, and the monster's face was my father's!

I sobbed and sobbed as I drew. For the first time in my life, I acknowledged to my conscious adult mind that I had been sexually molested repeatedly since I was old enough to remember; that it had been so painful to remember that I shut it out for years. Finally, I felt all these painful feelings from the past that I had never let myself feel, and it hurt so much I felt like I was going to die.

Afterward, I walked around most of the night, shaking my head in disbelief. I didn't understand how all these years this nightmare was locked out of my mind. I still had gaps in my memory, but I knew it was real. I could never split this painful part of myself off again. I was awake, and the nightmare was still there - it was *true*.

In my next session, I brought my drawing of the nightmare. I was terrified to tell Ramona that I had been sexually abused by my father. I had never told *anyone*. How could I if I'd kept it hidden even from myself? My powerful experience with disclosure eventually motivated me to write down the things that made the difference between life and death; success and failure; taking a step forward or hiding forever in the shadows. I titled this document *Guidelines of Disclosure of Sexual Abuse.*

God, I felt safe with her! I felt that I could say things to her that I'd never shared with another human being. Because of that, with all the courage I could summon, I disclosed my childhood of incest and sexual abuse.

Before our session ended that day, Ramona asked my permission to consult with a professional incest therapist. She told me that she was not trained in child sexual abuse. My heart sank.

"Don't worry," she said quickly, "I know someone who is." She suggested that I make an appointment, and I did.

After I saw that incest professional once, I went back to my therapist and told her, "I have to stay with you if I'm going to heal. You are the one I trust." She told me that was my choice, and *choice* was something I'd never had. It was a choice to continue working with her though she wasn't skilled in that area. I made the choice to do just that.

As I left Ramona's office that day, I was so relieved. Yet, having disclosed the truth of what had happened for the first time, I felt the fear of my father finding out that I had "told" hit me full force. I took the train home, got in the house, and locked myself in the bathroom. I was petrified! Remember, my father said he'd kill me if I told anyone. I truly believed that my father would soon be at my door, ready to kill me.

Photo Collages

The photographs on the following two pages feature moments from childhood and teenage years. Notes for each photo are below.

Photo Collage 1

Upper Left – Me at age 15 taking care of my siblings. I called them my children.

Upper Right – From Left – Mom, Brother Jacques, Me, Sister Doris holding Antoinette

Lower Left – My first day of school – happiest day of my life. I loved my school bag I was proud of it. I had a seersucker little blue dress. My sister Doris was starting second grade with her little pink seersucker and fancy shoes. My mother said I was too much of a tomboy for fancy shoes.

Lower Right – From left – Me, Jacques, Luc and Doris. Jacques' little red fire truck was a rare toy for us. We are standing in front of the little red house.

Photo Collage 2

Upper Left – 1964 in front of the canteen. I loved these girls. My father was standing in the door. These girls became my family and to this day we are close friends.

Upper Right – 1965 at age 15 in front of the canteen. I am holding my little brother Adam. My sister Antoinette is standing next to me with figure skates that were too big for her.

Bottom – The opening of the canteen in the summer of 1964. Andrea and I next to her cousin's convertible. He had come to visit from Connecticut.

Collage 1

Collage 2

Chapter 23

The following week, I had a question for Ramona. "Why do I remember so little about the actual details of my abuse?" Ramona explained that the reason I didn't remember all the details was that I had *protected* myself from the details. That was the first time I ever heard the word *dissociation*.

"What is that?" I asked, "How could I not be there for my own life?"

Even with professional help, it took me a long time to understand how dissociation is the mind's way of saving us. It creates "the empty space"; a space in which the details are gone. The sexual abuse inflicted upon me by my father disappeared; my body disappeared, and *I* disappeared. The feelings remained. Dissociation affected my intimacy with men, and my relationships with my children, my work, and even with God.

My mind continued to protect me. When I tried to remember the details, it was like a white wall with nothing written on it. No matter how hard I stared at it, I couldn't make the words appear.

These dissociated memories were the most difficult part of my life to reclaim. I wanted recovery; one must want it more than anything to go through this process and, in that process, I believe that God handpicked every mental health professional with whom I worked. I decided that I *had* to remember! I assured myself that I was ready. And as I kept doing my work, I started to remember things.

My father had a brother who died when I was very young. He was handsome, like my father, with blond curly hair. When my father called me in to "love me", even at a very young age, I had a feeling that something wasn't right. I couldn't remember what he did with me; what I do remember was wishing that I were a boy - because he never called my brothers, not even once.

When my father called my mother's name, she would immediately say to me, "Go see what he wants, Gaetane." I hated her for that. Taking the first step up the stairs to him, my mind would go blank. I remember white sheets. Nothing more. It was always the same.

During this time of searching, I realized that my friend Andrea had been around my house almost every day. She'd come in the back door and she'd sit in the old wooden chair that was against the wall in the kitchen, with the old towel-holder and round mirror on the wall behind her. If I was hanging out with her when my father called me, that's where she'd wait for me. It was right near the stairs that led up to the bedrooms.

Suddenly, there was someone else who might remember what I couldn't! Right then and there, I made up my mind to disclose my secret to Andrea. I went to visit her upstate just as soon as I could.

"I'm in therapy," I told Andrea, "and there are things I can't remember. I need your help. I'm counting on you to remember so that I can remember. *You* were there, Andrea. You would sit in the kitchen and wait for me. You're the only one who can help me remember."

When I told Andrea what I knew about the sexual abuse we cried together for some time. She told me that her mother must have known because when I had left Canada, she knew it was the best thing that could happen to me.

Yes, of course, she remembered being there in the kitchen. I asked her if she remembered my father calling my mother, and my mother sending me upstairs to him. She remembered that, too.

"What happened then?" I asked, excited yet scared that she was helping me remember.

"You'd go upstairs."

"For how long?"

"Not long."

"What did I do when I came back downstairs?" I asked.

"You cleaned and talked nonstop!"

This was interesting to me because I still went on cleaning sprees. This, by the way, is a big incest signal. I had no idea at the time that what I had been doing my whole life was the result of dissociation. I suddenly remembered that even when I was small, after an encounter with my father, I cleaned everything in sight.

"But what did I *talk* about?" I asked Andrea.

"Boys, music, fashion. But it was different because you just talked *nonstop*. I couldn't get a word in."

So, in my dissociated state, I was not able to have a two-way conversation. I was not able to be present with another person – not even my best friend. The state of "not being there" continued even once the danger was over. Where my memory got triggered to shut off was very clear: taking that first step on the stairs. Coming *out* of dissociation was another story. Andrea helped me so much. I wasn't alone anymore. She'd been the most generous, loving friend and continues to be so.

Ramona raised me like a child through therapy. I had to learn it all like a baby learns, except it was even more challenging because a baby is a clean slate. Me, I had to unlearn my beliefs; I had to unlearn reacting and learn to create; I had to unlearn running away before I could learn how to stay.

I lived with only a head and a face. I saw my body physically and yet, it didn't exist. I had no idea that I'd left my body behind in dissociation years ago. I was in New York, seeing so many beautiful women. It was baffling to feel that I wasn't like them. Well, how could I be? I had no female body; I had no body at all.

Around this time, I took a job as an OB-GYN medical assistant. I was afraid and excited at the same time. Perhaps I would turn out to be a normal woman with all the body parts of a woman; perhaps I wouldn't.

Eventually, the issue of me not having a body came up in my therapy, and our conversations revealed new possibilities. It was scary, but I started getting it: I had a body and I had all the parts a woman should have. The issue became how I *felt* about "down there." I didn't just feel unclean; I felt filthy. My children had been forced to pass through all that filth, which made my pregnancies very stressful emotionally. I *knew* I was filthy because I could *feel* it. I'd felt it for years.

Ramona recommended a gynecologist who specialized in helping sexual abuse survivors reclaim those parts of themselves that they'd lost. I was terrified but agreed to see her.

This gynecologist told me I could ask her anything and that she would keep me safe. So, I told her how filthy I felt "down there."

"Nothing could be further from the truth," she assured me. "I'll show you."

Show me? I couldn't even give this body part a name, and now I was going to look at it?

As I lay with my feet in the cold, hard stirrups, she kept reassuring me that I was going to be okay as she examined me. Then, she positioned a mirror in front of me and asked me to look at my cervix in the light.

145

"Look," she said. "You are so pink and clean."

I could not believe my eyes, but it was true! For the first time in my life, I saw that I wasn't filthy. I saw that I had a vagina and a cervix like other women and that it was clean. I started to sob and kept sobbing. It was the beginning of acknowledging that I was like all other women. It didn't happen quickly; it was a process. I came out of the doctor's office in awe and very curious. Slowly, I started to notice my physical shape and connect to the body I had left behind so many years ago.

I learned a lot about my potential, my capabilities with Ramona. She said to me, "You are so strong. All that you are was used for negative energy, and when you turn that around, I can't wait to see what you do with all of your strength!"

What I chose to do with my strength was contact the Canadian social services department of mental health and report my father for his many crimes of domestic and sexual abuse, and to ask about having him arrested. My courage and strength for coming forward were praised, but I was too late. Too much time had passed; it had been almost 20 years since I left Canada. They told me that if other family members would have pursued it at the time, we could have had my father put in jail. But that didn't happen, no one came forward, only me.

Disclosing to my husband wasn't an option for me. I knew it wouldn't be like my disclosure with Ramona, or even Belle, who, when I told her, was furious at my father. I knew it wasn't something he wanted to hear. It wasn't something that people talked about back then. It was taboo. It was shameful and disgusting. Plus, I was afraid he wouldn't believe me. So, I didn't say anything to him.

But one day, John asked me why I was going to Manhattan for therapy. "Why isn't Al-Anon enough?" he asked me. He couldn't see why I needed additional therapy, all the way in Manhattan every week for months now. By then, John was sober. He'd been attending AA for a while. He was "in program." To me, us both being in recovery seemed to invite a certain level of emotional honesty, and that is the moment when I disclosed to him that I had been sexually abused by my father; that was why Al-Anon wasn't enough; that was why I needed this extra therapy.

It was my worst nightmare come true. He simply didn't believe me, and that was the end of that conversation. We never talked about it again and I don't think I ever forgave him. It was just a few months later that I told John I wanted a divorce. I had been attending meetings for two years and therapy for a year. By that time in my recovery, I was finally able to face my feelings and to honor them. I had a support system in place to take some action and finally make the decision to get divorced. The message that I thought came from God, the message that John and I were meant to be together forever, had gotten weary and worn. *Not at my expense*, I thought, *Not at the expense of my life.* It was painful to acknowledge that my husband was wrong for me; wrong for my recovery; wrong for the happy life that I was trying to find.

Why did it take so long, you might ask? You might recognize my patterns as you read them here, so why didn't I recognize them as they were happening? The truth is that during those years of marriage, though I was sad with a husband who had no interest in anything, we traveled quite a bit and did a lot of camping across the U.S. in a Volkswagen camper with a pop-up top. It was so different for me and it was fun. I'd also gotten an education and found jobs and there were people around me who valued me and my contribution. Some patterns are more difficult to recognize, and some tolerations seem worth the effort for the belonging and acknowledgment that went along with them.

When I told John I wanted a divorce, he was angry. He remained angry even as he granted me a divorce and bought me out of the house and let me leave with our children. He was still angry when he eventually remarried. I could understand his anger and I felt a lot of compassion, but I knew I had to leave. It was more important to have compassion for myself.

Chapter 24

Despite all my feelings of guilt over abandoning my husband, I was happy when I moved! It was the winter of 1984 and I found the cutest little house. My son was in school now and doing very well. But my daughter was still cutting school. Elizabeth was only fifteen and I was scared. We were constantly arguing. I didn't know what to do.

One of the hardest parts of my journey was having no answers; and often looking to others for answers. I sought answers through someone else like I was a shadow. Just call me a walking, devastated human being, trying to find my way in the world with no clue about reality and the truth of life, let alone how to handle a troubled teenager.

My sense of internal guidance was very limited. I thought the people in Al-Anon were smarter than me; I thought everyone was smarter than me at that time. I trusted that they would know how to guide me and that I should listen to them. Well, they convinced me that my daughter was doing drugs and that she should go to this new half-way house that was just opening.

Elizabeth living with her father was not even an option to me; I didn't think he was responsible enough to handle an out-of-control teenager. If she went to live with him, I was sure she would just keep cutting school and get deeper into drugs. So, I insisted Elizabeth go to the half-way house.

My daughter protested that she was not on drugs, but I didn't believe her. That's when she threatened to run away. In my best unskilled motherly way, I became cruel, taking bad advice from people who I swore knew better than me. I told my daughter, "If you run away, don't come home. I will not let you in."

Well, it turned out that my daughter was not on drugs. She didn't run away, and I sent her to the half-way house. God only knows why she went along with it. Today, I know that Elizabeth would have done better in private therapy, or family therapy with me. I'm sad about what happened. I can't change what I did, although I often wish I could. These are the consequences of not having any self-esteem. My daughter suffered because of it.

I would talk about my suffering and the suffering of my family in therapy and my meetings. The biggest difference was that, at my meetings, I focused on only the alcoholism and domestic violence; but I had to be very selective in disclosing my sexual abuse. At some point, I decided I needed to tell my sister, Eileen. After all, she had become a social worker. She was the one sibling who I felt I could talk to. Guess what - she didn't believe me!

Around that time, I got the news that my uncle George was in the hospital dying. I had spent a summer with him when I was so young; he was the one who had shown me what the love of a father should be. I knew I did not want to disclose my sexual abuse to him, but I wrote him a long letter to thank him for his love; for showing me what a father could be.

My aunt Debbie told me that my Uncle George would bring my letter to the hospital with him when he went for his treatments. He even had my letter when he died! I'm so glad I wrote it and that it meant so much to him. He truly did love me, and I am grateful for the love of this amazing father figure in my life.

Meanwhile, I was living in my house, my son was in school and my daughter in the half-way house and I continued going to my therapy and my meetings. In addition to Al-Anon, I would attend ACOA meetings for Adult Children of Alcoholics. I finally decided I was ready to share the rest of my story at ACOA; my whole story of growing up with a violent alcoholic who had also sexually abused me for years. I had seen a lot of people share their stories. In all the stories people shared of their lives affected by alcohol, no one ever spoke of being sexually abused as a child. I was terrified to share this information, but these people had been so supportive.

When I told my story for the first time, it brought a lot of people to me. I was the first person to ever disclose childhood sexual abuse at this Al-Anon group in Queens. It encouraged others to come forward and as it turned out, I was not alone. I discovered that I had a lot of company and support. Because of these support meetings I attended, a series of other doors opened, each a passageway to my healing. One suggestion was to attend an incest awareness workshop. Once I had opened the floodgates of my secrets, I joined quite a few other groups as well.

It was at ACOA that I met Dave. He was so tall and handsome! But I was freshly divorced, and I didn't really notice him in that way; he was just another addict telling his story of recovery. Dave's story went like this. He had grown up with two brothers in Queens, in a very bad part of a poor neighborhood full of drug dealers and addicts and crime. He had been very young when he started using alcohol and drugs. He had never been abused by his parents, but he had been abused by drug dealers. Many of these drug dealers were black, so Dave hated blacks. But he also seemed to hate Jews and Hispanics and just about everyone who wasn't white or Italian.

He'd become a heavy user and had gotten involved with some bad people over the years; he mentioned the mafia. When he drank, the story went that he became wild and crazy. He'd beat people and leave them for dead and he didn't care. Meanwhile, he was still stuck in this terrible neighborhood. It was typical to stay in the neighborhood in which you were born and raised, and his family never wanted to move.

There was an Italian family in the neighborhood, and Dave ended up marrying one of their daughters. He said he'd been using a lot of cocaine at the time and he would get so paranoid that he would sleep with a rifle under his pillow. "I don't know how my wife let me do that!" he said. He was never violent towards her, so maybe that's why. At any rate, they divorced.

At the point in time when he told his story, Dave had been clean and sober for a couple of years. He was deeply involved in his recovery, attending ACOA, AA, and NA, and even volunteered with violent alcoholics in the prison system. It was a huge transformation.

I saw Dave a few more times at ACOA. He was hard to miss because he was so tall! When we first met, he told me that there was this fat Mafia hit guy who wanted to kill him and that he had to watch his back. The fat guy was in jail but that wouldn't stop him from sending someone else after Dave to kill him. After hearing his story and hearing about this hitman, you'd think that would have been a clue as to how bad these men were that Dave had been involved with and that there was something wrong with this picture. I started dating him anyway. I was still clueless.

We started dating over the summer. I had just gotten a divorce the previous year; I hadn't been looking for love, but Dave told me that he was. I could not deny that I was very attracted to this man in so many ways. He was very intelligent and liked to be neat and organized like me; plus he was very funny. We laughed a lot together! And we had amazing passionate chemistry. I felt safe in his arms. Before I knew it, I was in love with him – in love for the first time in my life since I was 14 - and when Dave proposed to me, I said yes.

By then, my daughter had met Dave a couple times and knew his story. I knew she didn't like him, but I was in love with him. I went to see her at the half-way house and told her that we were getting married. My daughter was 16 years old and had grown up in New York; she was street-smart. As soon as I told her, Elizabeth got very angry at me, very scared for me. She said to me, "Oh my God, Mom, are you crazy? You can't marry this guy! He is the biggest *drug* addict - he shoots drugs up his arm! What about AIDS? Aren't you worried about that?" She was so upset that she was crying.

Here was my wise daughter who had never been a drug addict, yet because of me she was living in a half-way house for drug addicts, and at the same time had to warn me against marrying a drug addict. "Mom, he is crazy, and he is dangerous. *Please* don't do this," she begged me with tears in her eyes. But no matter what she said or how much she begged me, nothing she could do would change my mind.

At the time, I thought that being in recovery was about making all those bad things people did go away. I thought being in recovery made him a better person. I thought he was "cured." I stubbornly believed Dave had turned his life around and there was no going back for him to that old way of life. I let myself be blind to his history of drug use and violence. I was truly in love with this man who was generous, funny and protective, and he loved my little son Jonathan. He loved kids in general! And we had this wonderful, passionate chemistry together that was thrilling to my new female body. Being intimate with Dave, I never wanted to dissociate! Dave had also known from the get-go at ACOA where I shared my story that I had been sexually abused, and he was very supportive. He was supportive of a lot of things. We were both young, and we were like lost children who found each other. We were very much in love and it felt too good to let go, despite my daughter's warnings.

Plus, I absolutely loved Dave's family! Dave was the only addict in his family. His two brothers were both such good people. I especially loved their mother Betty. She was a real mom, very family-oriented, making every birthday and holiday such a big and special event. She threw me a wedding shower, and when I became pregnant, she threw me a baby shower. She treated every one of us like we were so special, even her opinionated mother who lived next door, and her own alcoholic husband. Though Dave's father was an alcoholic, he never got mean or violent – he was a jolly drunk. Betty was so generous with her love; she was there for anyone who needed her. I was so happy to be a part of her family. She was my mother-in-law, but she became like a real mother to me.

It was late October when I married Dave. By then, I had been married and remarried a few times, but the difference was that this time, I was in love! With this marriage, I knew it was over between me and John for good. Right after we got married, Dave and I moved with my son Jonathan into the bottom of a two-family brownstone apartment in Woodhaven. We also had an extra bedroom for Elizabeth, who had worked so hard to graduate from the half-way house and came to live with us.

Dave knew all about the movie *Goodfellas*. It was one of his favorite movies. *Goodfellas* is the story of a young man who grows up in the mob. He works hard to advance himself through the ranks of organized crime. He idolizes the life of the mob and loves his life of money and luxury, but he is oblivious to the horrors that he causes. Dave said that he knew these people; that some of his friends were in the movie. He would watch the movie with my kids. I had no idea about anything, except what he'd told me about his ties to the mafia. Dave still had a friend who'd been in the mafia, but he was in AA now, and they would spend time together. Sometimes, Dave would come home with merchandise that had fallen off the back of some truck. One box was full of fur coats!

"We should sell them," Dave suggested. So, there I was, walking into my job at the medical center in a fur coat with extras to sell, and we made some money. I would also sell Nintendo games, shoes, and many other things that "fell off the back of a truck."

It was my street-smart daughter once again who told me about how things really were. She told me, "Mom, these are stolen!"

"Stolen?"

"Fur coats don't fall off the back of a truck, Mom! They were stolen!" Then she added, "You could go to jail for selling them!"

After that, I stopped bringing the fur coats to work. I had no idea. I laugh about it now, but I was so naïve. I had no knowledge how out of whack it was; that these things didn't happen to everyone. My husband was a misguided person in a lot of ways and I was ignorant about so many things. I gave birth to our son in September of 1986. We named him Paul.

My daughter walked around angry making it clear that she didn't like Dave. It wasn't long before they got into a huge fight that breaks my heart to this day. Somehow, Dave had found out that Elizabeth had cut school again, and he confronted her about it. My daughter got angry at him, shouting, "Don't tell me what to do! How dare you! You're not my father!"

Dave snapped. It was the first time I'd ever seen his rage; it was like he went crazy. Now, Dave was a huge man and very strong, and he physically picked up my daughter and literally threw her out of the house onto the street and slammed the door closed.

I was in tears and in shock; it happened so fast! I turned around and looked at my baby in his cradle. Paul was only a few weeks old and I was faced with the most horrible choice a mother could ever be forced to make. I knew in my heart that if I tried to leave with my baby and Elizabeth, Dave would take our son away. I couldn't bear that pain of losing my newborn baby; so, I did nothing. I was weak emotionally and raging with post-partum hormones and I'd just had a procedure for carcinoma found on my uterus after my son's birth.

The truth was that this incident triggered a deep wound from my father – casting out one child and keeping the other, how he played favorites, how my mother was helpless to stop him. I wasn't aware of this consciously; all I could do was think of my daughter and cry. I cried for hours and days that turned into weeks. I kept holding my baby like he was going to be taken away, too.

Elizabeth didn't come back to her empty bedroom and no one could console me. I was heartbroken. My daughter ended up living with a friend. Her friend's mother was a widow with four children. I'm sure this woman was in no position to take on Elizabeth as a fifth child, but that did not seem to be her point when she came to speak with me one day. She asked me, "Why isn't your daughter living with you? Elizabeth is such a good girl!"

How did I respond? I cried. It was all I could do in those days. I was so heartbroken, and my hormones were all over the place. I didn't know it was possible to feel any worse than I did. When she said this, I knew it was possible. I was devastated.

This is perhaps the hardest part of my life. Harder than poverty and hunger? Harder than long-term sexual abuse? So much harder, I assure you, because this is my child we're talking about. I abandoned my child, and this is a wound that has never healed; it wounded me, and it wounded my daughter; it wounded our relationship. I sob as I write about this wound. Saying "I'm sorry" feels so inadequate, yet it's all that I can say. As for Dave, he never said sorry at all.

Elizabeth eventually went to live with her father. I never had to wonder why my daughter hated me so much. I abandoned her and broken her heart; it didn't even matter that I also broke mine. It was like losing my brother Luc all over again, how he got kicked out of the house. I repeated what I knew from my mother; I *allowed* it.

Soon, we needed to move because my oldest son, Jonathan, suffered from a very bad sinus problem. His room was in the refinished basement, and there was an issue with mold that affected his breathing. We moved to a three-family house on Pitkin Avenue. I hated it. I'd walk around and everyone I overheard used all this foul language and seemed to have a nasty attitude. But we lived closer to Dave's family in Ozone Park, so that was something. After a few months at Pitkin, my brother Luc offered Dave a job in Massachusetts. I never wanted to leave New York. I loved New York, but my husband needed to get away from it all. It didn't matter that he just started a new job. He liked the idea of moving out of the state. He had never been able to get away from his family, his upbringing, his old mafia friends, whatever. I finally gave in.

Besides, I knew that my therapy with Ramona was ending. Sadly, her mother was dying and needed her help. To this day, I am so grateful to her. She was like a midwife to my spirit, and she had helped deliver me from so much constricted darkness and brought me into the light. I didn't know it at the time, but I still had so much left to learn - and unlearn.

Chapter 25

It was 1987 and I celebrated my 40th birthday in Massachusetts with a party that felt quite different from the very first birthday I ever had when I was feeling undeserving and unsure of myself. And Paul had his first birthday as Jonathan turned 9.

Soon after we arrived in Massachusetts, my mother visited us from Canada. I wish I could say this was a happy visit, but once again, my mother could not stop talking about my father. "He asked me to tell you he says hello. He misses you, and he'd love to see you!" I didn't want to see my father ever again and hearing about how he missed me made me feel sick to my stomach.

"Please stop talking about him," I had asked her many times over the years.

"He always asks about you - please go see him," she asked again.

After she left and returned to Canada, I was overwhelmed with feelings. I wished that my mother and I could have just enjoyed each other's company without the conversation turning to my father. I felt bitter and angry about how, after all these years, she was *still* sending me to him!

"Gaetane, your father wants to see you," she had told me my whole childhood and adolescence. "Gaetane, just go. Go see what he wants so he'll stop calling me."

Though my father would call my mother's name, she knew what he really wanted: *me*. And when she sent me to him, I blamed her; after all these years, I still blamed her. The saddest thing is that my father did this purposely. He single-handedly destroyed the love I had for my mother so that I wouldn't see that he was the evil one. Now, she was still sending me to him like the handmaiden of the devil himself. Of course, I was angry at her. Getting sent to my father was a trigger to dissociate, to feel a fear so profound that it turned me into a white sheet and only a ghost remained.

I found myself completely triggered by a rage and hatred so strong that I wrote a letter to my mother and ended our relationship. In a rage, I told her about the sexual abuse; that my birthright had been taken from me; that I never wanted to see either of them again; that I would *never* be touched again! In tears, I wrote, *Please, just go away and leave me alone.*

I know now that my mother only did what my father told her to do; she did *everything* that he told her to do. She lost me because of it. I decided to completely stop going to Canada. It was a door that I needed to close for as long as I needed to close it. As usual, my husband was supportive of my decisions, and I was so grateful for his support.

Over the next year or so, we did a lot of camping and had fun together when Dave wasn't working. Dave was very smart and a good worker for my brother and we grew close to Luc and his family. When my brother had originally moved to Massachusetts, he had met and married a woman named Geraldine, who was very tall and pretty and so young. They'd had three sons by then, plus Luc had stayed true to his word and found the son he'd had out of wedlock in Alberta who was my daughter's age. To her credit, Geraldine had accepted him as her own son. Our boys would all play together. I found myself missing my daughter, thinking she should be here with us.

And while I liked the house in Springfield, I came to realize it was a rough neighborhood when Jonathan started to have a difficult time in school. My son was one of the few white children at his school and there was some bullying that was going on. I wasn't sure what to do about that. He missed his old school and I missed my old neighborhood and my old network of people and meetings. I just couldn't get into the recovery network in this new location. The few meetings I went to, I felt very uncomfortable. I tried seeing a male therapist for about a year. He was nice, but over time, I completely lost my recovery routine, and with that, my support system.

The worst thing was that my husband ended up getting fired by my brother's supervisor. Dave had been a very good worker; he was educated and very smart and he had worked so hard and was responsible. Dave was completely blindsided when he was told that he was fired, and he flipped out. He drove out to Luc's, and almost ran my brother over with his truck!

The falling out between Luc and my husband was complete and total, causing a huge rift between our families. In the back of my mind, I had worried that it wouldn't work out with my husband working for my brother – but things had been going so well. When Dave got fired, it seemed that my instincts had been right all along. I had feared it would be Dave's fault, but it was my brother's fault. I couldn't forgive my brother; I couldn't even talk to him. Geraldine tried to talk to me, but I couldn't even talk to her. Luc was my closest sibling and we loved each other a lot, so this fallout was very painful. This was another part of my family I lost because of Dave.

After being fired by my brother, Dave and got a job at the Air Force base. Over the next year, the bullying situation with Jonathan got worse and worse at his school. The school bus would pick him up and drop him off, but while he was in school, he would get bullied. He was being hurt by someone. Bullying awareness wasn't a topic of conversation back then. I couldn't believe it when Jonathan came home from school one day in tears and told me that he had been thrown in the garbage! Nothing like this had happened in New York.

The happy times in Massachusetts were becoming less and less. Meanwhile, Dave's father had developed lung cancer, and when Dave started talking about moving back to New York, we picked up everything after two years in Massachusetts and left. I didn't even say goodbye to my brother and his family.

When we got back to New York, I spoke up and made it clear that we had moved too many times; I didn't want to be moving anymore. This time, I was going where I felt that I would feel abundant, and I loved Richmond Hill. The neighborhood was rich with big trees that were old. It was the most beautiful neighborhood I'd lived in.

Dave and I rented an upstairs apartment in a beautiful Victorian house. We ended up doing a lot of work on that house; we worked well together. We were partners and a good team.

By then, Belle was no longer living in Richmond Hill. She had moved to New Jersey with her new boyfriend, and I couldn't stand him. He was a cheater, a womanizer. I tried to warn her, but it didn't matter. I didn't see much of her after that. I also didn't see much of my daughter, who had gone away to college; our relationship remaining strained and difficult.

But I was so happy to be back in New York! It was such a relief that Jonathan was in a school where he was loved, and no longer abused. That made me happy. After all, I'd been building a life that would end generational violence and sexual abuse; but I'd had no idea how to end the bullying my son had endured. To see my son abused by his schoolmates and not be able to do anything about it had been terribly painful for us both. And it was wonderful to be reunited with Dave's family again, though his father's health was deteriorating.

In contrast to my life in Massachusetts, I started doing a lot of recovery work again and going to meetings. I also returned to my old job at a Medical Center, where I liked the people. Working with doctors, I was very conscious about my health. Having experienced so much hunger, I knew what good food was; what was truly nourishing. I never let my kids have soda. My food regime was healthy, and I exercised regularly but not obsessively. I was in the best physical health of my life - finally the "right" weight - and I felt good about how I looked. Looking good was a form of control; to look perfect on the outside because I felt so imperfect on the inside. But looks were just as important as health to me. I was afraid to end up sick and dying like my patients who had not taken care of their body, or even like my mother.

Meanwhile, I was still smoking cigarettes. I tried to quit about 5 times and it would only last a few weeks or a few months. I had been smoking for 25 years. It was an absolute roller coaster trying to stop using this addictive substance that I knew was bad for me. It affected my emotions, my mind, and my body. I had mood swings from anger to tears, with cravings when I was awake, and dreams about smoking when asleep. Some of these dreams were nightmares, and some were pleasurable. I joined Nicotine Anonymous for support. Many times, all I could do was call on my higher power to help me. *Please God, help me to quit, help me to honor my body.*

How did God help me? He sent a patient to the medical center where I worked. This man was in a wheelchair because of smoking. He'd lost one leg and he was afraid of losing the other one. He was only 54. Every time I lit up, my legs hurt. I knew I really needed to quit smoking. I did – on my daughter's 21st birthday. I just stopped, and it was the hardest thing I've ever done.

While working at the medical office, my mother-in-law Betty called me. She told me she was having severe chest pains, and I told her to get herself to our office right away. When she got there, we hooked her up to the EKG machine that shows an electrical reading of the heart's activity. I took one look at the results and reported it to the doctor. I knew by then what a heart attack looked like! We called an ambulance immediately.

When Betty passed away, our entire family was shocked. Her husband had passed from lung cancer two years before, but no one had expected Betty to die when she did. After his mother's death, Dave stopped going to recovery meetings. He continued to work full time, but he was devastated. We were *all* devastated. Betty had been an angel to all of us.

I could feel my husband slipping away. He registered at the College of Aeronautics to study to become an aircraft mechanic and didn't tell me until afterward. It was the first time my husband had not included me in a major decision or even discussed it with me.

Dave's parents had loved him so much, and now they were both gone. He also lost his older brother around the same time. It hit Dave hard though he kept up all his activities: working full time and going to college. He never stopped to grieve. We saw each other less and less and he became distant and depressed. I became deeply concerned about him and about our relationship. I knew his life had not gone the way he hoped it would, but I didn't know what I could do about it.

All I could do was continue my own recovery. I was ready to continue this part of my journey head-on with a professional incest therapist. It was my old friend Belle who referred me to a mental health center in Queens.

When I showed up for my appointment, the first thing I asked at the reception desk was, "Do you have anyone on your staff who works with incest survivors?"

The receptionist brought my inquiry to the director of the mental health center. I filled out an evaluation questionnaire, spoke with the director for a few minutes, and she assigned me to a therapist who worked with victims of childhood sexual abuse.

I loved my new therapist! Brenda was very kind. My life felt confusing. When I began working with her, that increased threefold, as I tried to learn about the brainwashing that happened while growing up living with a perpetrator, my struggles resulting from the lies, the betrayal, the seduction, and the mental and emotional abuse. I had to put together the pieces of how this traumatizing experience affected my life, and the influence it had on my inner messages. My therapist understood. She knew what to say and how to listen. She had information and great resources. She encouraged me to get involved with recovering survivors and to speak out - and to my surprise, I did.

At some point, I told her that I'd barely spoken to my daughter since she was 16. Brenda looked at me and said, "When you have children, they are yours for the rest of your life. You don't let them go at sixteen."

In the family I came from, you *did* let family members go, at just about any age. The age was just whenever the falling-out happened. At five, my older sister had been sent away to live with grandma because she was "difficult." At age thirteen, Luc had been sent to lumberjack camp to earn a living for the family, and then was completely kicked out a couple of years later because my father was violent towards him. At nineteen, I left my family, my language and my entire country behind.

After John's mother approached me in the bathroom, I did not see or speak to her again. I left my husband, returned and remarried him, then divorced him again and he was still angry with me and we didn't speak unless we had to. When my little sister came to live with me and I kicked out her beatnik boyfriend, I allowed her to leave with him. I still wasn't speaking to Luc since he fired my husband in Massachusetts; I cut him off, and his entire family.

I never spoke to my father after leaving Canada, and I still wasn't speaking to my mother since I sent her that letter telling her how she and my father ruined my life and to leave me alone. I never even heard back from her and that was fine with me, I thought. Moreover, my husband Dave and I hardly talked anymore in the heart-to-heart way we once had.

These broken relationships and the fragmentation of my family seemed like a natural part of life. I sent my daughter away to a half-way house when she wasn't even on drugs; My husband kicked her out of our house, and I continued to allow our relationship to stay fragmented. When it came to my daughter, I could see that what I had done was wrong by others' standards. Yet, that was part of my belief system. Years of unlearning and I was still making the same mistakes.

I can't even express how difficult it was to change how I looked at things; to turn myself inside out. Those years, it was all about me; the victim; the survivor. It was difficult to look at the pain of others and the pain that I was causing my children. All along, I tried to change my life and I came back to the same thing. Now I was inflicting my wounds on my children, as I continued to make the wrong choices.

In therapy, I worked to understand the ins and outs of a person impacted by incest. I learned that it permeates every part of your life. It becomes part of your DNA; every day; every decision. Recovery was a very painful part of my life, hurting myself and others in the interim. Knowing your children still suffer from your wounds is its own pain. Your children leaving you to survive; repeating your own pattern of leaving your parents to survive when you thought you were changing all that and creating a better life for them is a sobering experience.

Chapter 26

I had been seeing Brenda for a couple years when I got a call from my youngest sibling, Adam, in 1992. He told me that our mother didn't have long to live; that she'd had another major heart attack and all she had left was about 15 percent of her heart function. He also mentioned, on a happier note, that his wife was pregnant with their first child.

My brother's message registered with me and yet it didn't move me to take any action. I hadn't seen or spoken to my mother for years, and I still wasn't ready to forgive or release at that point.

It wasn't until later that year, right around my birthday, that I suddenly knew that I needed to go to Canada, and I needed to book a trip that day. It had been nine years since I was there, but this was clear in my mind that I obeyed without much of a second thought. It was one of those strong messages that I got from time to time and I did as my inner voice told me.

I booked a trip to Maine because my brother Adam would pick me up; I'd only be about an hour away from *Riviere-Verte*. I found out that Adam's wife had just given birth to their first child on the same birthday as Paul, so it felt like a special trip to make. I had no intentions of seeing my mother, but I'd been thinking about her through these long, nine years of silence. Even after Adam had told me she didn't have long to live, I had no intention of seeing her. As far as I was concerned, I was going to spend my birthday in Canada with my siblings, and I also planned to see my Aunt Debbie.

I called to tell her I was coming. I asked her if she knew about a picture that used to hang in the bedroom where I would stay when I slept over Grandma Smyde's house when I was a little girl. The picture was of a beautiful guardian angel watching over two children playing near a cliff; this was one of the familiar guardian angel pictures in which the children were crossing a treacherous bridge or playing near a cliff. I had thought of this picture a few times over the years; it had been special to me. My aunt told me that she had the picture; that I could have it.

This was my plan as I flew up to Canada. When I got there, instead of Adam picking me up, I decided to rent a car. Before I went to Adam's, I stopped at my Aunt Debbie's. She gave me the special guardian angel picture. I put it in the back seat of my car and went off to Adam's.

At my brother's house, I met his wife and their little girl for the first time. It was emotionally difficult. Seeing Adam and his happy new family brought up all sorts of feelings for me. I could also feel some anger coming from Adam. He tried to hide it but was there, nonetheless. I knew he was angry because I hadn't come home when he told me how sick our mother was, and angry because I still didn't plan to see her though she didn't have long to live. He was also angry because I had not gone to his wedding. He was disappointed and hurt. It was a complicated homecoming.

Not long after I arrived at Adam's, I heard the door open. Much to my surprise, the visitor was my mother! Apparently, my brother was not going to allow our mother to pass out of this world without seeing me, even if I didn't want to see her.

She came in through his kitchen door. Her eyes were sad; the saddest eyes that I've ever seen and yet her face lit up with a smile when she saw me. She was thin and weak. I was sure that Adam had prepared her for my visit because she wasn't strong enough to withstand any surprises. Now, we were face to face and it was clear that she was dying. I knew at that moment that she had been waiting to see me one more time before she passed away.

We looked at each other and said hello. I could tell she was so happy to see me. I understand that more than ever now that I have children. I let myself go numb. If I let myself feel too much, I would have fallen apart.

I asked her how she was doing, and she talked about her diabetes. She said she finally understood the impact of not taking her medications for so many years and not losing the extra weight she had carried around; how this had led to her heart damage and had made her tired her whole life. I could see how weak she was and knew that it took a lot for her to be there. We sat and made small talk as we ate cake. We didn't talk about much that I can remember. It's not the words, but the feelings that are still clear in my memory; they were sad and heavy. Mom still had a sweet smile, but it was the smile of a broken-hearted woman, and quite literally that was true. There was almost nothing left of her heart. Over the years, most of her children had been sent away or had abandoned her, and with each one of us, went a piece of her heart. But it was my father who was the real heart-killer; he is the one who had destroyed her and all of us, breaking her heart and our family to pieces.

For the first time, my Mom did not mention my father; did not tell me he said hello or missed me; did not ask me to see him. For once, it was just about us – a mother and a daughter who loved each other after the hell we had been through.

When I left, my mother walked me to my car, and she saw the picture of the guardian angel and the children in my back seat. She smiled and told me, "Gaetane, that was mine when I was a little girl." I hadn't even known it was hers!

My Mom stood by the car and waved as I pulled away. That was the last time I saw her. My mother died on October 24, 1992, three weeks after my visit to Canada. I returned for her funeral. The picture of the guardian angel watching over the children is the only thing I have left of her, aside from her "mothers" ring that contains the birthstones of all nine children. It was hard to sit at her funeral and grieve for her. It had been nine long and difficult years of silence; of being apart. We had barely managed to say goodbye. She was the mother that I had, but never truly had; the mother that I knew, yet never knew; but wishing that I had. It was the saddest funeral that I'd ever attended.

At the funeral, I saw my brother Luc. It was the first time I'd seen him or spoken to him since our falling out in Massachusetts. We were both grateful to see each other. I found out that Luc had just been diagnosed with diabetes. It felt as if Mom had died and left him her disease. We were at the funeral home when my father showed up drunk in the middle of the morning. He approached my sister Eileen. It looked like he was asking her to do something and she refused, shaking her head. I still don't know what it was that he wanted her to do, and it doesn't even matter. She said no, and he went crazy. What did he do? He ran up to our mother's coffin and started cursing at her corpse! It seemed like he wanted to beat my dead mother; even in death, she was the one he was angry with and wanted to hurt.

"*Christe merde!*" he shouted at her dead body. I'm still astonished at the rage he showed towards my mother, and his rage and violence no longer had the slightest bit of power over her. By dying, she took his power with her. Now when someone said no to him, there was no Loreen to stand in for him, no slave to hold hostage. She finally left him. She had to die to do it. *She finally left him.*

My father was enraged! If the police weren't called and if they hadn't taken him away, he seemed wholly capable of killing all of us. He was handcuffed and taken to jail. And all of this happened right in front of my mother's proper family. This was my father, *Le Diable*. Some things never change.

How to shake off the sadness? I couldn't. I got to understand through my many years of healing that my mother died a victim of domestic violence; an unknown victim because everything was a secret.

Adam told me that he'd asked Mom before she died, "Why didn't you ever leave him? We asked you to come live with us so many times. Why didn't you just leave?" She replied that my father told her many times that if she left, he would find her and kill her; then he'd kill himself and all of us kids would be alone. Other times, he threatened to kill our entire family if she left him; he'd kill all their children. She believed him, so she stayed, and she lost us anyway because of him. Adam had stayed close by, so he could keep a watchful eye on her. But he couldn't change anything about her life; all he could do was be there for her as the old man continued to sneak around, stealing the family's money out of the canteen cash register.

I came to realize that my poor mother was afraid that my father would go on a killing spree. All the times that I was angry at my mother for sending me to him or hiding when he came home drunk - all of that was so she could stay alive for us. What would have happened if he had killed her? We would have been left alone with him. How long would we have survived then?

It took me years of therapy and healing to understand my mother's journey: who I thought she was and who she really was; the unbelievable emotional and physical abuse she had suffered in our home and likely in their bedroom; how I'd thought that my mother was weak and didn't care enough about us to make him stop; how I'd hated her for not taking care of us, for being incapable of taking care of us; how all she was ever allowed to do was take care of him at any cost. I finally understood how my mother had lived her life at gunpoint for the sake of her children and had done what she had to do to stay alive for us. It took enormous emotional energy for her to do so; it took her whole heart.

I've had so much loss in my life, and there is an element of sadness after each stage of healing. I choose to focus on life, not loss. I know that my life continues to take new turns, crossing yet another bridge under the wings of the angels.

Back in Queens, I had a very supportive recovery network going, including meetings I would attend at the church around the corner. At one of these meetings, I met Marty. She was short like me, chubby, and had the kindest blue eyes. It turned out that Marty lived only a few houses down from me - from then on, it was tea time and long talks for us! She would also read Tarot cards for me from time to time when I most needed it.

Marty had her hands full with three young teens after her husband left. It had not been a happy marriage or a happy childhood for them. They were good kids; they were just troubled and got mixed up with other troubled kids. Marty loved her kids, and she worked hard to support them and be a good parent. I was a witness as Marty went to family therapy, Tough Love programs, and finally had to involve the court system to help her two older kids.

Over tea, Marty often mentioned California; where she grew up. She smiled when she talked about the nice weather and the cool, foggy ocean and the lighthouses. "Someday, I'm going to move back there," she told me. She thought she'd wait for her kids to graduate before she moved back to California so that they had a choice, so that they could have a relationship with their father. Meanwhile, her two oldest children were not even speaking to their father.

I told her, "Just go! Bring your kids! They can come back to New York if they want to. Maybe California will be good for them. Maybe they'll stay there with you."

One spring, Marty told me she had seen needles and crack vials in the melting snow on the sidewalk. She told me she was done with New York; she decided to move back to California with her kids. "It's time," she said.

The same year that Marty left, Dave's uncle's house went up for sale, and Dave and I bought it. It was on Long Island, in a place where no one got involved with their neighbors on the block; no one hung out on their stoop, and there were no block parties. Even so, we bought it, and I really missed the friendly neighbors in Queens and Brooklyn.

It was lonely. For me, and for Dave. By then, both of his parents had passed away and one of his brothers had died suddenly at only 49 years old of a heart attack. He was deeply depressed. This was the first house we bought together, and I wish I could say it was a lovely house; that I loved it; that it felt like coming home. But I hated this house from the moment I stepped into it. I call it the Brown House. It was full of brown energy with wood paneling on the walls. And the house was so small, it felt like the brown energy was closing in on you. It reminded me of the outhouse! Even the windows were tiny.

The place had some seriously bad energy and needed so much work.

The schools were excellent, though. Both of my sons were in school there. Elizabeth was still away at college and our relationship was still difficult; some things take years and years to turn around.

Although Dave and I did a lot of work on the house to make it appear like a happy home, it never was one. Things got worse as time went by, especially when Dave's grandmother came to live with us.

Dave's grandmother had outlived both of Dave's parents; she lived right next door to them when they were alive. She was 92 and dying of a heart condition and refused to get a pacemaker. She needed help; she needed to come and live with us. It was a disaster!

This woman caused crisis after crisis within the family. She was poisonous, doling out money to buy the family's love. She had money from working on Wall Street and from her husband who had died of battle wounds as a soldier. Her husband had been Catholic, and I was Catholic, but she was anti-Catholic. She called herself a born-again-Christian, but she had quite a mouth on her. She'd smile to my face, but then I'd hear her gossiping on the phone, saying how we mistreated her. As soon as my husband came home from work, she'd be calling him upstairs to wait on her hand and foot for every little thing. This went on for a couple of years. There was never a moment of peace with her in our house.

I should have known how it would be with Dave's grandmother because her reputation preceded her; so much so, that my late mother-in-law had confided in me, "Never live with her, Gaetane. She will destroy your marriage."

Dave's grandmother passed away and, as it turned out, Dave and I didn't need any help destroying our marriage. By then, I knew that something was seriously wrong. I didn't even want to think about losing the life that I had worked so hard to build - again. I wanted to hold on to a happy, safe life that was no longer happy nor safe. It was a false sense of security, and there was nothing there anymore between me and my husband. We lived separate lives.

I knew that my therapist didn't care for Dave. It was obvious whenever I mentioned his name. Looking back, Brenda knew that he wasn't good for me, but she never came out and said it. Instead, she focused on encouraging me to speak out about my story and, to my surprise, I did. Speaking out led me to The Incest Awareness Foundation. Through them, I got involved with a group called Parents for Megan's Law. I even traveled to Albany with them to speak to politicians and lobby for the passage of this law, which would require convicted sex offenders to register with local police and have their information made available to the public. As I was trying to find my place in the world, this was one of the causes that spoke to me. We would also speak in courtrooms to lawyers and judges about how sexual abuse affects those involved.

I also got involved in studying something called "Life Coaching" with a training organization called Coach University. I worked with doctors to focus my niche on business coaching. I traveled to Montreal for coaching conventions and met a lot of people from all over the globe. I met wonderful friends, including my friend Jeannine; friends I still have today because of this training.

I was still working with the medical group. I got promoted and I was feeling good about it. It seemed I'd broken a work pattern finally; once and for all.

Before I knew it, I was celebrating my 50th birthday! I invited Andrea, and it was so good to see my oldest friend. My kids were there, and some friends from Richmond Hill. The most special thing was that Belle surprised me by coming to my birthday party all the way from New Jersey. It was the last time I saw her because she passed away a couple of years later from an asthma attack. I was heartbroken when she died. She was truly heaven sent. I will never forget the sound of her laughter and I think about her with a smile! I miss you so much, Belle! With love, from The Canadian.

Chapter 27

One day in the summer around that time, I was sitting on a beach with my coach-friend, Jeannine. I had never really talked about the hunger I had, and I don't know why I told her that day. By then, I'd talked about incest and abuse and alcoholism, but never the hunger. Even in my therapy, I hadn't talked much about the hunger and poverty; I would just mention it in passing. They knew, but that wasn't where we put our attention. It was never the focus.

In an unguarded moment, I turned to my new friend and told her the rest of my story – the part about the hunger. I told her about drinking my brother's baby bottle, the 100 pennies, everything.

There was a moment of silence.

Jeannine finally said, "Gaetane, I'm so sorry that happened to you." This classic response is written into my guidelines for disclosure, and it means so much when it is heartfelt. But what Jeannine said next really got my attention!

She told me how her husband had begun an organization to end world hunger - with none other than the late Harry Chapin, himself. I couldn't believe my ears, especially because I love Harry Chapin's music! He was such a favorite of mine. I never went to concerts, yet I had gone to his concert. Jeannine explained that Harry and her husband had just founded this organization with a goal to defeat hunger through charity by using grassroots efforts and rallying celebrities and leaders to help promote the cause. Her husband was now the CEO!

I can only marvel and be in gratitude for such synchronicity arranged by God; to speak about my experience of hunger to someone whose work leads the struggle to end hunger in the world was a gift beyond value.

After this, Jeannine encouraged me to volunteer and speak about my experience. I helped raise funds during a "Hunger-thon," and even spoke on a radio show. Because of her, I started to share the story of my hunger. I talked about the 100 pennies I dreamt up for myself when I was starving, only to be faced with an empty donation box for "pagan babies" in faraway countries. My story got such a huge reaction! One woman let me know that she'd gone home and told her children that story. Speaking about my experience of hunger added yet another dimension to my healing and my purpose.

Despite these successes in the public world, the turning of the century marked some of the most painful years of my private life. At an age when most women are settling into a life well-lived with a family grown and established, mine was anything but settled. It started when my daughter was visiting us after John's mother had passed away. Dave knew that John's mother was the woman who had approached me in the bathroom so many years ago coming in when I was taking a shower, eyeing me up and down, and that was the last time I had seen her. I had no respect or love for John's mother; I had spoken badly of her to Dave. But over the years, John had maintained a relationship with his mother to some degree and had included our children, even after his mother had moved to Florida.

When my daughter expressed some sorrow over the death of her grandmother, Dave made some smart remark that Elizabeth shouldn't be sorry about this crazy lady dying. It was something I might have said to Dave; I just would never have said it to my daughter.

When Dave made this comment, Elizabeth got upset and Jonathan, who was now 19, stood up for his sister. He yelled at Dave, "Don't talk to her like that!"

Dave started punching my son! My husband was twice as tall as me and so strong, but I jumped on him so fast and I was hitting him and the next thing I knew, Jonathan packed a bag and left to live with his father a few blocks away. Once again, things had happened so fast that I'm still not clear on what happened.

Dave could go for years without being angry. But when he got angry, the world came crashing down! He would simply snap. Because of Dave's instances of rage, I had lost my daughter, my brother, and now I lost my eldest son. But I had been raised that way - groomed to tolerate insanity - so it didn't really make an impact though it turned my life completely upside down. After losing Elizabeth and Luc, I knew the pain that was ahead. I just couldn't believe it was happening again.

I'd been kidding myself when I thought that I had found that life that I talked about; that "other life." Really, it was very similar to the old life: a mess. I was in deep emotional pain over losing my son, yet I would not let go of my ideas about marriage. I had to ask myself some tough questions during this time. Was I addicted to Dave? Was it an addiction to love? I couldn't lose his love; that grip he had on me was all my heart knew for the last 15 years. If I let him go, did that mean that I was worth nothing again? Who was I, without a man in my life? I would be a single mother with a boy who hadn't even started high school. I couldn't stand on my own! I'd had my job forever and it still didn't pay enough to be on my own. Plus, I could not face the loneliness that being alone would bring. This was the truth and I believed all of it. It was part of my core and I lived feeling scared.

I tried to make excuses for my husband. *He had experienced the death of so many family members including his young brother; he was really depressed.* I struggled, holding on to what was left of our pathetic marriage. *We'd had so many good years in the beginning; the love had been real.*

That summer, I went camping with my husband and our son to one of our favorite places in the Berkshire Mountains. It was a beautiful sunny day when a staff member from the campsite came and asked to speak to me personally. That's when I learned that my father had just passed away. It was July 29th. The last time I had seen my father was from afar on one of my trips to Canada. I got so scared when I saw him that I started running away. He saw me and laughed. That was it - he just laughed.

I thought I should call my brother Luc. I knew that my father had slowly been wasting away since my mother's death over the years. He never took care of himself because my mother had done that for him. He became more and more ill. I'd heard he'd been looking like a skeleton, completely malnourished and still drinking. That was all he knew how to do.

Beyond calling Luc, there didn't seem to be too much else I could do. I knew that I wouldn't be going to his wake or funeral. It wasn't because I was angry with my father; it was because I had made my peace with him internally, or so I thought.

After receiving this news, I felt sad and chose to take a walk by myself. The smell of the forest was incredibly pungent. I walked to the edge of a beautiful mountain, right to the edge. I sat down and looked out over the mountains that were so huge. It was only then that I started to cry.

My tears startled me, and I asked myself, "Why am I crying? I should be happy that he's gone from this earth. Now he's no longer a menace."

But instead, as I sat on this cliff and remembered my father, I cried for the person my father could have been. I felt incredibly sad for him. He'd never had a chance at life. He'd been kept out of school because his father wanted him to work. When he was a little boy in a lumberjack camp, his father beat him every chance he got. He repeated what he learned from his father.

He never learned to be a real father; a dad. I never had a dad; none of us did. My father did what he knew, which was abuse, attack, drink, and lie. That was all he knew. He couldn't stop repeating the generational pattern that was beaten into him as a child. Someone, as damaged as my father, should never have had children; should never have been allowed around children.

Even as an adult, he'd never learned to read or write, and he was frustrated because he could never go anywhere without my mother; he had to ask her to read for him and even to sign documents for him.

He'd never had a chance at a better life, and it could have been a great one because my father did have his gifts, as we all do. His major gift was dancing and music. This will surprise you, but he also had a great sense of humor – not with us, but with other people, especially his friends. He could be very social. Since we lived in such squalor, you'd think he'd be disheveled, but no. He had that kind of pride in himself. He was very handsome and strong and looked like a model with not a crease on his clothes. Maybe it was pure vanity; some of it was, I'm sure. He couldn't read or write, but to dress nicely and dance well was important to him and he came by it naturally; these were his personal gifts.

Despite my father's lack of education, he wasn't stupid. He was ignorant about a lot of important things like basic human decency, but in ways, he was very smart. He'd been one of the best hunters and trappers around. The stories that followed him recounted his skills as a lumberjack as well; that is when he worked and wasn't "burnt out."

My father was happiest when he was in the wilderness. He could spend days by himself hunting, trapping, and fishing. Sometimes, he'd tell us stories about the wildest of these animals; animals so wild that no human being could approach them. He learned their calls and they would come to him. He would go for days in the cold of winter and he would come back with some animal that he hunted. Sometimes he would go hunting with his friends, but he preferred to be alone. This was where he belonged. He even looked different when he came back home. His clothes still fit like a glove right down to his hat. Even in the wilderness, he took pride in his appearance. Still, he looked different when he returned; lighter somehow.

Once home, he was like a caged animal with a wild and fierce streak, like the animals he was so fond of. Whether he was drinking or not, he could be an absolute brute. And yet, my father had been gentle with me. I saw how my father was a little boy caught in the age that incest became part of his growing up. I know he was sexually abused because he became that little boy whenever he called me to him. He was never violent; never rough. Was this part of being a perpetrator? Earning my trust with his charm? I think it was something else. Was this a cry for help and a cry for healing?

He was so violent with everyone else. Was this the only safe space for him to express his gentleness and love? I realize now, with no doubt in my heart and soul, my father was a little boy with me and he aged along with me as this secret continued. The teenage years were the worst because he became a teenager, too. He was never my father, not even for one second. Incest was like being peers; not with someone older, or a father.

The night before I got married, my father came into my room and told me how much he was going to miss me. I can see him now, standing by the bedroom door. I knew what he was going to do; it made me sick and yet there was this little girl inside who loved him. I knew it was wrong, and yet I loved him. The pain of loving my abuser had shattered my mind into dissociation. Years later, I was still picking up the pieces.

I sat on the cliff and felt compassion for how my father had been destroyed as a boy. But he is both the victim and the perpetrator in this story. The most confusing and difficult part was that my father had destroyed me and every member of our family, and I was *still* sitting there having compassion for him. I wept, holding the tension of these opposites: the man who did what he did, and the little boy who did what he knew; the little girl who was abused and yet loved her father who had no clue about how to be a father, just like his father before him. Being able to separate my father's sickness from his essence allowed me to see a light in him that I couldn't see before; it allowed me to feel compassion instead of hatred and pain. The awakening I had on that cliff was that, if it was my purpose in life to end our family's generational incest, then that meant healing my soul, and my father's soul, too. This healing can only come from forgiveness, and forgiveness can only come from compassionate understanding. I believe that there have been moments of grace that saved my sanity, and this was one of them.

The telling of this awakening, the sharing of this intimate truth, is very, very difficult. I never wanted this story to be about the physical acts of sexual abuse; that would be too raw, too ugly, and too capable of hurting those I love who may read this book. This is an emotional sharing and it's about the emotional and spiritual scars. Everyone's story is different and this one is mine, and if the telling of this awakening brings even one person closer to peace, then its telling is not in vain. For me, writing about and sharing this truth has turned out to be one of my greatest healings. I see who my father was all along, and I forgive him. Of all the years of healing, that's my peace — the peace of forgiving the unforgivable.

That day on the mountain, I asked God to please release my father's soul into the wilderness. "Return him to nature," I asked God, "Give him peace, finally." That day, I let him go where he belonged - to God, with his soul set free forever in the wilderness. Offering my father's spirit and soul into God's hands, releasing him into the place where he was the happiest, was a release for me, too. It allowed me to release the old story.

All this light, and still, my life continued to fall into darkness. It can take years and years to write the new story. It can take a lifetime. You can forgive all you want, and it truly helps the process of recovering peace. But the damage is done, and all you can do is keep picking up the pieces.

Chapter 28

So many personal breakthroughs, and yet my home life went straight downhill in the strangest way. It started when Dave bought a couple of small geckos for Paul. But it was really Dave who was involved in this new quirky addiction: reptiles. Don't ask me why. Before I knew it, we had reptiles all over the garage; many kinds of snakes and other amphibious creatures. You couldn't turn around without bumping into something with scales. On top of that, these reptiles' diets involved mice and rats, neither of which I hoped to ever see again.

My husband also began to hang out with young people - I have no idea where he met them. He bought rock n' roll guitars that cost thousands of dollars apiece. He couldn't even play guitar! He tried, I think he even took a lesson, but mostly it seemed that he just liked to admire these fancy guitars. I was in debt by then, having long since discovered credit cards. Notice that I said "I" was in debt because Dave never got into credit cards; he would save up all his money and then buy something like another guitar or reptile. He didn't even know I had credit cards, so the debt was mine and mine alone. I eventually told him about it and it was still my burden to bear. Once Dave was in this phase of hanging out with young people, he never discussed anything with me; he just did whatever he wanted.

Worst of all, his attitude towards me began to change. He would get nasty and secretive. I was baffled by his behavior! He was no longer the funny, openhearted person that I believed he was. Besides his new obsessions with guitars and reptiles, I noticed some other compulsive behaviors. For example, he could spend hours and hours on the computer.

I knew something wasn't right - I thought he might be drinking - but I was naïve. I began to suspect that when he visited the reptile shop, he smoked pot. Really, all I knew at the time was that Dave hadn't gone to a meeting ever since his mother died years ago. Recovery is an ongoing personal journey; it was his choice and I couldn't make it for him. All I could do was continue with my own process.

I returned to my programs for money and debt, and for support as a family member of an alcoholic. The reason I got out of debt was that Dave remortgaged the house; at least he was generous that way. I'd go visit my Canadian friends Andrea and Julie often because I knew I'd find love and nurturing in those visits with them. At home, I was living in total insanity. I wanted it all to go back the way it was, I thought I loved Dave that much.

On New Year's Eve 2001, Dave decided to leave me and go out with his new young friends. He finally came home at 3 in the morning. I was still up and waiting for him. That's when he told me, "I don't want to be with you anymore; I don't want to be here anymore."

Happy fucking New Year! Seriously? I was not prepared for that or how much it would hurt. I blinded myself to how he had become a teenager again, the way he was so focused on his music and his friends. Frank Zappa had been his favorite artist and now he was listening to him all the time, like when he was a teenager.

Dave left right after that. He moved out to live with his brother; his one remaining family member. Before I would consent to a divorce, I made Dave agree to let me keep our house until   Paul graduated from high school, which would be another four years. By May 2002, we were in the throes of our divorce; by summer, all the paperwork had been signed and submitted; by December, the divorce was final, barely a year from start to finish. This was such a painful year for me as my family fell completely apart. What cut the deepest is that Dave had started a new relationship with some woman who had 2 kids.

I will never forget when he called me that December to ask me a favor to help his fiancé get into the country; I learned that she wasn't an American citizen and for some reason, the immigration authorities wanted to see *my* citizenship papers. Our divorce was barely finalized, and Dave had a *fiancé* already? How could he replace me so easily? How could he not even consider my feelings, to ask this of me? Once again, it was all about what *he* wanted.

"I am *not* going to help you with this," I told him.

He said it would take so much longer for them if I didn't cooperate.

"I don't care how long it takes!" I replied. I could have killed him. I thought Dave loved me, cared about our family. We'd been together for 15 years, and overnight he had a new family. He abandoned and cast out my daughter, my brother, and then my son. Now, he was abandoning the son we'd had together, and he was abandoning me. He turned out to be just like my father, the way he could cut off relations just like that.

Dave re-married just a few days after the divorce. He jumped right in to take care of his new family - it didn't matter that he had to go all the way to another country to do it. Even when I heard Dave's last brother died, I still couldn't feel sorry for him. Dave tried to have a relationship with Paul, but our son was not interested in seeing him. Neither was I.

This was such a hard time for me. The next four years I continued to grieve. My heart was broken. My *family* was broken. All I could do was keep connected to my 12-step friends, people who were going through the same thing I was - all of us divorced and lost - doing a lot of therapy and going to meetings.

I had to reflect on what happened. Looking back on my choice to marry Dave in the first place, I thought about how I'd acted and saw a full circle; I was just like my mother. She'd been warned not to marry my father; warned that he had a history of addiction and violence; warned that he was dangerous and would not be a good husband or father.

It was so bad, my daughter could see him for who he really was, and I couldn't. I had to face how Dave was so very much like my father. What is it about this type of man? Why are they so seductive? I saw that, on some level, my situation was the same.

It's just one more example of how what you live is what you are supposed to learn. I had to admit that I married a man like my father. It's all I knew! You do what you know. Though I feared my father, and he was dangerous, I never gave it much thought because it was a natural part of my life. It was what I saw all around me growing up. Even unconsciously, I gravitated towards what I knew.

The man I married had been different before I married him; I thought he was cured of that life. Long after he stopped his recovery and was acting out, I was still so invested that I just kept on going even when our relationship was in shambles and crawling with reptiles. That's how much I wanted this to work. *He's not that man anymore,* I tried telling myself as I cried myself to sleep alone. *Was it somehow* my *fault?* That was the question that kept me up at night.

During this difficult time, my therapist received a job offer to become a director and she let me know she was leaving. *Seriously, could anything else go wrong?*

For 11 years, I had called her "my incest therapist," but she was so much more than that. Brenda asked me, "What will you do when you are no longer a victim?"

No one had ever asked me that. It had never occurred to me that I would one day live as anything other than a victim. "I don't know," I told her.

I knew she asked me that question because she saw my potential and she had more hope for what I could do with my life than I did at that point. She told me that one day I would be helping other victims become survivors. For years, she had encouraged me to speak and network, to create goals and pursue them and, once again, she encouraged me to write this book.

By then, "my book" was an old conversation that went something like this. In therapy, when I disclosed a particularly profound experience or insight that came up for me, my therapist would say, "You have to write this. It belongs in the book."

I didn't want to write a book; it was too personal. To write a book was to re-live my painful life and expose all the filth my soul had experienced. My experiences of sexual abuse were very difficult to even talk about. How could I possibly write a book about it? Just saying to my readers, "I was sexually abused but am not giving you the details," would never be enough.

"You can write it on your own terms," Brenda assured me. She helped me to understand that it could be an emotional sharing of my shattering and the journey of recovery that could help others to recover.

"I have children," was the biggest thing that kept coming up for me – meaning that this is another scary disclosure and I don't know what they'd think about it, or me, or what any of my other family members would think about it, or me. Brenda would remind me that I'm doing this for them, to stop the generational patterns that permeated our family.

Meanwhile, I had to remind her that English was my second language. Write a book in English? I couldn't do that. Do you think she accepted that as an obstacle? Of course not! Writing a book was so far out of my comfort zone for many reasons. And for every reason that I had to not write a book, Brenda had a reason why I should. For example, my story also has a lot of love in it – and humor! Shouldn't people know about that?

When I think of Brenda, I see her encouraging, confident, patient smile. She encouraged me to live my life not as a victim, but as myself, in all my power and strength. At that point in my life, my power was such a fragile thing! By then, I was a certified coach - yet my personal life had completely fallen apart.

I was extremely emotionally vulnerable after my divorce. I knew I still needed professional help, so I found a new therapist. Her name was May and she eventually became a Buddhist nun. Sounds promising, right? Well, names and titles can be deceiving. With this woman, I had the most psychologically dangerous therapeutic relationship of my life that would test everything I had learned in my recovery and therapy.

I don't think this woman liked me from the beginning. From the most compassionate standpoint, I think I triggered something in her. To put it kindly, she was extremely unsupportive of my feelings, observations, and my entire reality.

She was the devil's advocate for everyone but me, and she would give me such an attitude. She was very condescending.

For example, I would talk about my experience of being surrounded by Dave's rats and strange reptiles, and she would say, "That's okay, that's just *different.*" As if the real problem was *me.* At that point, I only suspected that Dave was smoking pot at the reptile shop, but I can only imagine how she might have justified *that* behavior.

And when I talked to May about being a survivor of sexual abuse and the devastation of having failed relationships with men, she asked me, "How can you expect to attract the right man, with the sexual energy you carry around? What kind of man do you think you're going to meet with all that?"

She seemed accusing and hostile and there I was, newly divorced and now a single parent abandoned and replaced instantly by a man I had truly loved, confused and hurt, needing support and encouragement, and I got no understanding from this woman; she had *zero* compassion for me.

Maybe May was just "confronting my shit" and she was too advanced for me with where I was in my recovery - or maybe she was just plain toxic. I literally felt like I had to stand up for myself against this woman who was supposed to be supporting me. I had to stand up for my reality and validate it against the opinions of this "professional."

Thank God I was strong enough in my recovery to see that she was not good for me. So far, I had been blessed with wonderful therapists, and I knew the difference. These therapists witnessed my journey through the some of the deepest emotional pain that any human being can suffer. Because of my experience with these professionals, I stopped seeing May after just a few sessions. But my experience with May scared me away from therapy for a few years. Instead, I went deeper into my speaking networks and, finally, I began writing. I joined a writing group and that was a whole different kind of network for me.

Chapter 29

I quit my long-term job at the medical center. Now that Dave was gone, I needed to make more money. This was another loss as I liked the people there and I had been there on and off for almost 20 years.

Another thing that needed healing was my relationship with my brother Luc. It had been 13 years since we'd spoken, besides briefly at our mother's funeral and through our siblings. Luc had been my closest sibling, so this rift between us was painful. It broke my heart to miss all that time with my brother, and for what - a marriage that didn't last.

But the way that my husband lost his job seemed inexcusable. The supervisor who fired him led Dave to believe that it was my brother's doing. Apparently, he was only the messenger. Still, I was the one who needed to apologize to Luc, because I was the one who cut off all communication and left without even saying goodbye.

I called my brother and asked to come to see him, I asked if we could talk. I told him that Dave and I had divorced. He said, "Of course, come."

When I met Luc and my sister-in-law at a restaurant in Massachusetts, I told them I was sorry. We all suffered because of this fallout.

"And the children suffered," my sister-in-law made it clear. "They never got to know each other as they grew up over the years because of you."

She dished out some heat at that restaurant, and I had to take it because it was all true; it was all my fault. I'd been blind, and I'd hurt everyone in my blindness, even our children.

"*Especially* our children," she corrected me.

Yes, it is especially the children who suffer, and that is the saddest part. All I could say was that I was sorry; that's the whole reason I was there. And it filled my heart that they accepted my apology.

Inevitably, the subject of the way Dave got fired came up during our conversation. It took me thirteen years to find out the truth behind why Dave was fired - what my brother would have told me if I had only asked him if I had only allowed my sister-in-law to tell me the other side of the story when she had tried so long ago.

Well, imagine my surprise when Luc explained to me that, yes, Dave had been a good worker for him, responsible, and smart and that he had great ideas. Dave had been *so* good, in fact, that Luc's business partner had become very jealous and felt threatened. Well, this partner had the supervisor fire Dave as if he was acting on Luc's behalf - as if it was Luc who wanted Dave fired - when that couldn't be farther from the truth. It took me thirteen years to hear my brother tell me that he had never told his partner to fire my husband. Imagine finding this out after so many years of unnecessary heartbreak in my life!

There was another reunion I needed to have. This one was in Canada, and I brought Elizabeth and Paul with me. I was really looking forward to this quality time with my family, but something unexpected happened during that visit.

When I arrived, my brother, Adam said to me, "You'll never guess who I ran into! Remember Matt? Well, he asked about you and I told him you were visiting. He asked me to ask you if he could come and see you."

I was shocked, happy, and afraid all at once. Over the years, I had tried my best to forget Matt; getting married, getting divorced, and repeating that pattern. I feared that our relationship had ended because Matt wanted nothing to do with me. This feeling of being rejected wasn't new to me; I often felt this way about myself.

But this just didn't feel *true when it came to Matt*. When you fall in love with someone at 14, people write it off as "puppy love." I knew my whole life that it was more than that. I didn't know why it ended, but I knew our love had been real. No one could ever change my mind if I trusted them enough to share the story in the first place.

For many years, I'd still had this deep love in my heart for Matt. *What if...?* kept coming up for me. Each time I visited Canada, I would say to myself, "This time, I will call him." Every time I visited, I thought of him and wanted so much to see him, though I knew he was married with children. His love that had engulfed me at such an early age never went away. I wanted to thank him for his love and tell him how much it had meant to me back then and over the years.

Yet, each time I would go to Canada, I never called. I never had the courage. I'd leave Canada, missing him deeply and not saying anything about it, except to one or two trusted friends or a therapist. I'd never had the opportunity to get any closure with him.

I told my brother, "Of course, I'll see Matt."

I was excited and nervous! I was finally about to see this boy who was now a man; the boy I had never forgotten. What might happen?

When we met, he was still handsome, and he said, "Gaetane, you haven't changed. I would recognize you anywhere."

The first thing Matt wanted to know was if I had left Canada abruptly because of him.

Honestly, I was taken aback. I didn't realize that he'd been questioning that all these years, thinking maybe he'd done something that caused me to leave.

"No, I didn't leave because of you; I left because of my father; because he sexually abused me." I told him the whole story about getting married just so I could get away from my father.

Matt's eyes filled with tears and he said he was sorry. It was what he said next that really made my heart beat so loud. After all these years, he said to me, "If I were on my own right now, I'd take you with me."

But he wasn't on his own; I'd known this for years. Matt told me his story. Like me, he had married at a very young age, but for different reasons. He married his wife when she became pregnant; they'd been together ever since. He told me they weren't in love, but he felt it was his responsibility to take care of her. Now, they had two grown children and a young grandson.

Matt told me how he would take his grandson ice skating in the winter like we used to do many years ago. He said that when the skating rink plays this one song, his grandson asks him, "Why are you smiling, Grandpa?" Matt would tell him, "It's because I'm thinking of someone special who I used to know."

We talked about my mother, and he told me about his mother - how he would find her passed out on the floor sometimes, and that he was still angry with her about her addiction. I never knew this about his family.

Matt got to meet my daughter and youngest son, who were with me on that trip. Elizabeth knew about Matt; I told her about him when she was little. Matt said that he'd told his daughter about me. After almost 40 years, I finally knew our love was mutual. After we left, Elizabeth told me, "Mom, he is just as nice-looking as you said."

I know that I must accept our separate fates. Even as the young love of my life, we took separate roads. When I think of how my other marriages ended up, I wonder if God kept us separate so there would be a beautiful love in my life that happened before I healed all the pain, hurt and behaviors that made being in a healthy relationship impossible. I asked God to help me to accept our separate fates with peace. If it is God's will, let it be so.

This is a chapter of my life that needs to finally be grieved and to be placed in my memories as a beautiful love story. The most beautiful part is the innocence; the struggle to figure out the difference between normal sexual, passionate, love feelings versus the vulgar touch of incest. It took years to finally figure it out; feel it and love it. All the other feelings, the deep, deep pain of incest was felt, too; the feelings that easily took over my innocence and wanting; at least, my yearning to be innocent, which I believe is my gift as a human being. It took a lifetime of figuring out and feeling those parts of me. There is deep sadness in the loss of innocence because I didn't do anything wrong. The painful, searching years; the love for Matt, wondering if only, if only, on and on.

Matt was the one man in my life who showed me what kind of love was possible between a man and a woman. This was one of the most beautiful gifts that God ever gave me. This was how God showed me the difference - that what I'd had with Dave was not true love because it had not endured. Still, I cried over Dave despite this truth - and I cried new tears because of it, too. There are gifts and pain in revelation.

Back in New York, my son continued high school, and my journey of recovery took me to new places. I'd spoken several times publicly about child sexual abuse but as part of a group. Now I needed to speak on my own. It was 2003 when I first took my voice public at the Holliswood Psychiatric Hospital for a whole crowd of mental health professionals. When I walked on stage, I paused only a moment to gather my emotions. There was no time to be shy; my message was too important.

I started my speech with the alarming statistics I had researched about child sexual abuse. In 2003, these were the numbers: 1 out of 3 girls, and 1 out of 6 boys, were sexually abused; 93% of juvenile assault victims knew their attackers, therefore only 7% of the predators were strangers; 58.7% of these predators were acquaintances, and 34.2% of these sexual predators were actual family members, and less than 12% of sexual abuse was reported to the police.

And then I told them, "*I am one of those unreported statistics. My father sexually abused me from the age of 3 until the day I left home at 19.*" I told them, when I tried to stop my father, how he warned me that no one would believe me; that if I told anyone, no matter where I was in the world, he would find me and kill me; that I believed him and had literally become my father's property; that I had lived in fear every single day of my life. I explained how these mentally ill abusers have power over their children because children are the most vulnerable of human beings. Children depend on the people in their lives; they often have no voice; no one to protect them. A perpetrator will threaten a child that if they tell, they'll be killed, or people who they love will be killed.

I also shared some startling discoveries about others who were victimized by my father. I learned as an adult that our neighbors, a family of 12 children, also lived with sexual abuse. Their father had sexually abused all of them. I had no clue what was going on when I knew them. Though I was being sexually abused myself, I didn't recognize it. I learned that some of the children committed suicide in later years.

I even shared that, within my own family, none of my five sisters ever reported sexual abuse. They didn't say it happened, but they also didn't say it never happened; they didn't say anything at all. Even within my own family, we couldn't talk about these things as children or as adults. So many victims keep their own secrets. This is how deep the silencing can be: my father was dead, and he continued to rule my family from the grave. That's the power of these abusers.

I spoke about how sexual abuse committed against a child's body is also committed against the child's soul. The crime my father had committed permeated my entire life - my mind, my body, my soul, and every choice I made in my life. There was more research to show how the impact of child sexual abuse is all-encompassing. It leads to dissociation and confusion about the self; depression and anxiety; sexual problems and all sorts of interpersonal dysfunction; mental illness; alcohol and drug abuse; crime; suicide. And it was not just the victims, but society at large that had to deal with these issues resulting from childhood sexual abuse and the perpetuation of a generational cycle.

"How does one heal from a crime like this? Is there hope? Yes," I told them. Personally, I was blessed with an abundance of faith, which helped me stay strong and eventually seek out help and support. And there were several other factors that had helped me in the healing of my incest and sexual abuse. I spoke of the importance of a good therapist, especially one trained in healing sexual abuse.

I shared how helpful art therapy had been for me because, sometimes, we are able to draw that which we cannot verbalize. For children especially, the most powerful therapy can be art therapy because children have no words for these atrocities; they can only act out their feelings. But the subconscious has a language of its own and it can speak through art, and children are brilliant artists. That's when the truth comes out and they can begin to understand.

Lastly, finding a powerful, strong group to support us is essential to the healing - groups can be very empowering for others, and had empowered me.

This speech at Holliswood launched me publicly as a speaker; as a voice for children of sexual abuse. It had all started with the Al-Anon meetings, listening and sharing, then networking, then private therapy and art therapy, all the way up to political lobbying and public speaking. My life and family had fallen apart around me time and time again. It was the people in my life and my commitment to recovery that held me together, and my determination to create change for myself and in the lives of others. In many ways, I was the classic "wounded healer."

And I had so much left to heal! I would do anything suggested for my healing. I had spent so many years in various forms of therapy, but after my divorce, I started getting into bodywork. I went for some massage therapy for the first time! The thought of letting someone touch my body this way was petrifying. My massage therapist was a young girl who had just graduated from school, but I had some trust in myself by then and I sensed that she would be respectful and professional.

The first few times during these sessions of deep tissue massage, I would have flashbacks of my father touching me.

"Please stop," I'd ask her, and she would.

But as time went on, it felt good and I could release a lot of the energy that I was holding; I cried at times. The deep tissue massage helped me heal on a physical and emotional level.

I also did some chiropractic therapy. My chiropractor was a gentle soul, inside and out, and the process was so gentle. There was no cracking of bones on the table. Instead, the technique is called networking and is about aligning the spine as a channel of energy from the individual to the planetary consciousness, rewiring the brain using precise touch along the spine.

She would work on me so lovingly, and I cried so much. I said, "I'm like an ocean."

Throughout my bodywork, the tears ebbed and flowed. My body got healthy and I released deep levels of stress. I reclaimed my body a little at a time. It was a long process. Each time I connected to my body, I could take better care of it. Looking back, it's difficult to believe that I had lived so disconnected from my body. Being sexually abused permeates all parts of one's body; physically, emotionally, and spiritually. What catastrophic damage! It takes a village to help make someone whole again.

I was starting to feel strained financially and emotionally. I returned to Debtors Anonymous but was exhausted from working on myself and my situation. I decided that what I really needed was to bring some *fun* into my life. I needed that balance. There'd been this love of life inside me and it was time for it to come out again. I guess once you hit bottom, there's nowhere to go but to pick yourself up.

I decided that I wanted to learn to dance. As an adult, I'd never been comfortable with the dancing I'd seen at clubs. It was all sexual moves and I was uncomfortable behaving that way. It felt shameful, and it left me lost socially. It was ballroom dancing that interested me because I thought that kind of dancing was classy and graceful. I signed up for lessons at Arthur Murray Dance Studio because I'd heard of it and knew it was famous. I spent a lot of money on those dance classes and, considering that I'd hit bottom financially, it probably wasn't the smartest thing to do. I later learned that I could have taken lessons at any studio for less than half the price. I thought Arthur Murray would be the best dance lessons around and I wanted the best.

In retrospect, it was worth every penny. When I danced, I got in touch with a part of me that absolutely loved music; not only loved music; loved moving my body. Arthur Murray taught me a beautiful way to move my body to music. My body came alive in my ballroom partner's arms. It helped me be free to go out into the world, dance and have fun. My favorite dance was the Viennese Waltz - it was just like floating!

Chapter 30

The day came that my son Paul graduated from high school. He had done well, and I was proud of him. This meant it was time to sell the house and split the money with Dave. I had to move again for the first time in years. A lot of work had gone into this house, but I never loved it. I made the arrangements for the sale of the house. Imagine my surprise when the inspector told me that, underneath the house, there were cat skeletons - many of them. Under my house was the place cats would come in our neighborhood when they were going to die. Even before I became a Feng Shei practitioner, I knew that the house had some bad energy, but this was so creepy and disturbing!

We made a lot of money with the sale. I was grateful to still be in Debtors Anonymous when all that money came my way. I took their advice and saved and invested my money; I had to be very careful not to spend it all or give it all away to rescue people as I would have in the past. I found the cutest little 3-bedroom cottage nearby. It had this wonderful old character but was newly renovated; everything had been fixed up and it was clean. My son stayed with me and it was a special place for us. Plus, I had an extra bedroom for my other children whenever they wanted to come and stay; they knew they were welcome.

Around this time, my daughter got married. Her husband was kind and smart and had a good business going. He was from England. I felt this was very appropriate for my daughter, who had been interested in travel and culture. The wedding was a small ceremony with dinner in Manhattan. Of course, John was there. He was still angry with me and would have never talked to me if I hadn't been the one to say hello. Our son Jonathan was still living with him.

Paul started taking classes at Queens College. I'd agreed to share the cost of our son's college tuition, but Paul wasn't really interested in getting a degree. It was very disappointing. Then, my son told me he wanted to move out and go live with his Aunt, who was the widow of Dave's deceased brother. I was confused and angry and my self-esteem was hurt by this. Once again, I was replaced. I never asked Paul why; I just let him go.

For a brief time, I enjoyed living on my own. But soon, I began dating.

Larry was kind, young and fun. The best part was that he wasn't an addict and yet I'd met him at Debtors Anonymous; that should have been a red flag.

It's just for fun, I told myself. I needed some fun in my life, and Larry was fun! In some ways, Larry was like Freddie, the man I had dated for two years and then married for one day because they were both very social. Larry liked to go out and I loved that about him. We would go see Broadway plays and go dancing. But that's where the comparison ended. He was nicer than Freddie and had much better manners. Larry was very respectful, and a real gentleman. He wasn't an embarrassment. And yet, like with Freddie, I struggled to return Larry's feelings. He was kind and supportive when I started writing - he was encouraging about everything - but I just didn't feel any chemistry or emotional connection with him.

I knew I could never marry Larry because I didn't love him, but also because he seemed very young to me. He lacked self-sufficiency. As we dated, it became obvious to me that he could not hold down a job. I had enough trouble holding down my own jobs since I'd left my long-term employment at the medical center. So, what did I do? I stopped going to my

Debtors meetings. I cashed in my investments, gave money to my children, and soon all my money was flying out the window. I even gave some money to Larry, to help him and his daughter, a decision I deeply regret.

The best thing I had going for me was that I started working with a new therapist, Lori. What was different about her was that she was more of a coach, but the most beautiful gift was that she was helping me with my daughter. After all these years, my daughter Elizabeth and I were still struggling in our relationship. I couldn't blame my daughter if she hated me for the rest of her life. I loved my daughter more than anything. I love all my children.

Lori, my therapist, promised to do everything she could to help heal the relationship between me and my daughter. Lori would say to me, "You can't give up on her."

And I wanted to give up because my daughter was so angry with me. It seemed like Elizabeth hated me and no matter what I did or said, it just made her angrier. I felt I was constantly defending myself - she never wanted to listen to my feelings or point of view.

In one session, my daughter said to me, "That's the problem, Mom - it's always about *you!*"

I heard her say that, from her heart to mine. For the first time in all these years, I finally heard my daughter. I realized she was right. I played the victim with her; it was about my abuse, my side of the story, my pain. I had never been there for her emotionally, and for the first time, I heard her pain. My daughter needed me to listen to her, hear her, feel her, put my feelings and defenses aside and be there for her. It wasn't about *me* being the victim - my daughter was trying to tell me that *she* was the victim. I should have known. Children are always the victims.

"Yes, it's true," I said. I cried a lot. I apologized. And the healing of our relationship began.

One issue Elizabeth raised in these sessions was about Dave. Lori had an answer. It was all about when I'd introduced my daughter to Dave so many years ago. I had been happy about this new relationship, and I had expected my daughter to be happy for me. Instead, my daughter had warned me against this man who was an addict with a history of violence.

Lori asked me if she could tell me a story and I agreed. She said, "Gaetane, I worked with lots of domestic violence victims." She told me that one of her clients was crippled and, in a wheelchair, because she had been beaten by her husband who was now in jail. As this crippled woman wheeled herself in that chair, she told Lori, "I love him! He really isn't that bad!"

Hearing this story, I knew what my daughter had been trying to warn me about. He could have hurt me; she could have been badly hurt and in fact, she had been. Dave's violence had been very rare, but it had caused me to lose my daughter, my brother, and then my eldest son – three people who mattered so much to me!

I had been in complete denial about who my husband was, and what he might be capable of, especially when it came to my family. Three times, I had put this violent bastard above my own family members and lost them because of it. And I tolerated it and was able to justify it, just because he wasn't a wife-beater. Remember, my father never beat me. I thank God that was not one of the many patterns I needed to repeat until I ended up in a wheelchair still in love with and defending a brute who had crippled me. This was a pivotal point in our relationship and my belief about him.

On July 29th, 2008, I left New York to attend a family reunion in *Riviere-Verte*. Eight of us siblings would be there, and we hadn't all been together since my mother's funeral in 1992. It was a fourteen-hour day of travel with a canceled flight and waiting hours to connect from Boston to Maine, so I had plenty of time to think about my family and how much they meant to me. Everyone arrived at my sister Eileen's house. It was an exciting and happy time to see each other again! The only one who was not with us was my brother Jacques. He was angry with two of our brothers; something about money.

This reunion was a turning point for me. I opened up to my siblings when I shared my guilt and pain for abandoning them. After talking about this pain all those years in therapy, it wasn't over. I needed to face my fears, face my family, and face myself. Finally, at this reunion, I did exactly that. For the first time, I told my siblings how I had raised them; how I had worked hard and taken care of them, so they would never go hungry like Luc and I had; how I felt I had abandoned them when I left Canada. I talked about all of it and told them that I'd been in therapy for years dealing with this alone and it was time they knew. I cried like hell. They cried. We cried together. Finally, it was off my shoulders, out of my body; all this guilt, pain and sadness about the abandonment.

The only person who didn't want to hear anything was Adam. I knew that Adam was angry and had been for some time. For Adam, everything had to appear perfect and life was far from perfect for him at that time. His wife had just moved out; he was loaded with rage. I found it ironic that he had been like my son, that I'd even almost adopted him, and yet he was the only one who didn't want to hear my side of the story.

I started a conversation with Luc, Adam, and Eileen about the fact that the rest of the family had no money; not even to buy food. I was ready to pitch in and help take care of them; no obligation. I suggested we go out and have a nice dinner together. Well, my brother Luc was concerned that he would have to pay for everyone if we went out to a restaurant. Now, my brother Luc had plenty of money from his successful business, but he thought he was going to have to pay for the whole dinner and that didn't sit well with him. Adam felt the same way. I did more than my share though I was unemployed.

My sister Eileen ended up taking care of most of the expenses of hosting our reunion, but not without consequence. After a few days, the victim in her came out. She was totally overwhelmed by everyone in her house. She wasn't ready for the intensity of hosting all these revelations in her house either!

One day, she announced to us, "I'll never have so many people in my house again." She felt that everyone was complaining that they had no money; that they were in pain and no one ever considered her - she was unmarried, a single mother, just starting a job with no one to help her.

This was more of our childhood programming coming out. If only she heard herself in the way that I could hear her. I heard the victim in her; in all of them. I recognized it because I had been in the victim place for so many years; so many therapy sessions. It had taken me so long to know when I was in victim mode and to know when others were.

Yet, in ways, I was still in victim mode. I'd been having a very hard time emotionally, especially as far as work was concerned. I truly believed that I would never have a job again. I also believed that I would never find true love again. I had repeatedly failed to find "that other life," maybe because I didn't deserve it. *Je ne le merite pas.* It's such an easy place to go back to for me.

After the reunion, Larry moved closer to my cottage into a big house without even a chair to sit on! Meanwhile, I had this cottage full of furniture where the rent kept going up.

By then, all my children had come and lived with me at some point and then left again, and each experience had been very special to me. In ways, maybe my cottage felt like an empty nest now, and then there was Larry with this huge empty house – an empty relationship – and it was irresistible to my programming. I moved in with Larry bringing all my furniture and set up the house. Larry and I split the rent, and I guess I expected that to change when his daughter was out of school and living with us. But it didn't. He really should have paid more. Rent had never been an issue with John or Dave, who'd had great jobs and were workaholics. But with Larry - even after all my generosity before we lived together - it wasn't until it came down to *rent* that I reached a tipping point regarding our fiscal imbalance.

Meanwhile, I had a new job, then quit. I was spending all my money and I basically hit rock bottom again financially. All the work I did and the money I earned felt good. Sometimes, the work was so enjoyable that I couldn't believe that I was getting paid to do what I loved. But when I earned it, I gave it away; time and time again, I earned, and I gave it away. I gave it to my family. I gave it to my husbands. Over the years, sometimes I even gave it to my father, the king of thieves himself! I gave my hard-earned money away to this man I lived with; to him and his daughter.

Pretty soon, I couldn't stand this "gentleman." I felt I was struggling to love him because he wasn't an alcoholic or addict. There was no chemistry with him. I couldn't *make* myself love him. I asked myself, "What am I doing here?" By then, the therapy with my daughter had ended and I had no private support system. I had to navigate this disastrous relationship completely by myself.

After a while, I simply couldn't stand him! I got so mean, angry, and nasty. Finally, I told Larry I had to leave. He was very sad, but I left anyway and took all my furniture with me.

Chapter 31

I had to find a new place to live. By then, I thought I knew what happiness meant to me and what "that other life" might look like. I knew that I needed nature in my life, especially trees. I'd loved hills and had grown to love the ocean. I needed sunshine, but I never thought that I could afford to live in a place that was close enough to all those things.

Ultimately, I settled for a house in need of love and life. The price was right, at least. This fit my caretaking, poverty, and I-don't-deserve programming perfectly. It was just a rental; I was done buying houses. I'd committed to this move. However, God chose this moment to intervene in my life. It began when I made a call to the landlady about the house, and I mistakenly dialed a wrong number.

Confused that the woman who answered the phone didn't know what I was talking about, I asked who I was speaking to.

She asked, "Who are *you* calling? Are you looking for a place to live?" It turned out that I had accidentally called a realty company here on Long Island! What a synchronous moment! I told her, "Yes, I *am* looking for a place to live," and our conversation quickly turned to what I was looking for and what she might have available. The realtor told me that she had the perfect place for me! The rent was so low, and it had beautiful *views*. "Did I want to see it?" Yes, I'd like to see it, I replied.

Once I got there, I saw large windows with a view overlooking the harbor full of sailboats. From the upstairs windows, all you could see was the sky. Right outside the door was a beach, a large park where there were concerts and so many beautiful trees. It was as if every element of nature was ready to nurture me. After 50 years of moving, I finally felt like I was *home*.

As I talk about patterns, one of the patterns that must be addressed is my constant moving over the years. It turned out that I moved almost twenty times from 1967 to 2009. Every time I made a move, it was because I thought the answers would be found somewhere other than where I was at the time. Moving was like running away; a coping mechanism. No matter where I ran, it never turned out to be the other life I was looking for.

I moved into my dream apartment. I loved it, yet, I was completely on my own with no partner to supplement my income, so I was terrified! My expenses were about three thousand dollars a month. I learned many lessons in a few months' time, including how to plan when and where I spent my money. Though my job as a manager was a struggle, I couldn't think of leaving it.

I made a quick trip to Canada for a funeral and when I got back, it turned out that I didn't have to wrestle about my job. I got fired again.

I've talked about being fired but not what it was like to be fired. One of my worst firings was when I was working at a plastic surgery office as a manager for doctors, medical assistants, and nurses. The only reason I was given was "low productivity," which didn't make any sense given my productivity there. I told them it was an absolute lie, but they didn't care. It was so degrading!

At another job, I'd had the courage to start working in management and I'll never forget the first two weeks. I could do the work. I had a big influence on the staff, motivating them to do their work. My boss told me that she couldn't believe the difference - even the administrators couldn't believe how the staff had changed. But I noticed how I started out with confidence, got acknowledgment, and then started to doubt myself. Once I doubted myself, I couldn't ask for help. How would it look if I asked for help? Shouldn't I know all this?! My relationship with my staff changed too because of this insecurity.

I had no idea how to communicate or resolve conflicts. I stayed in my head and fought this battle alone, expecting to get fired - and if I didn't get fired, I quit. Either way, I felt like a failure.

I finally asked, *Do I know enough about myself to change this pattern?* The answer came back, *pray and ask God.* So, I prayed.

Trusting in God was a big deal for me! God helped me get the beautiful home I lived in; though I believed that, somehow, I didn't deserve it. Let's face it - I wasn't working and I only had a little bit of money. It only made sense that, eventually, I would lose my home. Each day, the only hope I felt was from the beauty that surrounded me; the beautiful place in which I lived. That was it. That was all I had. I meditated in the morning and saw each day as fresh and new and full of hope. Yet, at night, the fear of losing my beautiful home would come back. I heard my voice saying, *Well, Gaetane, you'll be on the curb soon.*

Je ne le merite pas. I don't deserve it. And I'd get mad at God again, *not* trusting Him. *All I deserve is Hell!* I was better at punishing me than anyone else could ever be.

When I was fired again, I felt defeated. I could have used some therapy. Instead, I tried to do it alone. The thoughts in my head kept repeating: *I can't do anything right. I'm lost. What will I do with my life? I'm dying. I'll never be okay. I've had it!* I'd cry to God, "Just let me die!"

Then, I'd have a complete turn-around and say, "You know, I got all the way *here*. I've come *so* far. I *know* that You will not abandon me." This war between trusting and not trusting fractured my daily life. This is how I lived, in a paradox that was my insecurity and my trust in God, all rolled up in one.

Here's where I stopped to pray. What else could I do?

Please God help me now, I prayed. *I don't ever want to repeat any of my past patterns again. The pain of defeat is too big to bear by myself. God, I want to die; I want that part of me to die. Please take it and keep it. Renew my life and give me new eyes and new thoughts. I'm a brave, strong, determined woman. I can make things happen. God make me what you want me to be. Amen.*

After that desperate prayer, I received a call from my sister Grace. She told me that she wanted me to let go of the past; that she had called because God had asked her to tell me to let go.

Honestly, I felt offended. After all, who was she to tell me this? I'd had every kind of therapy I could think of for almost 30 years, and she was going to cure me with a phone call? I had just asked God to help me let go of this wounded part of myself, yet it was so hard to hear this message from my little sister because she'd had no professional therapy. I had no idea how much help I still needed; no idea that I was still in complete denial.

With the message that Grace gave me, I took a deep breath. Messages come from all sources. It's when we don't listen that we suffer the most. If I chose to believe her, believe that I could let go, then why was I still holding on? Why was I still struggling? Only fear could keep me in this place of suffering. Why couldn't I get it? Why did I continue to go against myself? Didn't I just go to Canada for my friend; *for a funeral?* Wasn't I worth something for doing that? Or was I still trying to equate my worth to my actions?

The call with my sister Grace ended with her telling me that I was stubborn, and once again, that I needed to let go. *Sure*, I thought. But letting go is easier said than done. My past kept hitting me in the face. I went back to therapy. Somewhere, during this time, I began to believe that I deserved; that I was deserving. *Je merite.* It was one of the biggest victories of my life. I looked at the guilt and the punishment that I had levied on myself for so many years. It was such a heavy burden to carry. It affected my relationships at every turn and my work. Had I turned a corner? I believed I had. And yet, my life was a mess – how could I possibly celebrate myself?

I realized that if I could find courage rather than living in fear, I could celebrate myself; finding the courage to believe that *I was okay*; that believing I deserved was one of my strengths. In an act of courage, I gave my resume to a company that posted an opening for a Clinical Manager. I believed I had a good chance of getting the position.

I even delivered my resume in person.

As I walked into the clinic, I ran into someone who had worked at the place from which I had been fired. "The place from hell," she remarked. She confirmed that it wasn't all about me; more people fired after me, and so on. What a gift!

I want to take a moment for reflection here. I notice that I have a positive ending in each stage of my recovery. Each time I say, this is the last time, I've got it now, and yes, next time, I go right back to the familiar fear and pain and all the familiar patterns.

So, it shouldn't have been such a surprise when my next job involved me in a medical scam. When I was hired, I had no idea that my boss had served time in jail for fraud! It was all about insurance money and a Ponzi scheme. He schemed and scammed everyone, including me.

The job didn't last long and when it ended, I was devastated again. I felt like giving up again. It turns out that churches are open just for moments like these when someone needs to talk to God and wants to talk in His house, on His turf.

I went to church and talked with God about the good person that I made myself into to be part of humanity; yet, I still lived with shame and the truth was that I knew that I couldn't really be that respected, dignified person if the victim still lived within me.

After church, I walked to the beach and had another conversation with God. It went like this: *God, I'm a liar. I will never be good enough. You love the saints and we both know that I'm not one of them. How can you talk through me? I'm dirty. Today I need answers. I know that I cannot go on living like this.*

When I got home, I found an email from my sister, Grace. She wrote, "I've specifically prayed for you lately. I pray that you find your true self once and for all! Just be true to yourself and the people around you. That's all that God asks of you. He promises that the truth shall set you free! Each day ask God to help you peel away one lie at a time which keeps you from being your true self; has kept you from being yourself most of your life! Have faith and believe in the person that you are! Then he will bless you beyond your wildest dreams! After all, it's about faith. Expect from God what is beyond all expectations. I love you."

This time I knew that it was God talking to me through my sister. Grace's email was my answer! I spent most of that day in this place of receiving God's message and cried and cried for that beautiful little girl who was so shattered and wounded. I understood then that with the deep pain that I carried, I could not have survived without the lies; becoming someone else; someone better than me was my way of surviving until I was ready to look at it all and heal.

Thank you, my sister; thank you for believing in me so God could speak through you and help me release more of those lies. Blessed are the lies for the protection they offered me and later, in releasing them, how they deepened my faith. Once again, I found myself in a place of choice; choosing to go deeper with God, having faith and believing that I'm a loving human being. God asked me to go deeper into my soul and heart, and especially my spirit to really find him and find myself.

All that faith didn't change my employment situation. There was still more to learn, so I kept getting the lesson! With my next boss, the issue was that she kept putting me off about getting paid for my work. Payday would come and go. I got so desperate to pay for the rent that I needed to ask my family for help! Asking for help is the hardest thing that I've had to learn. Help, for me, means that I am a helpless, non-productive human being. There was a lot of shame about needing help. The word "need" was a trigger for me because my family was in need. I had promised myself that I would never be like my parents, with their hands out, and whatever was given was never enough.

For most of my life, I'd kept that promise to myself. I was self-sufficient, never asking for a penny. I didn't even like to ask my husbands for money. At what cost, though? I'd spent so much money on therapy for so many years; just to help me get help. It feels ridiculous as I write it. Just the thought of asking for help from my children stirred in me the most uncomfortable feeling. I transferred a lot of my own feelings onto my kids. If I needed them, they would hate me like I hated my parents.

It took a lot to ask my daughter for help with my rent. I felt scared and ashamed to ask for help for fear that I'd be abandoned and hated. I was afraid she'd lose respect for me, and yes, she did. She was so disappointed in me that I never asked her for a thing again.

And, I still had to pay my rent. My employer couldn't pay me; she had no money to pay me what I earned, and it would be a few days before I got paid, or so she said. I knew my brother Luc had money; he had a thriving business, but I couldn't find his number. So, I called my sister Eileen for his number and told her what was going on with my boss not paying me; that I couldn't pay my rent though I was working.

My sister said, "Gaetane, I have only two thousand dollars to my name. I'm not working right now, but I want to lend you the money."

I told her how much it meant to me that she would offer, but, in the end, it was my brother Luc who lent me the money. When I spoke to him, he asked me, "After all your years of hard work, you have no money left?"

I had to admit that it was true. He didn't ask this to hurt me, but it hurt.

"You should move back to Canada," Luc suggested. "New York is too expensive. Go back home."

"I *am* home," I finally said.

Chapter 32

Christmas came and went. I missed my siblings and my friends. I missed working. All I knew was that 45 years later, I still somehow found myself with the same self-defeating patterns. As I listened to a Christian Ministries broadcast on the radio, the host talked about humility and pride. "What pride?" I asked aloud. I had no idea what pride looked like as I gazed out my window overlooking the harbor. God, it looked so cold out there.

I'd just joined a dating service and I remarked out loud, "I must be nuts."

I tried so hard to fight the loneliness, but it was rooted in my programming. All my life, I've had this deep sense of isolation. I never could connect it to anything. I would think, *Well, I like being with people. That's why I feel a sense of isolation when I can't be with people.* Over the course of my life, I tried to fill the intense loneliness by being with people as much as I could. Friendships, family, and therapeutic networks were one thing - but there was something else that I needed to fill this space: I needed to fall in love and *be* with a man. For so many years of my life, I tried to fill that deep hole in my heart with the wrong man. I had been brainwashed by my father, the original Mr. Wrong.

Soon after joining the dating service, I was again repeating the relationship I had with my father. My father owned me, left me and replaced me, then called me back, playing favorites. He gave me crumbs to keep me hanging onto what I thought was love. As a young girl, without the capacity to understand what was happening, my father's sexual molestation was interpreted as his way of loving me – of paying attention to me; of showing me I was special. In my cross-wired thinking, I continued to go after that which I knew.

How did looking for Mr. Wrong show up? I looked for a man who would eventually abandon me or give me just enough to keep me hanging on long after I should let go. I could stay with Mr. Wrong for years! Worse, there were men who told me right from the start that they were not available. Even knowing that, I chose to see them. Apparently, my looking for Mr. Wrong wasn't over. What did these relationships feel like? They were like a chase – I can't even call each a relationship – and it went like this. The chemistry and sexual energy were there, along with the excitement of him not being available or being available only when it was good for him - wow, big attraction! This one's for me for sure!

I found Mr. Wrong more than once and tried to keep him. His boundaries or walls were very clear. "I'm not ready for, nor do I want, a relationship with commitment - but I do want the sexual intimacy because I feel safe with you and I trust you." He was chase-able, and I'd fallen easily into the chasing game. And he was charming; very much like what most women would refer to as a gentleman. He became safe for me. He was very much of a perfectionist, and most of the time was successful at being his "perfect clean self." He had something that lured me to him. These were our roles in the chase; the game.

Mr. Wrong canceled plans often. What did I feel? I felt disappointment. Perfect! I waited for him to initiate a conversation about us. I waited for just about everything. When he made a move, I got excited. How I loved the crumbs!

This game was about wanting to be loved; the one thing that I knew I deserved from a man; from someone who I could count on - someday. This game was all about how he might love me, down the road, not now. I could *make* him love me. I was repeating what I experienced with my father, but I knew in my heart that no one could make anyone love another.

During one of these chases, I broke a personal record when it only took two months to realize that I was hanging onto Mr. Wrong. This was a big improvement, and any improvement was welcome after a long history of it being all too normal to feel disappointment, abandonment, being constantly let down and feeling like a piece of shit. For me, the game became deadly, taking me to a place that sucked all my energy again; wanting to be loved by someone and being told that's not going to happen.

When I meet someone like Mr. Wrong and I start the game, the excitement and thrill are there again, and I want it so desperately. It's a red flag for me. My part in the game was too powerful for me to handle alone. Only God could heal that part of my life. Being a female and born into a belief system that holds women as property is wrong and insane and has been the most difficult place to be for me though I know all the moves. Mr. Wrong was the perfect player and, oddly enough, he became my healer as he covered his tracks.

My own voice. What does it want to say? I want to make it go away. It taunts me about the relationship that I started with yet another man who could not be there for me; had nothing to give. This man was full of pain from his ex-wife and I stood in that pain and it was brutal.

He didn't want a real relationship because he'd had a relationship before me and she tormented him - at least, according to him. From what he told me, she only saw him when she felt like it. Well, doesn't that sound familiar? Doesn't that sound just like *my* pattern?

She was so unavailable that she'd even hidden him from her parents. How angry he was at himself, yet he refused to let her go. *She* was not available. Now *he* wasn't available. How perfect that was for me, as I sought Mr. Wrong. The wounded girl stepped in: *I will make him care!* My wiser voice told me, *Gaetane, you are so valuable, damn it. You are human. You will be dehumanized no more. Okay, walk away from the old life, just go and trust the process.* The message for me was not to give up my life for someone who did not care.

In truth, I was scared out of my wits. *Where would I go?* My inner voice replied, *Away. Walk away in love; love yourself. Have compassion for yourself. It's okay. You just didn't know that you were valuable. A place in you wanted to be loved so much that you did anything to have these unavailable men love you; men who are incapable of even loving themselves.*

Trusting God enough that I could say to this man, "I'm walking away because I need more than what you can give me," was *huge* for me.

Usually, at the end of the game, there was the rage, resentment, and revenge. I plotted to get even. Why? Because I was not able to change him; make him love me; make him pay attention to me; make him into a good and loyal partner. I became powerless and I got mean; full of "I'll show *you!*" when what was really going on below the surface with each relationship that failed was an unsuccessful attempt to rewrite my own story and change my father into a man who was a good husband, a loving father and a man with dignity who I could respect. My anger at not being able to influence that; that I couldn't be an example of what life could and should be for my siblings, coupled with my own fear of being alone, was something I just couldn't seem to get past.

The last time I acted out this game was a big moment for me - a scam, an internet scam, the internet dating scam where I was totally defeated by my own doing. I almost destroyed myself by getting involved with another man who was not available. He was the epitome of unavailable. I never even met him in person; our only contact was on the phone and through the internet. Mr. Wrong again – *so* wrong.

These scammers touch on a place where we are most vulnerable. This became another secret. "Don't tell anyone," he said. Secrets were special to me, so this was exciting!

They start out so charming. They are either divorced or widowed and they have a child or children that they are raising alone. They are looking for a *special* relationship. They travel a lot for business; typically, they've stolen someone's identity so you're seeing photos and evidence that this person is real. Even if you check on his itinerary, his address, etcetera, everything checks out.

He calls you every day. He knows how to get to what's most vulnerable for you. Knowing that you're spiritual, he'll quote the Bible. What a good man. How lucky you are to have found him!

After about three months of talking to you every day, sometimes from Europe or Africa or Asia, he has involved you in his personal life and his family. He may even have you speak with his child over the phone. He tells you about his son's birthday and even suggests what a nice gift might be for you to send to his son.

Then comes the time when he wants to visit you. Understand that he has your email address, your phone number, and now your home address. You are so excited to finally meet this wonderful man! Here's the deal, though: suddenly and tragically, there's a big accident, usually while he's in Europe or Africa or Asia. He can't make it to visit you. The accident was expensive; hospital bills and all. If you are seduced by now, you want to offer him money. Oddly enough, it happens again, and again. Accidents, hospitals, requests for money.

Finally, you get a call from his best friend, a lawyer. Sad news - the love of your life is dead! Go figure. Of course, you're devastated. The lawyer friend tells you that the little son is alone in the world now. What he really could use - is money. There comes a point when you just know; it's different from knowledge that something isn't right and yet you don't end it because there's hope. When you just know and after all the hope is gone, you finally tell the lawyer friend that you've gone to the FBI. That's when the lawyer friend hangs up and you never hear from anyone again.

Despite my shame, I could not keep this scam a secret. I reported the entire incident to the authorities. What they said to me was, "Good luck." There was nothing they could do. I also reported him to the state of Indiana, the state in which he claimed to live. Nothing ever came of it; I never got my money back; I never got any return on this financial and emotional investment. It was all a *scam*. It was what is called 'catfishing'.

Two years later, I got a call on my cell phone.

"Is this Gaetane?"

After talking to this scammer on the phone for months, I recognized his voice immediately even two years later. I gasped! A call from the dead!

This scammer told me, "I wanted to say thank you for welcoming me when I came to New York."

But he never came to New York, at least not to see me! I assumed that he was trying to rekindle a scam all over again with some other woman. He must have gotten his notes or numbers mixed up and didn't realize that our story had played out differently. How could he have forgotten about me so easily? Or was he just testing our old connection? I didn't know, and I didn't care. I hung up and he never called again.

Since then, I've received calls from friends asking me to talk to their friends who have had similar experiences. I tell my story and the facts all add up. Most of the time, I talked to them early in the experience and so I saved them all the angst that I went through.

This internet scam was the last straw for me. I was very discouraged after all the work I had done to improve myself. All my life, I had tried to fill this space. But I knew I needed to end the chase. I just needed to end the game, period.

It was the first time living on my own my whole life. I thought I would be lonely. But I needed to be alone and learn how to enjoy my own company. Even if I was *so* lonely. The pain of living without love became more intense than ever. A therapist once told me that when pain is this intense it's never about now; it's in the past. I was often angry, and I had no idea why. When something shows up, like sudden anger, I know that I've disconnected somewhere with something in the past.

I wondered what it could be. Was it because I was alone and divorced? Was that my fault? I wanted to disconnect from the conversation that went on in my head; I was sick and tired of fighting myself. It went like this.

So, I'm alone.

The other side would say, *Gaetane, accept this reality that is a huge part of your life.*

Instead, I wanted to cry.

Why was I wondering if my divorce was my fault? *It's not my fault! He became an insensitive, sick, snake-addicted bastard; one of the most unavailable men that you could ever meet!* I was angry after all this time. The marriage had ended, and I needed to end this conversation about how it might all be my fault.

So, what, if I'm alone?

Come on, Gaetane, why is that a good thing? Think.

Okay. It's a good thing because I'm not being abused by anyone.

Then, just as quickly, the other voice chimed in, *But you find ways to abuse yourself by calling yourself worthless.*

Well, wow. No wonder I was angry! Look at how I was choosing to show up for myself - as my own worst enemy. It allowed me to see that I was worth much more than how I was treating myself would indicate.

Here's what I knew: loving me was hard. I didn't know how hard yet since I was just starting to show up in ways for myself that were more positive; it was unfamiliar and awkward. I truly wanted to be kind and loving to myself and accept that my life was loving, quiet, and respectful. I lived in a wonderful place. I had the gift of time, so much alone time. I told myself that I should just use it and treat it as a gift instead of a punishment. This was a brand-new life; I needed to show up and say, *I'm here. Now what?*

Read, write, meditate, walk, exercise, pray, love, laugh, forgive me, and build a coaching practice using my gifts. Maybe even be a hero.

I was only just learning about me and what it takes to live a happy life and what makes me a human being. I was learning to love myself and getting to know myself intimately. I was learning to think on purpose, and with all the conversations in my head, the hardest person to get to know and be intimate with was me. What I liked and didn't like; just showing up for myself with patience, compassion, understanding, accepting the good and the bad and even the drama. God, I detested the drama. I could so easily get stuck in it. I got stuck in the conversations that turned me into a victim. It was so easy to go back to that because it was familiar. "No peace" was the norm for me and it was a peace that I was getting to know more and more and wanted with all my heart. I just wouldn't give up. There was no way I'd give up. I told myself, *I must never give up, even though it's hard right now.*

While all this was going on in my life, my ex, Dave, called me and asked if he could see me after ten years of separation. He said he wanted to "make peace." When I saw him for that first time since we divorced, he was sick and my attraction to him was completely gone. I felt a sense of relief, knowing that part of my life was over. Healing came at the most unexpected times. Later, I learned that when he came to me seeking peace, he had cirrhosis of the liver. I realized that he probably thought he was dying, and this was his way of making amends. But he didn't say sorry; he had never said he was sorry about anything.

But he was not dying. Not just then. Dave received a new liver, a new hip, and healed Hepatitis C. All these medical issues had come from his chosen lifestyle. Yet, even after a liver transplant, he did not return to recovery, and even worse, he was still drinking. Once I knew, I felt sad for him, knowing that even with all those second chances, he continued drinking. The sober person that I once knew; the fun and generous person that was Dave was no more. The sadness was mostly for our son. My son had been abandoned by his father overnight. Now that Paul was living with his father, they were repairing their relationship. Dave helped our son finish his degree in engineering. I still worried that Dave's lack of self-care might separate them again and I missed my son!

I made a conscious choice to live alone. No matter how lonely I got, I knew that the pain of being with Mr. Wrong went deeper than the pain of being alone. When I finally stopped dating is when I ended my addiction to unfulfilling relationships. The ocean was my favorite place to purge my addiction to my father.

I know I'll come out of this, I would tell myself. *Right now, I need to stop all the bullshit.* I turned to prayer, meditation, church, writing, and my networks of support. Living on my own, I was never alone. I was lonely at times and yet, God was with me. *I was with me.* I had to learn to stay happy. I had to make that my choice every day.

Chapter 33

One day in the heart of winter, I got a call from my niece about her mother, my older sister Doris. Of all the siblings, I was closest to my sister. In her prime, she had been a fashion designer for wealthy clients in Quebec City and lived in a beautiful house with her first husband, a special unit police officer. My sister was bipolar, although we didn't know what to call it at that time. He had been warned not to have children with her because they would also be mentally ill. They never had children. After they divorced, Doris remarried. Her second husband was financially and physically abusive. She had her first child, my niece, at age 44, and got very ill.

She was prescribed anti-depressants, but she stopped taking this medicine and everything fell apart. Her husband spent most of her money and left her a single mother, mentally unstable and poor, with a child to take care of – or, to take care of her. My niece earned a living since she was 13. The last time I had seen Doris, I was shocked how she'd gone from a huge house with not a speck of dust to a hovel of absolute filth.

When she called, my niece asked me, "Please call her and tell her to go to the hospital."

When I called Doris, she cried. "I'm tired of life," she told me. "I can't live anymore."

From my own experience, I knew this cry for help could easily have been caused by living in a family filled with domestic violence and incest. So many women fall into this desperation when sexual abuse lives within the family. For my sister, it was depression and suicide.

"I can't be here anymore," Doris cried.

I implored her to go to the hospital. I had to convince her that going to the hospital was the best course of action. It was January or February when she went, and I heard that she fell on the ice outside the hospital and hurt her head! My poor sister. When she was admitted, the doctors were surprised she was still alive. She had been malnourished for so long and was in kidney failure.

Luc and I went to see Doris regularly in Quebec City over the next year as she went through physical rehabilitation. Most visits, she looked terrible, but she gradually got better. Her emotional health was a different story. Every time I'd call her, she'd answer the phone with, "What do you *want?*"

But when I called her on New Year's Eve, she answered the phone and said, "I'm so happy to hear from you!" We had the most beautiful conversation. After that, I told all my siblings to call her right away and I was glad I did because she died a few days later from a heart attack. I hope those last few days were full of peace for her ... peace and maybe a little happiness.

I gave the eulogy at her funeral. I spoke of how she came to help me when my daughter was born. I acknowledged that none of us siblings had known her very well – and that was the saddest part of all; that, and the mental illness that terrorized her and caused her such suffering.

So, how did I escape the depression and thoughts of suicide that were my sister's struggle? It's a miracle that I never lost my mind. My mind was strong and survived Hell. It knew there was another life. Don't get me wrong. My psychological health has been a serious spiritual struggle every step of the way as the next lesson presented itself. I had to choose to live in a healthy way if I was ever going to find that other life; a *joyous* life. Every day, I had to fight this battle. We all do.

One of the next steps I wanted to take was seeing Matt again. We hadn't exchanged any information the last time we met so I had no idea how to get in touch with him. When I got to Canada, I prayed. I meditated. I was scared. Who did I know who might have Matt's information? It turned out that one of my friends did and she eagerly gave it to me.

Why am I so scared? I asked myself. The answer came back, *I'm afraid of being rejected again.*

I spoke to God about it and asked Him. The answer came back, *whatever will be, will be.*

When I dialed his number, Matt answered the phone. I recognized his voice immediately and learning from my friend that he was still married, had a moment of anxiety, hoping that this call wouldn't cause any problems in his marriage because that wasn't my intention. We didn't talk for very long because we decided to meet in a couple of days when we both could spend time together and talk face to face.

When we met, I was calm and at peace. It was wonderful seeing him again! We both looked at each other with wonder, sitting on the porch that afternoon. I told him right away what I had wanted to tell him for so many years. It wasn't easy in French because I'd never said any of these words to anyone in French before, or any language: "*Je t'aime, toujours aimer et je vais toujours t'aimer.*" *I have always loved you, and I will always love you.* I just blurted it out. It took a lot of courage to say this, but I needed to say it for so long.

He cried and told me, "I feel the same way." He added that I was his one-and-only and that if he lived to be 104, this love would still be there. Then came the part that shifted everything for me about why we had *really* ended.

Matt asked, "Remember when we were together at Celine's house in the living room sitting on the couch together?"

Of course, I did! How could I forget it?

"We were only 14 years old," he said. "Your father came in and called your name and stood in the door and gave me that look of his that said *I will hurt you if you continue this*. He didn't say anything - it was clear from the look in his eyes."

Knowing my father, I know that he would have hurt this 14-year old boy if he tried to continue a relationship with me. Matt told me that it had happened three times! I had disassociated it completely. Matt went on to say that one day he had gone fishing with a friend who would also fish with my father and that friend had told Matt, "Please stay away from Gaetane, or her father will hurt you *bad*."

Two days after Matt told me this, I saw my friend Celine, who had been a close friend to both of us. I told her all about my meeting with Matt and she said that it was true that my father came into her house and yelled my name. Celine's mother had met him at the door and asked him what he wanted. He'd pushed past her and came into the living room and yelled for me again. My friend Donna said the same thing. Soon, I started to have memories. I could hear my father's voice. I know that my father didn't touch Matt because Celine's mother would have hurt him. She wasn't afraid of much.

It took a while to process this lie that the 14-year-old inside me had so easily believed: that Matt had wanted nothing to do with me because I was dirty and poor. It was such a big revelation that Matt and I had truthfully shared the beginnings of a very healthy relationship until my father destroyed it. My father had stolen everything from me – but I never knew he had stolen Matt too. For the first time, it was so clear how my father stole the absolute love of my life – the man I could have married, the life we could have had. It was just not to be. We could have never been together back then. It just wouldn't have been possible.

The most beautiful part was that the loving spiritual connection between Matt and I was still there. It was sincere, clean, innocent, pure; it was never tainted by my father's sick evil ways. I see the love of God so differently now, so clear. When something is from the divine and the soul, no one and nothing can take it away or destroy it. Evil cannot destroy love. But learning how my father had chased away the love of my life brought a whole new level of sorrow to feel, forgive and release. It was an important conversation that Matt and I had together that day.

Back at home, I got a new job and continued with my writing and networking. One very influential organization, Toastmasters, helped me believe in myself again. It helped me be courageous again. To stand in front of an audience and tell my story is powerful. To be received by those who do this for a living is an honor. I knew I wanted to speak about my life and about the children of hunger, poverty, domestic abuse, and incest. Learning to speak publicly was part of my preparation for this book so that I might go out and speak about it and share my story.

What I learned from this speakers' organization is that you must be yourself to be successful speaking about a topic as sensitive as mine. I realized my topic was too heavy for most audiences. I learned that I didn't need to speak about this part of my story every time I had an audience; saving that for the correct venues held great wisdom. I was getting to know my audience; I was getting to know my voice and range. I learned about storytelling and adding humor to my speeches. Humor got me through so much when I was younger, not letting that in did a disservice to my stories. I was learning to hold everything in my life more lightly.

Chapter 34

As I reflected on that last conversation with Matt, I realized that a healthy relationship with a man seemed out of my grasp. In the years that I spent alone, I had never found a man who could fill my pain or numb it. I was feeling happier by myself, but what I still wanted was a healthy relationship with a man.

Did I start dating again? No. I said, "One day, it will happen." I left it up to fate. I still had so much to learn in my heart and spirit what loving a man was all about and what it meant for a man to love me. I was sure this was part of God's plan for me. But first, I was still learning how to have a healthy relationship with myself, to enjoy my own company. I lived well, cooking wonderful meals and dining at my table looking over the harbor as I watched the sunset every night.

When I met Jim, I immediately liked his gentle spirit and his good nature. I met him at a brunch with other friends. Fate! I found out that he was a widower, after 34 years of marriage. So, what did I think? *He just isn't my type.* Yet, there was a connection between us that I'd never experienced before.

Big surprise – he wasn't available! He was in a relationship with someone else. So, we became friends instead, and this was so new to me. We talked a lot, getting to know each other. We'd hang out or go to a movie. We even wrote each other letters! We had common values and got closer and closer, becoming very good friends and laughing together.

After a year, we were getting too close for my comfort. He was never a flirt; and we would talk about his relationship openly, which I began to learn wasn't as perfect as I thought. But there came a point when I wasn't willing to continue this way with him. I knew our friendly feelings had grown into romantic feelings, yet he remained unavailable – which made him Mr. Wrong.

I finally told him, "If you want to have a relationship with me, I need to be the one and only woman in your life." By then, I had too much respect for myself to do anything less, and he accepted my decision. After I walked away, I missed him very much, but life is about truth. My truth was that I wanted to have a lasting relationship with someone who was genuine, whole, and respectful. Jim had all these qualities and more.

My relationship with Jim, even if it had been originally a friendship, allowed me to take a huge step, find my voice and tell a man what I wanted from a relationship.

Chapter 35

One lovely morning, I took a walk to the labyrinth near my home for some meditation time. Suddenly, I was confused. Where was the entrance? Then panic. *How do I get in there?* A lot of weeds had grown up since the last time I was there. I began the ordeal of trying to figure out where the entrance was. Why was I so confused? I knew where the entrance was. I'd been there a thousand times. Why didn't I trust myself today to find it?

I found my way to the opening and started to walk the labyrinth. As usual, the little butterfly that I call "Mom" came to visit me. When I call the little butterfly, it comes towards me each day. I say, "Hi, Mom." and I know that she is with me. Despite the presence of the butterfly, the weeds were still frustrating! Not only did I need to get to the center of the labyrinth, I needed to find my way to the center of myself and, of course, to God. Losing my way, being confused, meant that I couldn't really get to my soul with all these weeds interfering with my clarity. I've removed a lot of weeds as I walked through my inner labyrinth over the years – literally and figuratively. Some weeds were deep-rooted and difficult to remove; they would just break in your hand and the root would remain in the ground and the weeds would just grow back as they inadvertently got watered and fed.

What was my lesson? As I walked, prayed, meditated, and took a hard look at how I could find my way to the center, through the twists and the turns, the delays and repeats of life, I felt frustrated and sad about all the weeds I could never root out all the way. Healing seemed very hard again. My arms ached from pulling those very deep weeds; the ones that refused to let go.

God give me strength.

My body was tired of pulling weeds as I faced the fact that I needed to tend to my garden, emotionally and spiritually, once more. My heart, still bleeding somehow, could not open completely with all these deep-rooted issues that I needed to heal.

So now what?

Just be in the process. Only when I'm ready can I let go.

When I'm disconnected from my spirit and heart and can't connect with God or pray, that usually means that a storm is approaching. What storm? What is in the way of my heart and soul this time? It's usually the deepest weeds that show up, and it can take a lifetime to pull those weeds.

Chapter 36

That winter, right between Christmas and New Year's Eve of 2013, my unemployment stopped unexpectedly. My last job as a manager on Long Island had been another crazy, stressful job that had started out fine until my boss created a hostile work environment for me and everyone at the medical practice. Yelling, and not in private. I finally decided to resign. When I told him I was resigning, he offered me a different position instead.

I worked out the ending in such a way that I would get a severance, and the unemployment benefit should have lasted until February. Now, with unemployment gone, I was anxious and scared. This was all about the primal fear for survival I felt growing up in my family.

I began to ask myself, *why don't I have money?* I certainly earned money over the years; I'd had good salaries at every job I'd held. I'd also received large sums of money when selling houses after divorcing. Where had it gone? Why was it that, when I looked at my paycheck and saw the amount of money I made, didn't I get to keep it or save the extra? There were times I had worked so hard with long commutes, traveling three hours per day to Manhattan and back, with lots of stress at jobs and serious efforts and I still had nothing left to show for all these years of work because I had given it away! I didn't *get* the money, and I didn't get *why* I gave my money away until I was flat broke once again.

It didn't matter that I had dabbled in being self-employed for years now. I had no money, yet I made money: cash by elder care, Feng Shui and organizing, French tutoring, and vision board workshops. These jobs accumulated enough money - notice I can't even write *earned* enough money - to pay my rent and my bills. But there was never anything left over. I was starting again at zero every month. None of it made sense to me.

Even if I could barely afford it, I knew I needed to go back to therapy. When I'm lost in my pain, sometimes only then can I change it. I know that other things will happen. I believe that I will include professional help in my journey and that's not a bad thing; knowing that I can benefit from the help of professionals is positive and affirming. It was hard to *ask* for help, but it was an investment to *pay* for help; an investment in myself and my journey. Taking the next step, there was something for me on the other side of despair.

When I first began seeing my new therapist, I had no money and no medical insurance. I was still having a very difficult time with my anger, too. I found myself back in that place and being so fearful that I wanted to die. I wanted peace and joy, but these were the deep-rooted weeds that came back every time. I was so frustrated!

My new therapist was kind and wise. She saw that I was working very hard on my recovery.

One day, she looked at me and said, "Gaetane. You need to do work on a soul level now and I'm not the person to help you that way. But I know a woman who does this kind of work."

I replied, "There's no way I can afford to see her."

Without missing a beat, she retrieved her handbag and wrote me a check for a hundred dollars. I was too shocked to speak! I gave away money; I didn't know how to receive it. Yet, there was no refusing.

I called to make an appointment with this new type of "soul therapist" later that day.

Her name was Angelica. She told me that the word "work" and the word "need" would no longer be in my vocabulary. She asked me to replace the word "work" with the word "service," and replace the word "need" with the word "require." Changing those two words altered my way of thinking about these concepts.

"This world is about doing service and we must ask God every day how we can serve in the world," Angelica told me. "No matter what kind of job you do, whether it's cleaning the floor or being president of a company, it must be treated with the same gratitude and thanks."

That didn't make me happy at first. I was still holding onto my "victim mode," as my therapist pointed out. I was holding on to my years of 18-hour days peeling potatoes for a family of nine plus the customers, making cheeseburgers, hot chicken sandwiches, and French fries, selling soda pop and bootlegged alcohol, taking care of everyone and cleaning everything along the way and doing it all over again the next day.

The years of being hungry and poor and knowing how people treated us left me unable to bear seeing other children, especially my siblings, suffering that way. I never wanted them to feel that hunger and shame of stealing food out of a garbage can or waiting at a neighbor's house for them to offer food, of going without soap or toothpaste. I realized at the ripe old age of 14 that they would go hungry and be destined to live in poverty if I didn't take over caring and providing for them, and this fear that something terrible would happen if I failed gave me courage, tenacity, and the resilience to do it all. I committed with a vengeance and pulled from reserves of strength so deep it could only have come from God. And yes, doing this service for my family did bring me some sense of joy. The joy of being strong and courageous and providing for my family kept me going.

But this was not a truly joyful service because it wasn't an *exchange*. At the end of the day, I was just a workhorse, a slave. I felt like I didn't matter. I was invisible, a ghost. No matter how much I earned or how much they were given, it was never enough; it was like a giant hole with no bottom. I deserved to be paid for all my hard work, yet there were times I cried for 25 cents. I thought *I'm not a martyr or a saint; I'm human. How can I not keep any of the money that I made for myself?*

Even as an adult, I'd never been happy working for others. Either I was underpaid, overworked, mistreated, or I sabotaged a good thing. And when I made money, I gave it all away! If I didn't give it all away, I felt selfish, as if I was a bad person for keeping it. Giving it away brought some relief. I did this yet would suffer when I gave away all my money – it made me angry and worse, it brought me to a place of sadness so deep and hopeless that it's hard to describe. This was my familiar place and, though painful, I found my way back there. I kept myself just above poverty level; just able to pay some of my bills. The truth was that what I was taught and what I believed in my heart and what became my reality, was that the money just didn't feel like it was *mine*.

"Okay," I told Angelica, "Work is service, I've got that part. But connecting with money? It's as if it doesn't exist even though I know it does."

I realized it was dissociation all over again with money. Dissociating is a way of life for those who've suffered trauma or who can't consciously incorporate what's happened to them in life. When you dissociate from something, it's not happening; you feel nothing. Well, I had no connection with money. I had worked so hard my whole life, but to try and figure out my connection to money has also been a lifetime of hard work.

Just talking about it, I knew I was so tired of being a victim.

So, now what? Now that I know the old story, now what will I do?

I had to ask myself, *what is my money dynamic? How does it come to me? How do I make money? What energy do I exchange? What do I have to serve and exchange in the Universe? How would I exchange my energy for money energy? Do I believe that I have anything in me to exchange?*

These questions made me anxious to the point of hyperventilating. The first time I hyperventilated, I was 16 years old and thought I was dying. There was so much anxiety about bootlegging and caring for my family, it all hit me at once and I just couldn't breathe. Now, here it was again.

What is it that I bring into this Universe in exchange for money? If money is an exchange of energy, how do I create from this energy? What is in me that I can exchange money for service and be fulfilled as who I am? What is it that I can do for others that makes me personally come alive?

I'm creative! I realized how I came alive with passion when I was being creative – especially working with flowers, design, and writing. I also loved to present and speak to groups, to coach in private sessions, to do organizing and Feng Shui with my clients, and to make vision boards. I had been doing these things on the side for so long, but I finally acknowledged them for what they were truly worth to my soul and to the world. I was discovering my gifts and the many talents I bring to the world. All these things were so close to my heart and brought such a smile to my face! If I could do these things "for a living," I knew I would have a *real* life. And to think I could make *real* money through these forms of creativity was huge for me.

These deep questions and answers awakened my soul, and when this kind of spiritual awakening occurs, there is no going back. Each session with Angelica – and I only had a few sessions - added something to what I was learning about my soul. Part of her method was for us to sit in front of each other as she quietly meditated and prayed. In one session when I was sitting in front of her, I felt tears rolling down my face. The odd thing was that I knew that I wasn't crying.

"What does this mean?" I asked Angelica, "I'm not crying, and I have tears coming down my face." Those tears felt very soft at that moment.

She replied, "It's your soul that's crying. Your soul has been waiting to meet you." She invited me to talk to my soul. She suggested that I say my name and introduce myself. I finally met my soul and all the wounds from my father she had faced. I knew that the sadness of my soul was real.

Angelica said that I was healing all those old wounds. She also said, "If one dies without forgiving and loving, their children will have to live with all that."

When she said that, my soul deeply responded. I realized that forgiving came from the soul and could not be done without it; that God was involved. I so dearly wanted to make peace with my soul! We had to forgive all the perpetrators, and we had to forgive ourselves.

After a few sessions, I began to feel at home in my soul. This may not be understood by others unless they have also connected with themselves on a soul level.

I saw Angelica only five times. That's all. Afterward, I went back to see the therapist who gave me the gift of Angelica. I told her from my soul, "I love myself."

She got teary-eyed.

We both knew this was one of the biggest moments for me, being free to love myself. I've never been the same and I've never lived the same since. I could suddenly sense and feel deeply. I had clarity about my life and what's real. I felt safe. It took being at home in my soul for my home to truly became my refuge and safety. This is a gift and one of the biggest rewards of all the work that I've done over the years. What a journey! I loved it when my friends would visit my home and especially when my family came to visit but I was finally at a place in my life where I needed no one to make me happy.

I knew that one day, I would have a loving relationship with a man. I believed that this time it would be different because I loved and could take care of myself in every way with the help of God. It kept me positive. I believed that because I'd gotten to this beautiful place in my life - physically, emotionally and, most of all, spiritually- I'd arrived at that other life I had been seeking for so many years.

Around this time, Jim walked back into my life. It was a loving, respectful meeting of souls. He'd left the woman he'd been seeing after his wife died. He was completely and totally available to make me the one and only woman in his life, and all I could do was smile. Still, we didn't jump into a romance; that just wasn't our style. Instead, Jim asked me to stage his house that he was selling.

"Of course!" I said. With all my Feng Shui knowledge, I made that house beautiful and Jim was so impressed with how I had transformed his home. It sold after the first showing. The buyer even bought all the furniture - every single piece.

Our romance began more slowly. There was lots of planning. Sometimes, we'd go out dancing or take a train ride. At some point, it seemed natural to talk about moving in together. I told Jim, "I'm not going anywhere. I love my home. It's beautiful and the rent is incredible. It's big enough for both of us." Jim is a quiet type of guy, not intrusive in any way. I knew it would be very peaceful living with him, and it was - and it still is.

Best of all, we are equals! We are equals as people. It is not about dependence on work or money or happiness; we each have our own families and our own successful, positive lives. He would go away golfing for two weeks and still does. We have trust and a healthy attachment. We share the same values. We have common ground and yet also complement each other because I have a lot of energy and love to create and socialize, while he is more intellectual and loves to read. We both like to take walks together, even if I turn around after the first hour, and he keeps going.

I thank God for him. Do your work, and this is what happens. My relationship with Jim brings me a sense of wholeness, respect, dignity, and love. I'm valuable and so is he. He's added energy to my world; the energy of peace, partnership and fun; lots and lots of laughter together. We tell each other that each of us is a great gift to the other and how blessed we are to have found each other.

Loving myself and loving him seems natural. Everything around me and in my relationship flows easily and lovingly - no judgment - only acceptance of him and myself, finally. I love because it comes from my core self. This is where love lives and there is no need to be fixed or changed. This is where I'm created in God's image; we all are.

This book wouldn't be complete without this mention of this very important man in my life. Because of my recovery, I have a blessed relationship with a gentleman who is respectful, loving, and values who I am. As an incest survivor, that is big!

I carry many gifts at present because of the therapists that I chose. I believe that God handpicked them for me. I believe Jim was also handpicked for me. He took my beautiful life and made it even more beautiful.

Does this mean my Hell is over? No. Recently, I'd just come out of the shower and I heard Jim coming down the hall; I heard his footsteps. I imagined I heard my father's footsteps coming at the most vulnerable moment there was; when I wasn't fully dressed and able to hide in my clothes. Hearing those footsteps coming, I was so triggered and scared that I dove for cover. When Jim saw me, he immediately knew something was wrong.

"Just, please go," I said from behind the bed, "We'll talk later."

Jim knows my story and he is understanding with me; he is patient with me. That was all I needed to say. And we *laugh* together! We laugh so much that sometimes, we go to sleep laughing. We are so silly together.

This was a traumatic moment for me, but I want you to know that my life is so much lighter now. Days of suffering are very few. That's the difference. Now, it is only occasionally that a weed in the labyrinth of my soul requires tending.

Chapter 37

I made a trip to Canada to visit my Aunt Debbie for her 80th birthday. It was 2015, yet I walked into the 1960's. Seeing the suffering and the poverty, even seeing a photo of my sister Antoinette, took me back in time. My brother Adam was sick with a severe attack of what seemed like diverticulitis; the year before, it was his heart. Each time I heard the stories, I felt enormous pain, sadness, and anger. Hate and guilt came over me until I cried. I lost all sense of my present life.

Dissociation. Again.

This time, once I could distance myself, come back to the present from the 1960s, I believed for the first time that their miserable existence was not my fault; that it is not my fault, even today.

Talking with my daughter about not seeing her enough, she said, *"Well, you moved far away, Mom."* That's when it clicked; that I felt the same way regarding my siblings. What a lifelong punishment I inflicted on myself. It was all I knew; all I learned. It took years to break the ties of guilt until only the ties of love remained.

Having lived this story of deep poverty, I would discuss poverty with my own children. For example, we talked about people labeled as "poor white trash." I was surprised to learn how one of my sons holds a belief that the poor want to stay poor; that it's a choice. "Otherwise," he said, "they'd get themselves out of poverty."

Oh, really?

That led to a conversation about my own life and how I lived in that "poor white trash" world; a world that, fortunately, my children will never, ever know. When I heard my son talk that way, I couldn't help but think that they can't really know what it feels like; can't really fathom what it is to be poor; to be hungry and dirty and covered with lice. I know what it feels like. I also know what it feels like to be perceived as trash. It's more than that. I felt like trash; not even having the same rights as the "clean people," as I called them.

The separation of "them" and "us" only drives the wedge deeper and the void between us wider.

What I notice is that most people don't take time to look underneath the poverty, the hunger, the illiteracy and more. If they did, they would see that these little children are not trash; they are not their circumstances; often, the circumstances belong to their parents, and their parents before them. These children are not criminals, not drug addicts, not mentally ill - not to imply that all their parents are – but the children are innocent.

The deepest crime that is committed against these children is they are not the poor white trash or any other color of trash; born without brains or creativity. They are children; beautiful little intelligent creative human beings to whom a great injustice is being committed. The so-called "clean people" must pass by on the street and see beautiful little children, not trash; these children are poor and human beings with the potential to help shape our future. If they are lucky, some teacher may take notice.

As they grow older, if nothing changes, they are likely to become their circumstances, too, because it's what they've learned from their parents, their community and the world. I believe that we are all born with everything we need, and we learn to live poor; to live with less. Poverty was a way of life for me as a child, and my concern is for the children. Poverty is like cancer; nearly impossible to escape once it takes hold. The core beliefs that hold us in poverty are so strong, and the label of poverty and the belief system in which it lives, is attached to a place inside our bodies that should we try to remove it, we end up removing a piece of ourselves. We are left empty, not knowing what's to come in its place.

Living poor is a lifestyle, just like living rich is a lifestyle. Children of the wealthy or affluent tend to live a rich lifestyle because that is what they experienced and learned. I could say that about my own life and my parents. The difference is that I was fortunate enough to have a contrasting reference point in my mother's family; the clean people, the educated people. I was fortunate to have my mother's side of the family, so I could see that there was another way to live. I hold a belief, however naive, that anyone who is living in poverty without a contrasting reference point - one that connects them, somehow, to a hopeful way of life - will never be able to extricate themselves and rise above their circumstances.

Yet, we have a choice to some degree. Being raised one way is not a certainty that you will turn out like your parents - though it does create a space for this to happen, good or bad, poor or rich, or somewhere in between. Have people escaped from poverty? Yes, some have. Even those with the barest of necessities who believe that they can help their children create a different lifestyle do just that. It doesn't come easy though; changing how you think about how you live is hard. So, if you are lucky enough to have parents who are healthy, both mentally and emotionally, and live with respect and dignity, you will be raised that way though you are not rich financially. Then, you are not poor at all. You are richer than most of the wealthiest people in the world because you have a healthy mind.

This poverty issue also came up with my daughter. During one of our lunches, we talked about the little girl who had lived upstairs from John's parents when I first came to New York. Amy was her name; the little girl with tangled hair who loved to be held. I had not seen her since she was a toddler and John's mother had scared me so much in the bathroom that I never wanted to go back again - but John had continued to visit with Elizabeth, so she had known Amy as a child. Recently, Amy had found us on Facebook. Well, Elizabeth told me that she was going to see Amy and suggested I come.

"Of course," I said.

The visit revealed poverty and living conditions, the likes of which Elizabeth had never seen. After that visit, I think my daughter finally understood the depth of poverty I had been trying to tell her about. After our visit, she texted me, "Have you recovered, Mom?"

I told her it had been difficult to see.

My daughter said, "Mom, the whole thing is so sad. I just don't understand how people live like that today. I guess I'm an idiot for saying I'm poor. I'm so grateful for you because you taught me a better path."

I knew at that point that finally my daughter got it. It was validation, and by a person who mattered so much to me! Now, my children are starting to understand what happened in my life. It's difficult for them.

Recently, I experienced a flashback from childhood that is so relevant to my little girl and all little children of poverty. As a child, sitting at 12 o'clock mass, I had the desire to volunteer to bring the gifts to the priest. No one had volunteered to do it. Suddenly, a very loud voice inside my head said in French, *"Non, tu peut pas le faire. Vous êtes trop pauvre et sale"* - "No, you can't do that. You are too poor and dirty."

Remembering this thought so clearly, I could feel little Gaetane's sadness. She felt worthless. She could be there in church, but never be a part of anything; she was just there to pray hard so that God might love her. When my Grandma Smyde got angry, she reminded us that because my father was so evil, because he was a demon, because he cursed God and all the saints - that we, too, were all doomed to hell. God doesn't love people like us! She reminded us how dirty we were and that we'd better keep on praying if we wanted to be saved from hell. It was only later in life that my grandma spoke of "God's rewards."

How ironic that my grandma was an example of the clean people and a point of reference for another way of life; and yet also made me feel so godforsaken and worthless in her eyes, and in His. The worst part of it all was that it was my own grandmother speaking; my religious, clean and proper grandmother told us repeatedly that God could not love us because of our evil demon father. When children are dirty, it's usually because there's no money to buy the necessities like soap or toothpaste. That was partly my story. In addition, at least in my case, the dirt that I thought was me came from incest; the secret filth that I could never clean no matter how much I washed or prayed. If only I knew then what I know now: that little children are innocent and ever beloved in God's clear eyes.

It wasn't until Ash Wednesday of 2016 when I went to receive my ashes that some part of the old life – the clean people part of the old life – got dismantled for me as I sat in church. I had arrived early to pray before the service. Well, apparently, that wasn't going to happen. Family after family with all their children arrived, finding their seats around me. It was so noisy; it felt like a playground rather than a church. I couldn't think. I couldn't pray. I'm usually quite tolerant but on that day, I was a bit out of sorts about it.

As I sat observing everyone, I noticed that it was feeling very different to me than it usually did; *I* was feeling differently than I usually did when I was among "the clean people." Here's what I started to notice as I looked around me. I realized that I was no longer seeing people the way my Grandmother had taught me to see them. I thought those words she spoke to me so many years ago were written on my soul; burned into it. I thought there were clean people who God loved and then there were unclean people who God didn't love.

The reasons were many: the clean people went to church, they looked beautiful, and they were educated. They had enough food to eat and all the opportunities that life had afforded them. The others, well, they didn't go to church, or if they did, they were unworthy of God's love; they were dirty or unkempt, they were illiterate and uneducated. They were hungry because they had parents who took from them; fathers who were mentally ill and abused them.

As I looked around me, a shift began in my soul and my heart on a purely emotional level. I felt calm and very clear as this new perspective came to me: *There are no clean people.* Oh boy. I saw this large group of people around me for the first time. Were they wealthier than me? Maybe. But they weren't any cleaner than me or other poor people. These were just people, not clean, certainly not dirty, but just people. There was no such thing as "clean people" and God didn't love one group of people more than any other group of people.

What a feeling of peace that thought brought to me! Suddenly, my whole life and especially my childhood, became real. No more lies learned from my grandmother - and what a sense of freedom that brought! No one should have to get down on her knees and pray for God to love her because of her mentally ill father; no one should have to beg for God's love because they are poor.

Realizing that there is no such a thing as "clean people" was huge for me. And yet, this had been my reality. It created such a horrible belief system within my heart my entire life, especially as a very young child. Sitting there, I looked at reality with fresh eyes as a healthy adult and it was powerful. My reality was that I had lived for eight years with "the clean people." I felt God's love and protection because I lived among them; I looked like them.

I thank God that this belief system is dismantled with all its horror from my heart and soul. I guess I should be grateful that I never made it to the "clean people" level and thank God because I would have been disappointed if that's how my story ended. All those messages, learned from the time I could understand words, were vanishing one by one. I was no longer a victim or poor or unclean; none of that old story exists anymore.

I thank God that my children will not have to walk that walk of deep poverty and suffering. I broke that pattern. If I had not done so, the pattern would have been passed to the next generation until someone chose to shift it by moving and beginning a journey towards freedom. I paid a high price for my freedom.

Eventually, I told my daughter the story about the terrifying night my father had come into our bedroom with a gun and we were all hiding under the wool blankets in the dead of winter. My daughter lived her whole life with huge fears that just wouldn't go away. She was anxious. After telling her that story, she sent me a text the next day. "I can't keep living this way," she wrote.

"Sometimes God forces us to live a certain way," I wrote back.

She answered, "Apparently, and my physical body can't handle it. I mean, I can't be so full of fear anymore. I'm like you under the blanket with a gun at your head. It's over. The trigger wasn't pulled. The only real way to survive is to live and so that's what I hope to do. I must learn so I can live. This horrible fear holds me back! I am scared but I've got to live! Anyway, I love you for sharing your life with me. It helps me figure out mine. X!"

That's my girl. All I've done in my life, all that's happened to me, it's all worth it to see my daughter starting to embrace her life. What a reward! Grandma Smyde said that God would reward me some day. Maybe this is it. And it would be enough for me.

The journey of recovery is really the journey of reaping God's rewards.

It's awesome to live every day with dreams and goals. There is nothing to interfere with my thoughts and my heart. I look forward to an incredible future. I imagine me with all my gifts, living, and living my purpose; being there for those incredible little people called children with their beautiful smiles and incredible laughter; those little humans who are just loving beings.

If they have enough to eat, they can play as children and have the opportunities for a great education. That fills my heart with joy! Our children are the future of the world. They are ours whether we have children or not. Let's all keep them safe.

But how? What if each person took one child under his or her care? Could we eliminate hunger and poverty? How could teachers notice more of the subtle signs of hunger, poverty and abuse? How could I help feed these children three substantial meals a day? What would it take for me to be able to do that?

Unanswered questions, yes, and questions that will stay with me and may, one day, have answers. And one more, what would Jesus do if he were here today? These are the questions I ask as I walk to the harbor to catch the last rays of the setting sun.

Chapter 38

With my next coach and therapist, I talked about my relationship with God, about His clear messages. I talked about intuition - my knowing and not knowing - the clear voice I'd heard at the most important times in my life when it was dangerous not to listen. I told of hearing a clear voice inside my head when I was 16 years old; this was the first time I recalled hearing a voice so clear and strong inside my heart and head. I just *knew* it was *true.*

God spoke to me so many times in my life. It depended on whether I wanted to hear it or not. When I listened, it was good for me. God spoke to me; often, I didn't listen. I was fighting my demons. Discovering my inner voice and that my inner voice was my strength, I knew that it wanted what's best for me.

The messages were very clear and straightforward. It was *Yes*, or *No.* It was never "maybe." When I started with the "maybe," that was a red flag that I was off my truth. The thing about being stuck in the middle between the past and the future is that, when you're stuck, you cannot move forward. Often, the only logical path seems to be backwards to what is familiar. But when you stay out of the past, you can hear yourself think, *don't give up. Don't quit. Don't move away. Listen.* When I listen, I hear, *God has a wonderful life for you, Gaetane.*

At 16 years old, I was afraid of God; so afraid of him talking to me that I would have panicked or thought I was crazy. Now, I felt safe and secure, knowing that God loves me. Though I didn't listen, he still walked with me on this journey - the marriages, the dissociation from the emotional pain of childhood and then leaving everything and everyone time and time again. I had God's grace and a lot of hope. God gave me the courage, strength and grace to survive all the years of suffering that I could possibly live through. I made it!

We all serve God in some way even if our relationship with God is not that connected. I believe that we need to develop a deep close relationship with God. The peace of Christ surpasses all understanding. Every time that I asked for the peace of Christ, I had it instantly! My life shifted for the day. It's a choice. Choices in my life are easy to make when I have peace; then, I know what the right thing is to do.

I have come to know that God's rewards have been many throughout my whole life. God's rewards are with me. Yes, my young life was stolen. Because of the devastation of my life, without God's gifts and rewards, I would not be here on this planet. I know what easily could have been living in a family filled with domestic violence and incest: more violence, murder, suicide, drugs and alcohol, eating disorders, homelessness and other forms of financial devastation, prostitution, depression and anti-depressants, prescribed medication and self-medication. The list of outcomes goes on and on.

It took me years to see God's rewards in my life. I often said, "I'm still waiting for God's Reward."

"Tell me, where is it?" I asked my brother Adam, "Where is God's reward that grandma said I would get?"

Adam was visiting me in New York. He looked at me and said, "What about your health?"

I said, "What about my health?"

He was talking about my physical health, how I still had the energy of a young person. Even my children say, "I wish I had your energy, Mom."

I say, "Yes, my energy is good." But it's really my mental health that I've realized is my true reward. My faith, hope, and courage. Believing that there will be a way, with all the gifts that were given to me. That, with all these gifts, it is time to give back to the world. I look over the years and I know that I was given gifts of love to have survived the dark world I lived in. I want my angels to know the purpose they served in my life as channels of God's love for me. This love helped me heal; their love may help me to heal others. In the words of my first therapist, "With the intense abuse that I suffered, the only reason that I was sane was because I had people around me who loved me." And I had found the love of God.

The Virgin Mary, on the other hand, was a different story. I wrote early on that I could never identify with Mary; not as a saint and not as someone so holy because no one could be that holy. Looking back on my early life, I felt that I was good. I never drank alcohol or had sex with anyone except being molested by my father. I don't remember doing anything wrong, just loving and hating at the same time. My only sense of fulfillment was those kids, my siblings, helping to provide them with food, taking care of my sick mother, having friends who loved me and who I loved. Wasn't that being a good person? I often asked myself the question, "How do good people live?" Good people live with dignity, respect, and honor. Like me, they have compassion and are doing service in the world that comes naturally, from the gifts that are given. But I know that I'm not holy and certainly no saint, like Mary.

My anti-relationship with the Virgin Mary was another wound God needed to heal. It happened one day no different than any other day. I was at my computer writing and checking my e-mail in my porch office when I suddenly felt called to go to Mass.

When I got to church, there were a lot of cars parked and many people going into church; more than usual, I noticed.

I wondered, *why are so many people attending mass today?* Something had to be going on; it had to be a special occasion, some holiday or something. As I sat down, the mass began. When the priest started talking, it was only then that I realized that it was Assumption Day, which is about celebrating the Virgin Mary.

Oh boy, I thought. *What brought me here today?*

I listened to the readings. I had been called to listen, and I listened with an open heart. The priest told the story of Mary visiting Elizabeth when Elizabeth was pregnant. I began to think for the first time that this is a beautiful story of two women friends visiting each other. It was the first time that I thought of these two women as humans rather than saints.

Another shift came when the priest said we should ask Mary to pray *for* us rather than pray *to* Mary. That's what the Hail Mary prayer was really all about: "Hail Mary, Mother of God, pray for us now and in the hour of our need." It had nothing to do with praising Mary; it was about asking her to pray for us.

As the days followed, I prayed and meditated and asked Mary to pray for me for the first time in my life. I asked her to give me the courage to listen. As the weeks went by, I recited the prayer that Mary recited about proclaiming from her soul the greatest God and rejoicing in the spirit of Jesus. Finally, I understood why this message was shared with me.

I know in my heart and soul that Mary was not some sort of saint. She was just a human being and a woman chosen and blessed by God to perform a very special service in the world through her soul's journey. She was a woman who said yes. She accepted her calling. Mary accepted God's blessing upon her and she accepted that all she was doing was God's will. I'm only beginning to accept that I am on my soul's journey; no more special than any of my family or siblings' soul journeys.

Understanding this, my life is now filled with acceptance, forgiveness and the knowing that I'm just a woman blessed with a heavy-duty task. And I am saying, *Yes.* My strength and courage make so much more sense now. God is with me. Now, Mary is with me as well. Mary was one of the most incredibly strong women of faith that the world will ever know; she was a tremendous example to all women in all nations. If she is all that, then I am, too - and so are you.

Doing the work that God asked me to do felt like heroic work. The people who continue and complete their journey into wholeness are heroes in my eyes. If we truly understand heroism, we know it's not about getting it perfect. We are heroes when we work through our pain; stay with it. I thought that I could make pain go away or erase it - for years, I tried. Those years weren't lost but I would never be where I am today if I'd given up hope. Abuse kills you a little at a time. The guilt that it's your fault takes away years of energy and years of your life. It is difficult when you work and work and repeatedly, your face hits the floor.

In my case, I know without a doubt that dissociating saved me; it was a life-saver as well as my worst enemy and can still stop me from thriving in my life today. Dissociating is like hitting your head against the wall; trying to figure it out and you get so frustrated and discouraged at times. Every time I decided that I was ending something, I went through hell again; I opened that wound; that fear; the pain; the sadness. It affected a major part of my life; relationships with men; intimate relationships, work; my life with people; anything that touched me emotionally; deep in my core.

I learned to accept dissociative behavior as part of my life and accepting it as a gift and not a hindrance in my life allowed me to go on. Now accepting its reality, the gift is seeing when I disconnect; when something is wrong. All the signs point to it. I may keep saying, *I don't know,* and become frustrated and feel nothing; but I know that there is something, and, what it is, I'm determined to find out. I know that there is pain involved when this happens and when I'm ready to face the pain of whatever it is and the fear, then I say, *oh, this is what it is again. I've dissociated again.*

The pain is usually a time, during which I want to die and see no hope. But I really am dying; dying to my old belief system, my old self. I understand how and why people break down, people kill others; people commit suicide. I understand, because during these times, I feel like I want to die. I know a big breakthrough is coming when this happens, and it usually does.

I know that I am a hero; I took on "hero" at 16 years old; maybe younger, with the belief that there was another life. I could never have done this without the grace and love of God; a much greater power than myself. That gives me the courage and hope to keep going. I know that I'm chosen to do this work. By myself, I could never do this work. Sometimes, when I take a detour and fall on my face, I think that God isn't with me, but He is. It is all heroic work. Anyone who does this work and don't make it, I do understand.

Now, I'm here to help others, giving to the world what was given to me. I want to help people; people who I know are helping those who get stuck in dissociation the hardest part of sexual abuse and other extreme abuse. I want to help those who dissociate to survive and let them know that I understand how it gets in our way of living. One cannot live a life with great big blocks to their memory and emotions and go on without help. Therapists can help. I've been blessed that way and with others who supported me.

I've lived all these years, holding the word "Shame" as my soul's name as if that was my heritage for my God-given gifts. That name no longer applies. My new name, my soul's new name, is Fortitude. I am ready to acknowledge and own my gift and its legacy. Without it, I never would have survived all the pain and adversity.

I realize that my purpose is not to suffer; no child needs to be hungry, poor and abused. I know it's not God's will for us. Parents have the responsibility of caring for their children; to nurture, love and, at the very least, provide the essentials, like food, for their children.

I believe we are all given the gifts to live a great life. I know that I was given every gift to live mine. It was all there inside me. The factors that kept me poor and abused were human factors. My parents' inability to take care of me and my siblings helped to nurture my ability to survive those early years.

It took a long time, but I can finally say that I've made peace with my little Gaetane; the poor, hungry, abused child. Looking back over my life, I understand, and I see this little girl in a new light with new eyes and heart. From the moment that she was born, she was equipped with everything she required to have a great big life; a world filled with possibility; able to be anything and anyone she wanted to be. She was born intelligent, strong, quick, and good-natured with a strong character and wit. Most of all, she was born with this gift that is her divine nature.

The reason that writing about this experience is so important to me is that little children are born with such tender, open minds. We – notice how I include myself - are ready to learn anything that's taught to us, especially by our parents.

What our parents instill in our minds as infants and toddlers sticks in our minds for a lifetime. Incest is deadly; it's even more deadly when it happens as an infant or a toddler and that infant or toddler equates incest to love. It took me a lifetime to rewire my brain from that brainwashing. I've had a strong mind and been truly resilient. I've bounced back. I still feel that I'm a miracle just for being alive.

When I meditate and pray, I have another awareness that is deeper than before. The clarity that I received is that God never made me suffer and never intended me to suffer though there is suffering in this world. Instead, he blessed me with the gift to survive the suffering that was to happen. God does not make us suffer - we make each other suffer – and yet, we are given tools to be able to walk through the storm.

I decided to turn over the resentment and the hate that I still had towards my parents. The clear message was to be grateful instead of being resentful; to be grateful for the enormous abundance of gifts and strength that allowed me to survive at the hands of cruel people. There would not have been enough money in this world to buy my freedom and no amount of money would have walked me through all the storms that I had to walk through without my connection to God.

If money alone had been my gift, I would have died like my sister had died. No amount of money would have walked me through the pain and adversity. Instead, God blessed me with his grace, and gifted me with the strength and perseverance to see my journey through; no money can buy that. I now understand what Angelica was saying by turning that resentment into gratitude; the abundance of blessings that I needed to survive was given to me. Just recently, I see that money now comes easily to me; it's the true meaning of "Let go and let God."

To forgive someone is to release them and yourself from that bondage so it isn't passed on to the next generation. It's learning that God loves us for who we are. No judgment or penalty. I'm getting to know my soul. In my soul, the truth lives; in the *Yes* and the *No*.

Next, my soul said *Yes* to working with a spiritual healer who practiced an integrative (body, mind, spirit) approach. With this healer, I had an incredible spiritual journey and cleaned up my family energy. She is the one who really brought it home to me about forgiveness. She is the one who really explained that, unless I separated my father's essence from his sickness, I could not fully forgive him. Up until this point and time, I thought I had forgiven him. I was wrong. How can you forgive what you don't know? Unless I was willing to forgive fully – what I knew and what I didn't - and could release it once and for all, I would never complete this process of remembering, hurting, healing and letting go. I was told by my spiritual healer that until I was willing and ready to let go, I wouldn't see that spark of divine light in them; I would not be able to forgive.

I did what she suggested and worked with some resistance, but I got it. I understood. Fifty years ago, I set out to kill the daughter of an abuser; I was systematically doing away with myself, my past and all the people from my past. After much searching and healing, I realized that I am the child of my parents. Separating my father's essence from his sickness and my mother's weakness from her essence, I could see that spark of light in each of them that we all have as human beings. I finally understood that, by forgiving both my father and my mother, I was releasing their souls and mine. By releasing them to where their souls were going to be free, only then could I be free. I was their daughter. I released them both and forgave them. I decided to let myself live.

For a few days after that, I felt disappointed. So much had changed for me and yet I looked like the same person. The world hadn't noticed my transformation either. People spoke to me as if I hadn't changed at all. *Couldn't they see the transformation?*

I must admit that the disappointment didn't last long. I finally had a sense of peace and calm. I stopped looking for God everywhere knowing that God is in me; the real essence of Gaetane, not a make-believe person; the so-called good and clean girl I created, believing that somehow, I would be loved if only I could be someone else. I was myself, and I was finally free!

During this time, I had a dream – one of those dreams that stays with you - about the pain and the suffering that my family experienced. In this dream, I didn't want to be there anymore, and I kept saying that I had to leave. Doing this cleansing and releasing and forgiving on a soul level, allowed this transformative dream to surface. I instantly connected to it on a spiritual level.

A beautiful part of my new story is unfolding with the blessing of God. The Universe is waiting for me.

Most of all, I am an extraordinary, strong person with so much to give.

Chapter 39

The next time I visited Canada was different. It was July of 2017. I made a trip to Canada to see my Green River friends because all of us were turning 70; a big celebration was planned. I decided I wanted to spend some time alone while I was there. I looked online and found a little cabin I could rent for the week on *La Riviere de la Truite* – The River of the Trout. This cabin was perfect because it was right on the river in the middle of the wilderness with no internet, no TV - just peace and quiet. When I arrived, the smell of fresh cut wood was an instant revival of my senses. The peace that I felt there was instantaneous.

The cabin was painted green outside with a little porch, perfect for one or two. The owner said that he rented the cabins mostly to biologists doing research. There was the river right in front of the cabin, where I watched beavers building their dam. One large beaver and a baby worked nonstop, passing by the cabin very quickly with fresh branches in their mouths; something I had never seen before.

Inside the cabin was a small kitchen stocked with cookware, dishware, and a coffee press. There was a shower and plenty of towels. To reach the sleeping loft, I had to climb very steep ladder-like stairs. Upstairs were two twin-sized beds and limited head space under the A-frame roof made of tin and lined with heavy beams.

If you were more than five feet tall, forget about standing upright! Good thing I was a short Canadian!

At night, it was pitch black outside and so quiet. I was aware that I was the only person in the woods. I went to sleep, reading. There was a little light in the loft, but I read my book with a flashlight.

At morning, the sun would shine in through the little loft window, waking me up so gently with the birds singing and the sounds of the forest. I felt rested. I was in awe that the land where I was born and grew up could be this peaceful.

We had beautiful weather every day, which is rare in that part of Canada. Each morning I would walk down the dirt road to the river and sit on a rock, meditating and listening to the sound of the river.

There was, now and again, a sense of sadness that I never explored my beautiful country. Out there in the wilderness, I encountered my father's energy and essence. Was this how he felt? Had he sensed this deep peace of nature?

The week became a wondrous paradise; a loving place to be. While I was there, I met with my Aunt Debbie for dinner. She told me that she had found the letter I'd written to my Uncle George before he died in October of 1984.

Over the years, I had asked my aunt if she could give me the letter because he took the letter with him for his hospital stay and kept the letter with him until he died. My aunt looked for it many times over the years - she had finally found it! In fact, she had it with her, knowing I was eager to see it again and read it.

Alone in my cabin, I read this letter with intense joy. The letter was dated May 16, 1983.

Dear Uncle George,

I take time this evening to write a letter that is a long time coming. Today I received the news of your lab results and I felt sorrow and pain. I pray that God gives you lots of courage and peace and love.

Now I have something to tell you. It's been many years with beautiful and profound memories and you have been a big, important part of my life during those many years. When I was 11 years old, I spent the summer with you at Hautrive. I was a little girl who never had love or affection from her father. For two months in my life, I had a father. It was you.

I felt a lot of sorrow when I returned to Riviere Verte. I was at the age when I could understand that you are a good family man with a lot of love; you are a spiritual man, who loves God. I discovered at that age what it was like to have a normal family. I saw the love that you showed to your family. I saw the difference between a normal and a sick family. For me, your family was a dream that I always kept in my heart.

Today, I thank God for this light. It's painful that that light did not last when I returned to Riviere Verte. In my family, there was a lot of darkness: the sickness of alcoholism. When I was visiting in your home, I told myself that I would marry a man just like you; someone who was gentle and loving. Unfortunately, being as confused as I was, the opposite happened.

I thank you with all my heart, Uncle George, for giving me all of your love. It was at a time in my life that I needed to be loved. That's all for now. Write back if you're able to.

I love you very much,
Gaetane.

Being gifted this letter was yet another surprise and a miracle of sorts. I knew that my uncle came to visit me in my little cabin! I could feel him and hear his hearty laughter!

The reunion was an amazing gathering of familiar people, some of whom I'd not seen in 50 years. Being with these friends was the main reason that I returned to Canada and it turned out to be much more rewarding than I expected. It began with a feeling of peace and love about being in my native country. Being there with everyone speaking French felt right. What a full circle for me in my life! There was a finality to it that came from deep within my heart and soul.

Back home, I was just beginning to explore how I could bring my talent and experience together into a career of my own. I turned to art therapy through a process called Vision Boarding using an ancient Chinese art form called Feng Shui. I was ready to help women create a vision that would assist them in moving beyond survival. When trauma happens to the soul, your vision is taken away, your life is taken away, *you* are taken away. You must find who you are, and you need a vision of a hopeful future to move beyond surviving and into thriving. I still find this work rewarding; I still love being in the service of other women who've experienced trauma.

There was a time that I'd question my ability to be a teacher; I'd call myself undeserving of that role and title. Yet, I believe that I was chosen to be the model and teacher. I know that it has been my life's work on this earth. When I stop and think of it now; instead of thinking how I never did this or that right; I say I did my work and I'm successful at it - not perfect; successful.

I'm still creating. In this present and future, I look forward to serving others; doing God's will. My reality is my spirit; strong, open and willing to receive divine love. In living a new story, I respect and honor myself and recognize the difference between being loved and being manipulated. I've grown in ways that I never dreamt possible because of my willingness to walk through huge storms with the faith that I would come out of it whole, into the sunshine where there's a rainbow. From the moment I wake up in the morning to the time I go to sleep at night, it is with gratitude and thanks to God.

What marked the end of my old story? Was there a moment? I don't know. How does one write a *new* story? It's not about rejecting everything from the old story, though some things must be rejected. It's about choosing what you want to bring with you into the new story. To reject all my past life would be like rejecting my resilience, my faith, and all those who I carried with me in my heart. These also become the essence of my new story.

In my new story, there is love and kindness instead of hate and anger. There is joy instead of sadness; being present and living with ease rather than surviving. There is a naturalness to who I am that has full permission to come out and thrive. There is forgiveness for me and for others. The day-to-day struggle may show up and yet, it's received differently. It's just something that happens in life.

Recently, I had a dream. My dream was that I was standing on a very high place with my hands lifted to heaven. There was the most beautiful clear blue sky. The sun was warm, not hot. As I looked out ahead of me, what I saw was a long, long road - beautiful, clean, smooth, and on each side of the road was the ocean, clean and calm with blue water. Suddenly, it was clear that I was being invited into my future because I was ready to go. I looked down and was surprised to see that I was standing at the edge of a cliff! Suddenly, I was afraid that I might fall, hurt myself, or die. In my dream, I began to scream, "No, no. I *can't!*"

When I woke up, I wondered - *Why did I put cliffs and obstacles in my way?* It was a beautiful, serene dream until then. This won't take me into my new story. Fear, suffering, and sorrow don't get to come along. This dream helped me realize that it's time to take all that beauty, peace and calm with me; to walk forward; to leap.

And so, I leaped.

You probably thought this dream, this leap of faith, would mark the end of this book – I know I did. What a high note! What could possibly be better than taking a leap of faith? *It's always the landing, the next step.*

The thing is, over the years, there was one weed left that came up for me that I never resolved: I wanted to tell my truth to a priest. I spent my life going to church, for seventy years, and I never received the sacrament of confession; I was too ashamed. As an adult, I would look at the priests and think, "Maybe this one" or "Maybe that one." With my sensitivity, the choice of which priest was critical. But seeing these priests, it was just "maybe." In the language of the soul, this means *No.* The priest who made my soul say *Yes* had never appeared to me before. Well, God changed that before this book could end!

My soul waited for years before this priest finally appeared in my life. The priest my soul chose for confession was young and had a beautiful feminine spirit. He was handpicked by God. He was the one.

When I made my confession, it was Reconciliation Day in so many ways.

This priest received my disclosure and confession I had waited so long to give. He was very touched by my journey and told me how brave I was. "I'm honored you chose me," he said. The whole experience left me feeling clean. Just when you think there is nothing left to heal, you are offered the gift of the resurrection of your soul one step at a time; this is God in action.

At the end of my confession, what did God say next through this priest? He made me feel important. He said I needed to help people in the Catholic community with this problem, that this was important; they needed my help.

Imagine finding out that the clean people needed my help! That there were people at church struggling with this filth; the same filth I had been through. Here is where the journey, that black cloud, that curse, the one I'd been told I was meant to break by Joyce and Tony, began. After all those years, it was true that I have been chosen or called to walk this journey and break this curse — the curse of incest, poverty, violence, alcoholism, all of it, and everything that goes with it. It is going to stop here, and it is going to stop with me!

Because of my relentlessness about recovery, because of the encouragement about this book, I have come to believe that my story is not about being a victim, but about becoming empowered in strength and grace to take the next step. And then the next. My story is meant to help others heal and empower themselves. My story is for me, but it is also bigger than that because it is for the whole world and every single last one of its amazing inhabitants. It's for *you*.

My new story is in God's hands and now, reading this book, it's in yours. Pulling all those weeds in the labyrinth, somehow, *I* became the butterfly who would always know its way.

Gaetane Martin

Author Gaetane Martin has been interviewed on local and national radio about her story and her work. Her passion is speaking publicly about the issues of childhood sexual abuse, alcoholism and childhood hunger and poverty. She has presented at hospitals and mental health conferences on the impact of the trauma of sexual abuse and how to work with children and teenage victims. Contact Gaetane for speaking engagements or workshops around the themes of her book at http://www.gaetanemartin.com.

37780385R10166

Made in the USA
Middletown, DE
02 March 2019